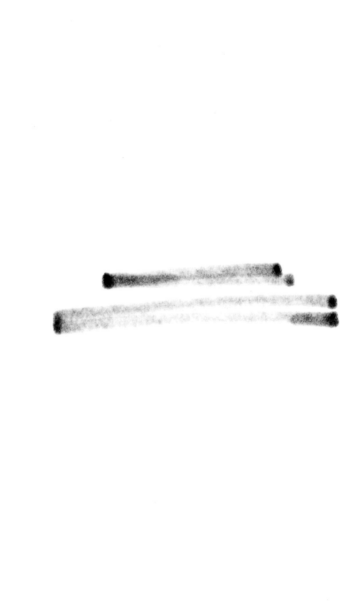

DÉTENTE IN THE NAPOLEONIC ERA

DÉTENTE IN THE
Napoleonic Era

Bonaparte and the Russians

HUGH RAGSDALE

THE REGENTS PRESS OF KANSAS
Lawrence

Library of Congress Cataloging in Publication Data
Ragsdale, Hugh.
Detente in the Napoleonic era.
Bibliography: p.
Includes index.
1. France—Foreign relations—Russia. 2. Russia—
Foreign relations—France. 3. Napoléon I, Emperor of
the French, 1769-1821. 4. France—Foreign relations—
1789-1815. I. Title.
DC59.8.R8R34   327.44047   79-28494
ISBN 0-7006-0201-1

FOR

MY PARENTS

CONTENTS

LIST OF ILLUSTRATIONS

PREFACE

THIS BOOK has three subjects. The first may be called, after a well-known work by Herbert Butterfield, Bonaparte's peace tactics. The second is a product of the first: it is a case study of the influence of political illusions on the interaction of Russia and the West. For centuries, these two uncomfortably juxtaposed cultures have tried to understand each other, both for good and for evil, and they are, in this age of détente, still hard at it. This study illustrates, by taking a close look at one episode in the process, what a Sisyphean labor it is. The third subject is the difficulty that the academic in the field of Russian affairs shares with the diplomat: the work of the scholar, like that of the statesman, where Russia is concerned, proceeds under special conditions. It is subject to special confusion. Perhaps Westerners are too ready to believe the worst about Russia in any case; the Russians have been astonishingly willing to encourage this disposition.

WHEN BONAPARTE came to power, he found France entangled in the toils of the Second Coalition and sorely in need of peace. He appealed to Austria and England to take part in negotiations. They both haughtily refused. Rejected thus, he turned his attention for the first time to the third of the coalition powers, Russia. In so doing, he began the formulation of what was to approximate, more than any other single scheme, the grand design of Napoleonic foreign policy. It was to prove that he was, with Talleyrand's assistance, as fantastically resourceful a diplomat as he was a commander. Within little more than a year's time, he would make supplicants of the two proud powers that had spurned his peace offers. It was an authentic virtuoso performance, perhaps the most successful diplomacy, and certainly the cheapest victory, of his fabulous career. In the long run, however, it was that very design, its Russian foundation, and the elementary misunderstanding on which it was based, that would prove his undoing. How that happened is the substance of this book.

PORTIONS OF THIS STUDY have been published previously, in rather different form, in the *Slavic Review*, the *Journal of Modern History, French Historical Studies,* and *Canadian-American Slavic Studies.*

My research has been supported by grants from the National Council on the Humanities, the Inter-University Committee on Travel Grants (now IREX), the American Philosophical Society, the Office of International Studies and Programs of the University of Alabama, and, especially generously, by the Research Grants Committee of the University of Alabama. The Russian Research Center at Harvard University and the Hoover Institution gave me the use of their facilities for a summer and a semester respectively.

I have benefited by various kinds of assistance from Thomas T. Hammond, George V. Taylor, Clifford Foust, Joseph E. O'Connor, Jacques Godechot, Harold Parker, John F. Ramsey, Robert E. Johnson, Norvin Richards, Catherine Jones, Romuald Misiunas, John Ehrman, G. E. Fussell, Walter F. Koch, Pat Tamarin, Carolyn Sassaman, Ruth Kibbey, Helena Koiner, Avgusta Mikhailovna Stanislavskaia, Nina Stepanovna Kiniapina, Vladlen Georgevich Sirotkin, Forrest and Ellen McDonald, my mother and father, my sons Terry and Jim, and my wife Kate.

It is only fair to add that I have at times been stubborn, and instead of taking all the kind suggestions that my friends and colleagues have offered, I have often done things my own way (now let them prove their devotion by sharing the blame). But I am very grateful to all of them, and I hope that they will be pleased with the book.

Translations of quoted passages are mine unless otherwise indicated.

1

THE SETTING

I have no idea of any peace being secure, unless France return to the monarchical system.—William Pitt

---

ON 18 BRUMAIRE the tired and corrupt French revolutionary government of the Directory was overthrown by a young general—he was thirty—who is now recognized as one of the prodigies of modern history. He is best known as a man of war, but his most crucial test in the early years of his new government, before his reputation reached titanic proportions, was to make peace. In the campaign of 1799, while Bonaparte's adventure in Egypt was deteriorating into disaster, the three powers of the Second Coalition—England, Austria, and Russia—first drove the French almost entirely out of the area they had conquered in Italy and then prepared to march into France itself. Though the French had turned the tide somewhat just before Bonaparte returned, they were by no means out of danger when the coup occurred.

Historians have debated whether Bonaparte's early peace initiatives were genuine—that is, whether they were bona-fide diplomacy or mere propaganda. The answer is impossible to determine. We cannot read his mind. It is commonly said that he nurtured his power on popularity. We know that he was popular and that the war was unpopular. We know that he had an awesomely disordered nation to organize. The political structure, state finance, the religious question—all demanded his immediate attention. For these problems, peace would bring a welcome respite. Bonaparte, as a good student of history, certainly knew that war was a mighty engine of unpredictable upheaval. He should have known as well as anyone that it provided opportunity for generals in the army to win military glory that might whet ambitions as large as his own, and at the expense of his own. The fortunes of war might force him to lead the army in person, as they did, and thus allow Paris to become his rivals' playground.

It seems fair to surmise, then, that he must have found the advantages of obtaining an early peace tempting, if he could manage to make a suitably glorious peace. His first steps toward it were, however, crude and ineffective.

On Christmas Day, 1799, he, an upstart Corsican usurper, addressed a personal letter to two of the crowned heads of Europe, the king of England and the emperor of Germany. The letters appealed in the name of humanity, and with, admittedly, no little rhetoric, for an end to the slaughter.[1]

THE BRITISH RESPONSE to Bonaparte's appeal was the business of the prime minister, William Pitt. Pitt was the second son of a famous father and former prime minister, the earl of Chatham. He was also, appropriately, a child prodigy, distinguishing himself in Latin and Greek, and by the age of seven he had decided to follow a political career. He was elected to Parliament when he was twenty-one. There he did not disappoint those who were expecting great things of him. His first speech was full of assurance and eloquence. Some said that it was the best first speech they had heard there; some said that he was not a mere chip off the old block but the old block itself.

Before he was twenty-five he was prime minister. People laughed when they heard about it. He headed a cabinet that lacked majority support in the Commons, but he bided his time, determined to call elections when his policy had put opinion in the country on his side. Within six months he had triumphed.

Pitt was committed, as his father had been, to reform. He tried to scrap some of the rotten boroughs but was soundly defeated. He accepted the defeat philosophically: he was noble but not quixotic.

As a public financier, Pitt won great acclaim, handling state funds with real genius. Millions passed through his hands, but he died deeply in debt, ignoring even legitimate sources of wealth. In sum, he enjoyed power, not money.

Pitt never married. Though he had a weakness for port wine, he was a decent and pure, principled and high-minded man. As such, he was not suited to deal in the affairs of—certainly not by the standards of—the statesmen of Continental Europe in a contest with the likes of Bonaparte and Talleyrand. Chatham is remembered as a great wartime leader; Pitt is not. It has been suggested, by way of vindication, that Pitt did not have an ally like Frederick II and that Chatham did not have an enemy like Bonaparte.

Pitt's initial attitude toward the French Revolution—and that of his cabinet and of George III—had been that it was a French, not a British, problem. When the war broke out on the Continent in the spring of 1792, Pitt feared that the Germanic powers were embarking on a monarchical crusade that would identify Jacobinism with patriotism in France, thereby escalating and prolonging the conflict. True, the French ambassador was sent home when Louis XVI was executed, but, after all, he had been assigned to London by Louis. It was the French who took the initiative and declared war, on 1 February 1793. Pitt would have had to go to war anyway, for by this time the French had overrun and occupied the Austrian Netherlands (Belgium). The Netherlands, the Baltic, and the Mediterranean were the three regions of Europe where the English were sensitive to their vital interests. Pitt insistently distinguished, at this stage of the conflict, between the issue of France's form of government and the issue of security for France's neighbors.

Pitt was sanguine about the impending war, as were many of his contemporaries, because France seemed to be in a condition of collapse. He expected to fight by a traditional British strategy—that is, by collecting colonial properties to throw into the balance against the Continental ones of the other side when a peace conference convened.

In the summer of 1793 the British government joined in alliance with Prussia and Austria. War aims were simply said to be restoration of the tranquillity and security of Europe.

The Whig opposition, led by Charles James Fox, soon began to accuse the cabinet of succumbing to the very vice of the Prussians and Austrians that Pitt had been so chary of in 1792—that is, Fox accused Pitt of fighting for the restoration of the French monarchy. In fact, the French, through their astonishing propaganda decrees, had altered the nature of the struggle. They offered to place the French army at the service of honorable democrats against corrupt kings everywhere. Pitt's policy soon reflected the new nature of the war: "I am ready to confess, that I can conceive an imaginary case of a peace being made with the government of France, even in its republican form; but I will fairly say also, that I have no idea of any peace being secure, unless France return to the monarchical system."[2] So far had the credit of the Jacobins fallen.

The British made war on French colonies and commerce and prospered enough to finance the great Continental coalitions, but their expectations from their allies were soon disappointed. The Prussians used their subsidies as much to plunder the territory of Poland as to secure the Low Countries. In April 1795, Prussia made peace and recognized the Republic.

The Dutch succumbed to a French invasion in the winter of 1795–96, emerging as a French satellite, the Batavian Republic. The

Spanish, tired of the war, were becoming alarmed at the growing naval supremacy of the British. They signed a peace treaty with France in July 1795. The following year, they joined France in the war on England.

These developments were quite discouraging for Britain, and several times between 1795 and 1797, Pitt tried to negotiate a satisfactory settlement with those French republicans with whom he had said that peace would probably not be secure. Not only did the French demand substantial restorations of British colonial conquests and refuse to concede what the British regarded as essential in the Netherlands, they were also intolerably arrogant. So the coalition continued, consisting of Britain and Austria alone now, until Bonaparte began the campaign in Italy which forced the Austrians to sign the Treaty of Campo Formio in October 1797.

France had, by this treaty, won the consent of all the powers on the Continent to her pretensions in European affairs. Then Bonaparte sailed for Egypt with an army. On the way there, he seized Malta. Meantime, France imposed more stringent control on the Dutch, extracted an alliance from her subjects in the Cisalpine Republic in northern Italy, intervened in central Italy to establish the Roman Republic, and brought Switzerland under French dominion in the Helvetian Republic. All of this occurred within nine months of Campo Formio. The French had conquered more territory more cheaply in time of ostensible peace than in time of war.

This series of provocations disturbed the Austrians and the Russians, and these two powers soon joined with the English to form the Second Coalition. Because one French army and its talented general were virtually sealed off in Egypt by the English fleet, the three allies had little trouble, in the campaign of 1799, in reversing their previous fortunes. The French armies were driven out of Italy, and plans for 1800 called for the invasion of France itself. It was in these circumstances that Britain and Austria received Bonaparte's appeal for peace.[3]

Pitt's response was now defiant, even contemptuous. It detailed the ravages of French armies in foreign countries and attributed the war to "the gigantic projects of ambition" and "the restless schemes of destruction" of the French Revolution. And it said flatly that England was now determined to make peace only after "the restoration of that line of princes which for so many centuries maintained the French nation in prosperity at home, and in consideration and respect abroad."[4]

THE AUSTRIAN RESPONSE to Bonaparte was the business of the chancellor, Baron Franz de Paula von Thugut. Thugut remains one of the most obscure of the leading personalities of that period. There is no biography of him. But obscurity has not protected his reputation, which was and is unenviable, to say the least.

His origins are very uncertain. He is variously said to have been from a family of peasants, cobblers, or weavers. His youth is a tissue of what the Germans call *Sagenbildung*, or myth-mongering. It is said that he was the youngest of five children who were left destitute by the death of their father-soldier and that Maria Theresa assumed the responsibility of caring for them. There is a story that she one day encountered him crawling on the stairs of the Hofburg and declared, "The name of this child [*Würmes*—also "worm"] shall be Thugut." The name, whether or not this is how he got it, seems to be a play on the German "thun gut"—"to do good." Another legend assigns him the name, "Thunichtgut"—"good-for-nothing."

Evidently, he was raised by Jesuits. In 1754, his talent having been recognized, he entered the newly established Oriental Academy, where he studied Turkish. Subsequently he entered the diplomatic service. In 1769 he was appointed ambassador to Turkey, where he served for seven or eight years. In 1780 he went for three years to Warsaw. He was assigned to Paris in 1783 and spent four years there, where he made the close acquaintance of Mirabeau.

In the meantime he became, as early as 1766, a clandestine agent of French diplomacy. He corresponded directly with Louis XV, and Louis was so pleased that he gave Thugut a pension of 13,000 livres per year and offered him, should Thugut's activities be discovered, an asylum in France. Thugut continued to serve the French until the death of Louis in 1774. All the while, his employers in Vienna remained as pleased with him as were those in Paris.[5]

In 1793, Thugut inadvertently profited from a considerable Austrian diplomatic setback. The venerable old Count Kaunitz, now senile, had just relinquished his political responsibilities to younger men. His successor, Phillip Cobenzl, allowed himself to be outmaneuvered by the Prussians, who left the Austrians out of the second partition of Poland. This was a real blow to their prestige. Cobenzl was retired, and Thugut was made general director of foreign affairs. The following year, he was appointed chancellor.

By this time, Austria was deeply involved in the Revolutionary Wars. Vienna publicly professed concern with two issues that had been provoked by the Revolution. The first was the threat to the French monarchy. An Austrian princess, Marie Antoinette, was queen of France. The second issue was probably the more important: the Revolution posed a threat to the German princes in the Rhineland. The archduke of Austria and king of Bohemia and Hungary was also the Holy Roman Emperor of the German Nation, and the protection of those princes was his responsibility.

Privately, the Austrian reaction to the Revolution was quite different. Austria approached the crisis in European affairs as a glutton approaches a buffet. Joseph II (d. 1790) read the omens of 1787–89 as being especially opportune. They fixed the attention of western Europe on France, partially paralyzing the powers with apprehension. Thus, Austria was freed for the pursuit of ambitious projects in the east. Joseph and Catherine II of Russia undertook their Turkish war of 1788 in greater security on that account. France, had it not been for the Revolution, would have opposed them. When the Turkish war began to go badly for Austria, the Revolution in the west began to appear, first, as a greater threat than it initially had and, second, as a greater opportunity. If the Revolution should weaken the French monarchy and nation without giving way to a government that would reverse the process, then Austria might have her way in western Europe more easily than she had been accustomed to having it. Vienna therefore sought to preserve the French monarchy in its crippled condition; she sought the opportunity of reconquering the two precious provinces that she had lost to Louis XIV, Alsace and Lorraine; and she sought to take advantage of the crisis as a happily unexpected chance to consummate her favorite territorial scheme—namely, the exchange of the Austrian Netherlands for the electorate of Bavaria. For Austria, the possession of the Netherlands was a burden. They had been assigned to Austria by the English in 1715 to serve as the outpost of a great land power and thereby prevent French expansion without jeopardizing English maritime interests. Bavaria, on the other hand, being contiguous to Habsburg territory, would be an invaluable asset to Austria.[6]

Thugut's own outlook was quite consonant with this somewhat sordid policy. Thugut hated both Prussia and the Jacobins. He sought the aggrandizement of Austria, and to the above list of desiderata, he added Venice. He proposed to make alliances with England and Russia in order to prosecute his policy. Thugut, who was extremely obstinate and persistent, was not well regarded by the foreign diplomats, either of Austria's allies or of her enemies. As the soul of the war party in Vienna, he was known as the "baron de guerre." Through all the vicissitudes of the wars—the partitions of Poland and the defections of the Prussians, the Dutch, and the Spanish from the coalition—he remained committed to his aims and to the English alliance. But when Bonaparte erupted into Italy and began to approach Vienna, the Austrians lost the will to continue. Thugut alone held firm. As Talleyrand reported to Bonaparte in the summer of 1797, Thugut alone stood in the way of peace. In the fall, even he caved in, but only under protest: "Peace, peace! Where is it? I do not see security in this treaty." The Treaty of Campo Formio was signed nevertheless.

The subsequent intervention of the French in Egypt, Malta, Holland, Switzerland, and Italy played into Thugut's hands, and the Second Coalition soon renewed the war and turned the tide. When Bonaparte's peace appeal of Christmas 1799 reached Vienna, the court was in no mood to treat with him.

His peace overtures having been rejected, Bonaparte was left with one obvious and one subtle alternative. The obvious one was to prepare for and to fight another campaign, which he did. The subtle one was more remote and more complicated. The Russians, it was noted in Paris, had begun to quarrel with their recent allies. The Austrians, pursuing territorial schemes of their own, had refused to restore Paul's favorite Italian princes in the liberated states. Soon afterwards, the English offended him over the rights of neutral trade. Perhaps the Russians, having deserted the coalition, might be charmed and maneuvered into the camp of the French?

2

THE PROBLEM

Whether the dispositions & wishes of the present french Government are so absolutely & universally pacific, as their professions indicate, may perhaps admit of a doubt, but a circumstance that entirely distinguishes the first Consul's policy from that of all his recent predecessors at the head of the french administration, is a desire not to be at War with all the world at once; of improving every opportunity to obtain peace with such enemies as France is least able to injure, and whose friendship is beyond all question more valuable to her, than the issue of any possible hostilities on her part against them could be. . . . Hence the address which has been used to effect a peace with Russia, to whom France has made every possible advance, insomuch as to offer a restoration without equivalent of all the prisoners taken in the campaign of 1799. . . . This has introduced a negotiation in which France has requested to know what further Russia required for peace.—John Quincy Adams

REVOLUTIONARY though he was, Bonaparte could not begin with a clean slate in an area as tradition-bound as foreign policy. His coming to power did not arrest the dynamics of the European state system. Behind him there was a long record of custom and convention, as well as obligation, which he could not suddenly slough off. The most pertinent aspect of the French diplomatic tradition in 1799 was that the very policy that Bonaparte sought to activate—France's Russian policy—was, and always had been, flawed in its foundation. The reasons are historical and psychological. Most simply, when modern French foreign policy was formulated, Russia was not a part of the European state system; and when the rise of Russia took place, at the beginning of the eighteenth century, thus drastically changing the balance of power, the French stubbornly refused to take the new situation into account.

Modern French foreign policy was a logical response to a specific crisis, which can be dated rather definitely. In 1519, as a result of a series of carefully planned dynastic marriages and the accidents of birth and inheritance that resulted from them, a single man, Charles V, suddenly fell heir to the enormous Habsburg empire. In a Europe where the modern nation-state was scarcely a generation old and the feudal fragmentation of power still seemed more natural, Charles inherited Spain, the New World, the German Empire, the Low Countries, and sizeable parts of Italy. A few years before, France had been roughly Spain's peer in political power. In 1519, France suddenly came to face the superpower of a supernational empire on her southern, eastern, and northern borders. As a consequence, she faced a mortal crisis.

France responded in two ways. First, she took advantage of the Lutheran Reformation in Germany by supporting the Protestant princes and thus trying to paralyze Charles's German Empire by fomenting civil war. Second, France looked for allies beyond the German borders. In the short run, France's most valuable allies were the Ottoman Turks. The Turks struck again and again in Hungary, thus diverting Habsburg forces away from both the Protestant princes and the French frontier. In the course of several generations, through many complications and vicissitudes, the French established the tradition of maintaining alliances with three major powers north and east of Germany—namely, Sweden, Poland, and Turkey. Though the harmony of these alliances was never complete and though there were significant defections from them, the tradition endured, and on the whole it worked.

By the middle of the seventeenth century, Spain was in decay. The Protestant princes of Germany, sustained by France and a powerful Lutheran Sweden, could hold their own against the Catholic powers of the German Empire. The Thirty Years' War, and the victory of France, Sweden, and the Protestants in the course of it, registered not only the success of French policy but also the eclipse of Spanish dominance in European affairs and the establishment of the hegemony of France in its place.

After 1648, France became the most dangerous threat to the European balance of power. Louis XIV (1643–1715) relentlessly pursued what he saw as his security and his enemies saw as the ruin of theirs. By 1713 a coalition of England, Holland, and the Germanies had contained the threat, and Louis's policy had exhausted France.

During all this time, Russia was, for France, entirely superfluous, a minor power rarely thought of, slumbering on the steppes somewhere east of Poland and therefore beyond the pale of civilization.

Then, suddenly, a revolution occurred, the Petrine revolution. The Romanov family had produced a prodigy. Peter I, who studied European models of technology and administration, worked desperately hard to transform his nation after the fashion of Europe, and he succeeded enough to make a decided impact on European politics and opinion.

Russians traveled in France, imported French tutors and actors, and soon made the French language their own preferred tongue. Paris was visited by Vorontsovs, Golitsyns, Shuvalovs, and other Russians who became famous not only for fighting each other and the populace but also for gambling and for chasing women. The French grew fond of them, and what they liked best in the Russians was their general gaiety and amiability and their tendency to lead a debauched and disordered life.

In more serious ways, also, the French image of Russia changed. Voltaire wrote his *History of Russia under Peter the Great*. Diderot, Alembert, and the brothers Grimm corresponded with Catherine II and served as her apologists in Europe, as did Voltaire. The philosophes and the public indulged one of their lovable banalities in finding in the Russians but one more example—along with American Indians, peripatetic Persians, and others—of the noble savage. If civilization corrupts and simplicity edifies, then the Russians were, for French sophisticates, a kind of Gulliver's travelogue come to life, and they provided the desired invidious comparisons with France's unenlightened despotism. The French had a willfully naïve and romanticized view of Russia as a land of simple people and good laws. The French intellectual community sold the French public its beatified "Russian mirage." Russia was à la mode, and Russomania was rampant.[1]

The reaction of the French Foreign Ministry to the Petrine revolution was just as extreme and just as foolish. But it was quite the opposite in nature.

Peter had embarked on a foreign policy of conquest and expansion, and the states that he most threatened were the three on the European border of Russia. He invaded Turkey, interfered in Poland, and defeated the Swedes. Thus, he had directly attacked one of the two fundamental pillars—divide the Germanies and ally with the borderlands—of French foreign policy. By forming a series of marriage alliances with German princes, he had at least meddled with the other.

At this decisive juncture, when the old balance of power was clearly foundering, Peter I, who not only had caused the reworking of the balance but recognized that he had, made the logical move. He went to Paris in 1717 and offered the French a sensational proposition. "Let me," he said, "supplant Sweden in your system." Russia had already supplanted Swedish hegemony in the Baltic. The decline of Turkey and Poland had also become evident. What Peter in effect was offering to do was to take the place of all three of these states in the French alliance system. In fact, Russia alone had the power to offer France a strong eastern European alliance in the eighteenth century. But the French knew that to accept Peter's proposition was to sacrifice their three former friends to the tender mercies of Russian imperialism; so they said no.

Whatever their reasons, whether the French were motivated by considerations of fidelity or whether they were simply too conventional to consider innovations, their refusal appears, in retrospect, to have been a tragic mistake. For the French no longer had the power, even had they had the will, to sustain the border states indefinitely against the growing might of Russia. That being the case, a Russian alliance would only have expedited the inevitable. But the refusal was a gratuitous sacrifice of French national interests. The French had the worst of it both ways: they succeeded neither in saving their clients nor in winning the support of Russia.

French diplomacy was spoiled for the remainder of the century. In the War of the Polish Succession (1733–35), Russia and France supported rival candidates for the Polish throne, and the Russian armies elected the Russian candidate. The lessons drawn from this experience began to produce a split personality in French foreign policy. Louis XV decided to try to woo Elizabeth I of Russia and the border states simultaneously and thus to mix incompatible elements. In the Seven Years' War (1756–63), France made a formal alliance with Russia against Prussia, and Russian armies thus had to operate in Poland, an experience that is sometimes fatal for the host country. Simultaneously, however, Louis put together a notorious device whose aim was to obstruct Russian influence in Poland and to confine Russia again to the wastelands of Asia. The French Foreign Ministry was unaware of the King's Secret, the name given to Louis's personal diplomatic secretariat. In attempting to do the impossible, the Secret naturally acquired an extremely low frustration threshold, and its agents reacted to the Russians with as much repugnance as the French public did with affection.

Louis instructed the baron de Breteuil in 1762: "The object of my policy in Russia is to remove her as far as possible from the affairs of Europe. Anything that can plunge her into chaos and make her return to obscurity is advantageous to my interests." According to the count de Broglie, another agent of the Secret, "The usefulness of liaisons with Russia is to prepare the means for annulling the dispositions of this power and of throwing her into an anarchy from which she will not be able to recover."[2]

Louis was asking the Russians to support him in the war against Prussia, but at the same time he was doing everything possible to damage all their interests. He wanted them to support the aims of France's foreign policy without offering them anything that would make their support profitable. This is a role that the Russians have never been known to play; so the Secret succumbed.

By the time of Catherine's second war with the Turks (1787), the French effort to protect their old allies from the Russians was reduced to giving advice to Turkey and Sweden not to get involved in a war with the Russians at all. Yet the influence that the French had by this time reflected their impotence, and the other two powers declared war on Russia together. Both of them lost. By 1789 the pursuit of irretrievable but expensive lost causes had contributed to and had aggravated the financial crisis that led to the French Revolution. By Bonaparte's time, Poland had been partitioned out of existence, Russia was playing a kind of satellite siren song in Sweden, similar to a familiar tune that it had played in Poland, and the poor Turk had acquired the unhappy status of "the sick man of Europe."

The envelopment of France in 1519 by Habsburg power has been described metaphorically as a vise, the two jaws of which—Spain and Germany—were designed to close on France. The metaphor is also useful for describing, in a summary fashion, the later evolution of the European alliance system. France reacted to her plight by erecting the same kind of vise around Habsburg Germany, the eastern jaw of which consisted of Sweden, Poland, and Turkey. When Peter the Great came along, he proposed that France make Russia the eastern jaw of the vise and that all of central and eastern Europe be enveloped in it. When France declined to take part in this scheme, an Austro-Russian device of the same kind was turned against the border states, and it did, figuratively, close on them. But the time would come when Peter's proposal would be taken up again, this time at the initiative of the French.

Russia at first reacted to the wars of the French Revolution by avoiding them. The almost universal involvement of the western and central European powers in these wars gave Russia for a time a virtually free hand in eastern Europe. As the wars dragged on, however, both sides sought to attract the support of Russian power, a power that might tilt the scales of the balance decisively. The coalition succeeded, temporarily, in 1799. In 1800 it was the turn of the French.

In the French Ministry of Exterior Relations, as it was then called, two different files were kept on each country with which France traditionally maintained relations. One of these, called the *Correspondance politique,* was simply a record of the diplomatic correspondence which passed between the two powers, official notes, instructions to ambassadors, and reports from them. The other, *Memoires et documents,* was something like an intelligence file. It was a motley collection, from the most diverse sources, of information on politics, the economy, the society—whatever seemed relevant about the condition of the foreign nation. It contained the impressions of seasoned experts, travelers, and crackpots alike. The two files were not always kept logically distinct or fastidiously organized. Catherine the Great had broken diplomatic relations with France when Louis XVI was executed in 1793, and there had been little activity with regard to Russia in *Correspondance politique* since that time. But *Memoires et documents* continued to collect fact and fantasy as before.

In the Russian volumes of these files, one idea dominates like an obsession. It is from a sensational document known to historians as "The Testament of Peter the Great," in which the father of modern Russia prescribed his scheme for conquering all of Europe:

1. Neglect nothing in order to give the Russian nation European forms and usages.

2. Maintain the state in a system of continual war in order to harden the soldier and militarize the nation.

3. Expand by all possible means around the Baltic and the Black seas.

4. Encourage the jealousy of England, Denmark, and Brandenburg against Sweden, and thus prepare Sweden for subjugation.

5. Engage the cooperation of the Austrians against the Turks so as to facilitate Russian expansion to Constantinople.

6. Encourage anarchy in Poland with the object of subjugating it.

7. Contract a close commercial alliance with the English, from whom Russian merchants and sailors can learn commercial and naval arts.

8. Conquer the Levant, in order to dispose exclusively of the commerce of the Indies and thus become the true sovereign of Europe.

9. Meddle at all cost, either by force or by ruse, in the quarrels of Europe, and especially in those of Germany.

10. Maintain an alliance with Austria, and engage her in ruinous wars to weaken her by degrees, meanwhile exciting against her the jealousy of the other princes of Germany.

11. Contract marriage alliances in Germany in order to gain influence there.

12. Use religious dissent to disrupt Poland and Turkey.

Finally, and most fantastically, he advised:

Prepare in secret . . . to strike the great blow. . . . Begin by

offering separately, very secretly and with the greatest circumspection, first to the court of Versailles, then to that of Vienna,
to share with one of them the empire of the universe. . . . This
project cannot fail to flatter them and to kindle between them
a fatal war that will soon become general, in view of the extensive alliances of these two rival courts, natural enemies, and
the interest that all the other powers of Europe will necessarily
take in this struggle.

In the midst of this general upheaval [*acharnement*], Russia
will be sought out by the belligerent powers for help . . . and
after having hesitated long enough to let them exhaust themselves and to assemble all her forces, she will decide finally for
the House of Austria, and while advancing her troops to the
Rhine, followed immediately by a swarm of Asiatic hordes
. . . , two large fleets will depart from Azov and Archangel,
bearing part of these same hordes. . . . They will appear un-
expectedly in the Mediterranean and on the ocean to discharge
these nomadic peoples, ferocious and greedy, and thus overrun
Italy, Spain, and France, some of whose inhabitants they will
massacre, some of whom they will enslave to repeople the
deserts of Siberia, and the rest of whom they will render unable
to shake off the yoke. All these diversions will then give complete latitude to the regular troops to move in full force and
with all possible assurance of conquering and subjugating the
rest of Europe.[3]

The ministry possessed at least four copies of this document. Three
of them were, appropriately enough, of Polish provenance. One was
identified simply as a copy made in Warsaw in 1794, though the original,
in Peter's own hand, was said to have been in the "special archives of
the Russian Emperors."[4] Another had a much more colorful history. In
1796, Catherine's lover and favorite—she was then sixty-seven—was a
young man of twenty-nine named Platon Zubov. Zubov, according to
annotations at the Quai d'Orsay, employed a Polish secretary named
Paradowski. Zubov was, in the fall of 1796, engaged in a careful study
of certain secret documents from the Russian archives. Allegedly, Paradowski's account of the contents of these archives was contained in
letters to his friend Sokolnicki. One day, Paradowski wrote, the prince
(Zubov) received some exciting news and rushed off to confer with the
empress. Paradowski took the opportunity to examine the papers on his
desk, and what he discovered there, of course, was the "Testament."
There was a "journal written in the hand of Leffort [*sic*], a confidant of
Catherine I," outlining "all the reveries of Peter I himself. . . . I was
not able to transcribe any of it for fear of being surprised; perhaps I

will find some more fortunate occasion for this." Which, naturally, he did.[5]

This is a most unlikely story. When have the Russians been so careless about state secrets? When have they failed to censor the mail of prominent foreigners amongst them? Francis Lefort, who died in 1699, was not one of the confidants of Catherine I, who did not accede to the throne until 1725; he was a confidant of Peter.

The third of the Polish versions is virtually unannotated. Dated 6 November 1797, it may be a derivative of the second. In an article that was long considered definitive, it was identified as the original French transcription of the "Testament."[6] But the 1797 version was the latest of the four, and the author of this article used suspiciously vague evidence, identified only as "family papers" in Warsaw, to attribute the "Testament" to one of his ancestors, General Michel Sokolnicki (1760–1816), an officer in the Polish legions of the French army. His solution to the problem of authorship is almost certainly wrong.

The earliest copy of the "Testament," and thus the one which might well have spawned all the others, is attributed to a character who is as intriguing as the document itself. The Chevalier d'Eon de Beaumont was a man of many facets—if in fact he was a man. He held a doctorate in civil and canonical law and left thirteen volumes of published writings. Scholar, lawyer, diplomat, and spy, he was also one of the most notorious transvestites of the eighteenth century. A contemporary drawing shows him, dressed in women's clothes, fighting a duel with swords in London; and he sometimes signed his name Mademoiselle d'Eon.

D'Eon was secretary of the French embassy in St. Petersburg from 1757 to 1760, and the last version of the document which we have to consider bears these annotations: "1725. Copy of the plan of European domination, left by Peter the Great to his successors to the throne of Russia, and deposited in the archives of the Palace of Peterhoff near St. Petersburg. . . . Nota. This piece was copied at Peterhoff by the Chevalier d'Eon de Beaumont and delivered by him to the Duke de Choiseul in 1760."[7] This document was later published in d'Eon's memoirs, and the most authoritative research suggests that he was responsible for introducing it into the French Foreign Ministry.[8]

It was in about 1759 or 1760 that d'Eon presumably supplied the "Testament" to the duke de Choiseul. It was soon reflected in the duke's correspondence. In 1760 we find him explaining to his newly appointed ambassador in St. Petersburg: "It was only in 1759 that the political system of the court of Petersburg began to be unraveled [demeler]. . . . the court of Petersburg has long had a well formed political plan [un plan de politique tout formé], from which it never deviates, . . . but which it develops only gradually and as events and circumstances furnish the occasion; . . . its distrustful and suspicious ministers join to the dissimulation natural to their nation the most methodical approach [*suite*]."⁹ The count de Broglie, champion of Louis XV's Secret, sounded similar alarms during Catherine's first war with the Turks:

> It cannot be denied that Russia will conclude this war in the most glorious manner, and that she will fulfill . . . almost all the projects of Peter the Great. The fruits that she will get from it are: the guarantee of commerce on the Black Sea; the independence of the Crimea [from the Turks]; Moldavia, and Wallachia, under her protection; the raising of revolt and of fanaticism disseminated among the Greek subjects of the Turkish Empire; also among those of this religion in Austrian territories; the submission of the Tatars; consequently the limits of the [Turkish] Empire thrown back, the borders of new Serbia become superfluous, and the troops that guard them free to act elsewhere; the submission of the Polish Ukraine, providing a supply post for war on the Danube and in Poland; the Cossack civilization . . . will furnish more good troops; the remounting of all her cavalry; an easy subsistence, and a despotic influence over Poland. In such a position, one may expect that she will be constantly ready to recommence [the war] with advantage, either to deliver the last blows to Turkey [or] to attack the court of Vienna.¹⁰

A year later, Broglie warned again:

> The crude but sublime genius of Peter I gave birth to the project, unknown to his predecessors, of taking his place among the great powers of Europe, and by virtue . . . of a strong and decided will, when he did not lack means and knew how to profit by them, he soon reached this great and glorious objective
> . . . . and as he would give the law to the North, so he would seek to do with all the rest of Europe.
> The Tsar had divined or learned from the Genevan Lefort what he then erected into a dogmatic system, dressed up in a mysterious jargon. . . . Power has passed to other hands; it has always remained the same [*sic*].¹¹

The old regime in France rested its understanding of Russian foreign policy on the "Testament," and this assessment no doubt contributed to the decided repugnance which French statesmen felt for Russia. Perhaps Bonaparte's government would take a different view.

THERE IS an ironic, almost star-crossed quality about the constellation of

17

personalities in Bonaparte's Foreign Office and the conformity of their attitudes toward the bogey of Russia in the eastern question.

Bonaparte himself was well known for his oriental predilections. Idle in 1795, he applied for an appointment as military attaché in Constantinople, but the French government thought that the appointment would waste his talent. Having conquered Italy in 1797, he became obsessed with French acquisition of Malta and the Ionian Islands, which would make excellent bases for operations in the eastern Mediterranean. In January 1798, in Paris, he allegedly daydreamed aloud, in a comment that is crucial to the Napoleonic legend: "I do not want to remain here, there is nothing to do. . . . I see that if I stay here, I will soon be forgotten. . . . I no longer have any glory; this little Europe does not provide enough of it. It is necessary to go to the Orient; all great glory comes from there. However, I want first to make a tour of the coast, to assure myself of what can be undertaken. . . . If the success of the descent on England seems to me doubtful, as I fear, the Army of England will become the Army of Egypt, and I am going to Egypt."[12] And so, capturing Malta on the way, he went off to Egypt on a mad campaign which he managed to misrepresent as a brilliant success.

One of France's most distinguished historians, Emile Bourgeois, interpreted Bonaparte's foreign policy entirely as the pursuit of empire at Constantinople.[13] Another, Edouard Driault, conceived Bonaparte to be in relentless pursuit of the reconstruction of the Roman Empire, eastern as well as western.[14] Not all the facts are consonant with such simplistic explanations of his complex policy, but no one doubts that the idea of eastern empire fascinated him and exercised a romantic compulsion over his mind.[15] The whole Ottoman heritage was, of course, of critical interest to the Russians, and whatever Bonaparte undertook there had to be done either in cooperation with them or in opposition to them.

The most formidable, or at least the most durable, figure in this story is also the most notorious—and deservedly so: Talleyrand. To students of European history, he is the prince of scoundrels. The pliable facility of his loyalty is legendary. His first career was that of bishop. Yet, early in the Revolution, he helped to mastermind the dispossession of the French Church. When revolutionary affairs became dangerous for him, he discreetly spent two years in New York, Philadelphia, and Boston, where he earned a living by selling real estate to other émigrés seeking refuge from the Revolution. Favored by a change of regime in France, he returned home to become minister of foreign affairs. He threw a big party to celebrate his appointment and, when asked what his foreign policy would be, announced candidly, "To make an enormous fortune." He did, taking twelve million francs in bribes within three months.

Talleyrand was a great rake. Neither a lame leg nor vows of celibacy embarrassed him. He had a sensational love life and a commanding presence among men as well as women. Reportedly lazy, he rarely drafted a document himself. His motto was "Above all, no enthusiasm."

He was also a great cynic. His beliefs reflect his deeds, or vice versa. "The only good principle," he said, "is to have none." Yet, he has been accused—uncomfortably, he might feel—of being a good, circumspect internationalist, whose moderation contrasts favorably with Bonaparte's megalomania.[16] Talleyrand paraded low principles as Bonaparte paraded high ones; yet he acquired the reputation of being an Anglophile.

Talleyrand was one of the kingmakers behind Bonaparte. The plot was laid at Talleyrand's house. Still, there is an ironic ambivalence, a quality of limited liability, about their relationship throughout. Their first common enterprise was the Egyptian campaign. Talleyrand wrote what might be called the policy paper on the scheme, arguing the virtues of colonies. He then read it to the French Institute and recommended it to Bonaparte. Bonaparte was ready immediately, and together they convinced the Directory. In spite of the failure of the campaign, Bonaparte used his correspondence to represent the adventure as a triumph. Fortunately for him, news of one of the few auspicious developments in the campaign—the defeat of the Turks at Aboukir—arrived in Paris at about the time he returned there. Yet, there is every reason that the expedition should have been a disaster. The very launching of it depended on the French navy, and that involved challenging the English where they were strongest. In fact, the French fleet played hide-and-seek with the English fleet all the way through the Mediterranean. They were almost within sight of each other several times. Nelson would have certainly found Bonaparte had the English frigates not been lost in a storm, and only the unlikeliest of accidents spared the French as it was. Once it had arrived in Egypt, the French fleet, Bonaparte's only communication with France, became a sitting duck, as Nelson showed in the Battle of the Nile, in which it was destroyed on 1 August 1798.[17]

Why should Talleyrand have promoted this kind of risk for his friend and benefactor? There is only one glimpse of documentary evidence regarding his motives. A note written by his mistress, Madame Grand, explained that he wanted thus "to favor his English friends."[18] By delivering to them a French army with an annoyingly ambitious commander?

Talleyrand probably first heard of a French project to conquer Egypt from the duke de Choiseul, France's foreign minister from 1758 to 1770. Choiseul certainly favored it, and Talleyrand was often a guest at his home, Chanteloup. It was there also that Talleyrand made the acquaintance of one of his subsequent colleagues at the Quai d'Orsay, Alexandre d'Hauterive.

Hauterive, like Talleyrand, shared the duke's consuming interest in the eastern question. In 1784, when Choiseul's nephew, the count de Choiseul-Gouffier, was appointed ambassador to the Porte, Hauterive traveled with him. Choiseul-Gouffier was to become a distinguished orientalist, and Hauterive had the rare privilege in 1785 of serving as secretary to the hospodar of Wallachia and thus seeing the politics of the eastern question from the inside. When he returned, revolutionary politics chased him, too, off to America, where he saw Talleyrand again. In 1798 he followed Talleyrand back to Paris, and in 1799 he became chief of the Second Division of the French Foreign Ministry (Northern Europe).[19]

Talleyrand and Hauterive were to a great extent students of the policy and the views of Choiseul. They, like Bonaparte, had an extraordinary interest in Ottoman affairs, but unlike him, they were both ardent Russophobes. In 1768, Choiseul had commissioned a special study of the political crisis in Poland. The man who produced the work, *History of the Anarchy in Poland,* was Claude-Carloman de Rulhière. He was much influenced by Jean-Louis Favier, one of the theoreticians behind Louis's Secret. Talleyrand was much impressed by the work, which he read in manuscript in 1783. He wrote to Rulhière one of the rare letters that survive in his own hand, a long letter, in which he commented in detail on the manuscript. Finally, he requested that he be sent a copy of the book when it was published.[20] The attitudes of Talleyrand and Hauterive toward Russia were quite traditional and thus consonant with the outlook of the "Testament."

Though as we have seen, Peter's "Testament" was probably introduced to the French Foreign Ministry around 1760, three of the four copies of the document are dated during the period of the French Revolution. It was Bonaparte who first published the "Testament"—a curious coincidence—in 1812, on the eve of the Russian campaign.[21] During the Consulate and the Empire, both the ideas and the phrases of the "Testament" circulated rather freely. Bonaparte once described the Russians, in reference to Poland and Turkey, as "a swarm of fanatics and barbarians."[22] Talleyrand described Russian policy similarly: "The entire system constantly followed since Peter I, regardless of the princes that occupy the throne, tends to crush Europe anew under a flood of barbarians."[23] In the opinion of Hauterive,

> Russia in time of war seeks to conquer her neighbors; in time of peace she seeks to keep not only her neighbors but all the countries of the world in a confusion of mistrust, agitation, and discord. . . . When one sees in history a certain uniformity of events in different epochs, one may be sure that this uniformity depends upon invariable causes. . . . if the estrangement and the bewilderment that deranges the conduct of the cabinets today should lead them to an irremediable state of dissension and result in the progressive degradation of the character and power of the governments, then the greatest reproach which future nations will make to us will be that we did not apply all our foresight and did not direct all our efforts to stopping the progress of Russia. . . .
>
> All that this power has usurped in Europe and Asia is well known.
>
> She tries to destroy the Ottoman Empire; she tries to destroy the German Empire.
>
> Russia will not proceed directly to her goal . . . ; she will not attack Constantinople; but she will in an underhanded manner undermine the bases of this decrepit empire; she will foment intrigues; she will promote rebellion in the provinces. . . . In so doing, she will not cease to profess the most benevolent sentiments for the Sublime Porte; she will constantly call herself the friend, the protectress of the Ottoman Empire.
>
> Russia will not attack openly the house of Austria. . . . She will take possession of Moldavia and of Wallachia. . . . [her] influence will soon allow her to take possession of Serbia. . . . Then there will be no more court of Vienna: then we, the western nations, we will have lost one of the barriers [that is] most capable of defending us against the incursions of Russia.[24]

Finally, if these comments show only the circulation, almost omnipresence, in the French Foreign Ministry of ideas that are common to the "Testament," there is one bit of evidence showing a more direct connection. In March 1812, the year in which the "Testament" was first published, Hauterive himself wrote a note of about two pages on one version of the "Testament" to explain that it was "a very curious manuscript of Peter the Great, that seemed to have been preserved in the cabinet of his successors as a kind of Gospel of the policy that was prescribed for them to follow."[25] Bonaparte's diplomats, then, knew the "Testament" as well as their predecessors had, and this explained, to their satisfaction, Russia's participation in the Second Coalition.

21

According to this view, Russia's entry into the war against France would have been provoked by Bonaparte's encroachments on the Ottoman Empire. In 1797 he conquered the Ionian Islands, lying off the coast of Greece. In June 1798 he captured the island of Malta from the sovereign Order of the Knights of St. John of Jerusalem. Paul I of Russia considered himself their protector, and he was deeply offended.

The Knights, an ancient nursing order of the church (often called the Knights Hospitalers), had been founded in Jerusalem during the First Crusade. In the late Middle Ages they became a military mainstay against the advance of the Turks in the Mediterranean. In 1523 they were driven off the island of Rhodes by Sultan Suleiman the Magnificent, whereupon Charles V made them a gift of Malta, an island of strategic importance. Though renowned for their stubborn defense against sieges —having turned back Suleiman's much superior force, for instance, in 1565—they succumbed to Bonaparte's attack in 1798 with suspiciously little resistance, and their grand master was widely accused of treason. The Knights were down on their luck and in need of a vigorous and powerful benefactor. So the formerly Polish, now Russian, division of the order undertook, on its own authority, to elect Paul as grand master. There was naturally much dispute about the legitimacy of this proceeding, since only a fraction of the order had done the electing and since the prince chosen was not Catholic. Paul, however, was flattered, and he accepted the honor.[26]

Malta was merely a stepping stone in Bonaparte's larger scheme. His landing in Egypt so alarmed both the Turks and the Russians that they buried their traditional enmity and astonished the world by forming—for the only time in their history—a military alliance. From October 1798 to March 1799 they drove the French out of the Ionians, and Russia became the backbone of the Second Coalition.

In France, Russia's policy was understood as an effort to preserve the Ottoman Empire as an exclusively Russian prey. Talleyrand wrote that Paul was following the system of his mother, Catherine II, which proved, Talleyrand argued, "that in the midst of the palace revolutions that have so frequently taken place in Russia, the fate of the empire seems to be to return constantly to the system of policy and aggrandizement that dates from the reign of Peter I."[27]

Clearly, Talleyrand and Hauterive held traditionally Russophobic views of Peter's "Testament." How, then, did their government swallow its distaste in order to initiate a rapprochement with the Russians? The answer to this question was provided by a canny Frenchman who had been thinking similar thoughts himself: How could France turn to her own advantage the policy of a power whose aims were what Peter's aims allegedly were?

MONSIEUR GUTTIN was a very obscure character—not even his given name is known. He is not listed in French biographical dictionaries. The correspondence from the Russian files of the French Foreign Ministry and a few notes from the National Archives provide the only sources of information about him; and they tell very little, simply that he had been an "inspector of manufactures" in Russia for twelve or fourteen years and had then returned to France in 1796.[28] What he was doing in 1797 and 1798 is not apparent. But about the beginning of 1799, he started to besiege the ministry with memorandums.[29] The nature and number of his proposals and the frequency with which they contradict and cancel out each other suggest that because he suddenly found himself unemployed, he sought to turn to advantage what was perhaps his only distinction—his knowledge of Russia and of the Russian language.

At first he dabbled in an armchair variety of grand politics, recommending to the ministry more or less simultaneously, though presumably alternatively, the promotion of revolution in Russia, the invasion of Russia's weakly held southwestern provinces, and a Franco-Russian alliance based on the partition of the Ottoman Empire.[30]

When these proposals were not well received, he advanced more modest ones. In France there were about six thousand Russian prisoners of war who had been taken in the campaign of 1799. Guttin offered his services to the government: he would indoctrinate these prisoners in revolutionary ideas, and they could then be released, well supplied with propaganda, among the Russian armies in Europe. The aim of the program would be to ruin morale and provoke desertions.[31] A little later, he was ready to employ the Russians to cut timber for the French navy.[32] Scattered correspondence indicates that these two proposals were entertained seriously for some time. Unhappily for Guttin, both were eventually turned down. He wrote an angry letter to Talleyrand; he was especially indignant because, as he put it, "I have not received anything, either for the state, or for myself."[33] He wrote to Bonaparte to complain about Talleyrand's conduct. He had been, he alleged, commissioned by Talleyrand to draw up and distribute propaganda among the Russian armies in Italy. When the Russian victories preempted the plan, Talleyrand had urged him to preserve his proclamations for future use, and now he wanted to be reimbursed for his expenses.[34] Apparently,

Bonaparte did not reply. The government must have regarded Guttin as something of a pest.

In the meantime, to complicate his situation further, Guttin had angered the Russian prisoners. He had visited them several times and perhaps had promised them too much. One of them, a certain Lewontoski, wrote to threaten him, in labored French, with legal action: "You promised us employment. . . . You says that you're more victim than we since you haven't received a cent. . . . Your bad luck doesn't make our good luck they have advised us to complain against you to the minister we will do it if you don't do us justice. Fraternal greetings."[35]

All of this business was as transient as it was comic. But one of Guttin's ideas endured, because it articulated, with sharp definition, ideas that, in a little less definite form, circulated freely in the auspicious atmosphere of the Foreign Ministry and because it was soon to be blessed by a happy coincidence of political accidents. There are at least nine different versions of this memorandum in the French archives. One is from 1796, one is from 1800 or 1801 (Revolutionary calendar, year 9), and one is from 1804; but most of them were done in 1799.[36] Some are short; some are long; several are crude and hasty. Two of them are methodical, well developed, and prophetic. "The objective of the ideas that we submit in brief to the government is to obtain for France a prompt, solid, and advantageous peace. . . . It is undoubtedly not necessary to prove in detail how defective the system that has been followed until now is: it has only served to alarm the powers, who have looked on the French republic as the enemy of all the old governments." France's neighbors were not prepared for a real reconciliation. They had grown habitually suspicious of the Republic. "Let us then look farther away and seek the alliance of a great power, which, by its geographical situation, believes itself to be, and may actually be, safe from our armies and our principles. . . . Russia is incontestably in this position . . . ; her alliance is the only one that might lead the French government to the end that it must desire, to a durable, advantageous, and stable peace." Guttin averred that Peter I coveted the Black Sea "up to the canal of Constantinople. It is this same ambition that animates the Russian nation today and that determined Paul I to enter the coalition."

Guttin proposed to tempt the Russians to forsake the coalition and to join France by offering to satisfy the ancient ambitions of Peter I, if Russia would share the spoils with France. These two powers, united, would dictate the law to all of Europe. The Turks would be expelled from the Balkans. Decrepit as they were, they would be unable to resist. Russia's share of the spoils might be European Turkey "up to the left side [côte gauche] of the Dardanelles and the Bosphorus; but France would reserve to herself, on the opposite side of the straits, enough territory to assure her of the exclusive commerce of the Black Sea." The Russians would also be offered some coveted but unspecified islands in the Mediterranean to serve as their commercial outposts. France would keep her frontiers of the Rhine, the Alps, and the Pyrenees. "The Republic, supported by the Russians and established in Egypt, would take possession of the great islands of the Archipelago [the Ionians]. Russia, from her possessions in Asia and on the Caspian Sea, could assist the [French] army in Egypt and, in concert with France, carry the war into India."

The one possible sacrifice for Russia—and not only for Russia—which Guttin proposed to ask for in exchange for all these rich gains was the resurrection of Poland. Grand Duke Constantine, the second son of Paul I, was envisaged as king of Poland, under a special constitutional provision that would prevent any union with the Russian Empire. Thus, "the influence of Russia would be no more to be feared in Poland than was that of France in Spain after the War of the [Spanish] Succession."

As for the other powers of Europe, Holland, Switzerland, and Italy were to keep the republican satellite status that France had given to them. Austria was to be dispossessed of Poland, what she retained of Silesia, and Italy and was to be compensated modestly by some unspecified Turkish provinces. Prussia—for reasons that soon will be apparent—was to get generous treatment, including the right to annex Austrian Silesia and the north-German coastal territories of Bremen, Hanover, Mecklenburg, and Lübeck. Finally, French and Russian domination of the Balkans, Egypt, and the Mediterranean islands, in addition to Prussian acquisition of most of the northern European port towns, would put an end to England's naval supremacy, at least in European waters, and would permit the navies of France, Russia, Holland, and Spain to cooperate in an invasion of England.

Guttin was confident of the Russians' reaction: "One must suppose the Russians to be stupid (which they are not) to refuse such propositions."[37] Essentially, what he proposed was that France offer the Russians a truncated version of the "Testament" or a highly elaborated version of what Peter had proposed to Paris in 1717. There was one epic addendum: the attempt to break the English stranglehold on the seas by coalescing all the maritime powers of the Continent against her. This would be a French initiative to squeeze all of central Europe in a Franco-Russian vise, thereby placing England at the mercy of the whole Continent, leagued together.

Talleyrand reacted to this scheme with his accustomed cold sobriety and Russophobia. He observed that the plan dwelled almost entirely on results, "without indicating any means of execution." He spoke of the insurmountable obstacles that such an enterprise would encounter, especially when one recalled that "Paul's hatred for the Republic has reached such extravagance and seems to exclude all possibility not only of reconciliation but even of communication." As for the restoration of Poland under Constantine: "What a fate for poor Poland, to be delivered to the despotism of a Russian monarch." In such an event, no conceivable treaty clause could prevent Russia from annexing it. Furthermore, Russia would not take part in Guttin's concept of a partition of the Ottoman Empire, because she would not wish to share with France what she wanted entirely for herself; and the current conjuncture of politics would be in favor of Russia's choosing Austria for such an enterprise anyway. On French acquisition of Mediterranean islands: fifty ships of the line would be better than Russian collaboration. Paul would not consent to the republicanization of Italy: Guttin did not seem to understand that Paul was the declared enemy of republics. Talleyrand elaborated:

> An alliance with Russia such as is described here is impossible. . . . and if it were possible, there is no good that could come of it. How could one wish that the republican government of France and the absurd despotism of Russia might unite to govern Europe! There is no community of views and of interests between them. . . . The Republic, in allying with Russia, would encourage [barbarian] invasions . . . , and the country of the enlightenment would become the accomplice of the triumph of ignorance.
>
> If we must negotiate with Russia, it would be to arrest her undertakings, not to serve them.[38]

In brief, Talleyrand advised the government that the project was neither feasible nor desirable. But, for once, Talleyrand guessed wrongly. For the feasibility of the project was transformed when the coalition that had looked so formidable in the summer of 1799 began to disintegrate in the fall. And as for desirability, Guttin was to have the last laugh.

THE FIRST and fastest fissure in the coalition was between Russia and Austria. Paul's motives in joining the coalition had been fervently conservative. After the Franco-Russian armies had driven the French out of Italy, Paul naturally expected that the legitimate princes there would be restored, especially the grand duke of Tuscany and the king of

Sardinia. But Vienna refused to do so. The Austrians also declined to carry the campaign to France, as they had formerly agreed to do, preferring instead to pursue their territorial designs in Italy. Paul felt betrayed. He wrote to Emperor Francis that he refused to sacrifice Russian soldiers for the aggrandizement of Austria; thereupon he recalled his army.[39]

The reasons for the Anglo-Russian break are not nearly so tangible and clear. In the diplomatic correspondence there are no substantial disagreements whatever.[40] Paul was admittedly disappointed by the failure of their joint campaign in the Low Countries (August–October 1799). The Russians blamed the English, and vice versa. But that did not cause the break between them; for the Russian troops wintered in the Channel Islands, awaiting new instructions. In the meantime, Paul took offense at the conduct of Whitworth, the English ambassador in St. Petersburg, with what justice it is hard to say. The Russians had surreptitiously procured the key to the code that Whitworth used in his diplomatic correspondence; hence they were able to read his most private opinions. Whitworth himself thought that his warm support of Austria, which was in disfavor in St. Petersburg, contributed to his own fall from favor.[41]

In fact, the Anglo-Russian break was probably not Whitworth's fault but was the result of indirect causes. The English were simply faced with the problem of choosing between their two allies, Russia and Austria, and the choice that they made—a natural choice, almost a necessary one—reflects considerations, not of the relative merits of those allies, but of English interests. The English understood quite well where the merits of the case lay and on whose side justice was to be found. Their ambassador in Vienna warned that the whole object of the Austrians was to take for themselves the conquests that the French had made in Italy.[42] But justice was not their sole concern. Any consideration of self-interest or of the relative reliability, not to mention durability, of the two sovereigns and cabinets concerned—for example, the simple fact that Austria could not disengage from the French armies at a whim, as Russia could do, and had done—militated in favor of Britain's choosing Austria. So long as the Prussians remained neutral (as they did, stubbornly, from 1795 to 1806), it was only in the Habsburg quarter of Europe that large Russian armies could operate effectively, not in the Low Countries and the Channel Islands. When Paul withdrew his support from the Austrians, he thereby forfeited his usefulness to the English and thus made their choice inevitable. Once the choice was recognized, Paul's reaction was equally inevitable and ugly. Deceived by Austria, he now found himself deserted by England, and quite without provocation on his part. The development of the crisis after this point was the function of a quality with which Paul was richly endowed: a vindictiveness encouraged by self-righteousness and ferocious suspicion. In February 1800, Paul asked the British to recall Whitworth, and in June he ordered his own ambassador in London to retire from the post.[43]

Talleyrand registered the dissension in the coalition immediately, and his reaction made a travesty of his previous critique of Guttin. Our first glimpse of his change of mind was occasioned by an inquiry from Bonaparte; for it was at about this time that England and Austria rejected Bonaparte's peace proposals. The First Consul, disappointed, asked Talleyrand about the prospects of help from other quarters: "What advantage would it be possible to draw from Prussia in order to hasten the general peace . . . ? And to decide her to place herself at the head of the Northern League, which would curb the excessive ambition of Russia?"[44]

It is surprising to find in Bonaparte such an amateurish outlook and such a garbled understanding of recent history. The Northern League to which he referred was the League of Armed Neutrality of 1780. It was headed, not by Prussia, but by Russia; and the excessive ambition that it curbed was not Russia's but England's, specifically her abuse of the rights of neutral trade. Bonaparte's note reveals not only a complete misunderstanding of the events of 1780 but also a remarkable ignorance of Russian politics. He apparently had no ideas of his own about the mysterious nation that was to have such a decisive part in his future.

Talleyrand's response put the matter into much more practiced perspective. For five years, France had been seeking Prussian diplomatic intervention in vain. "The policy of the Prussian court, consists entirely in this: that it sees with pleasure the continuation of a war from which it stands aside, and that it [seeks] the advantages . . . which it promises itself from the mutual exhaustion of the great powers which surround it." Talleyrand saw more cause for hope in another capital. "I cite Petersburg," he continued, "and on this subject I must submit to the First Consul some important observations. . . . Until now, the possibility of entering into direct negotiations with Russia has been completely missed; no attempt has been made [for several years]. . . . Undoubtedly the difficulty is great, but the benefit would be substantial."[45] Talleyrand, then, undertook to tutor Bonaparte in the Republic's Russian policy. Signs of the collapse of the coalition soon became unmistakable, and the interest with which Bonaparte followed them shows how quickly he responded to Talleyrand's lead.

On March 30 he noted that reports from Germany suggested that there had been a conclusive break between Russia and the coalition powers. On April 4 he observed that the Russian troops on the Channel Islands had embarked, apparently for home.[46] At the beginning of May, Bonaparte left Paris for the Marengo campaign, and Talleyrand's reports to him were full of news of the Russians. In Berlin the Russian ambassador gave a dinner to which the English and Austrian ministers were not invited. There was similar news from Copenhagen. "Everything confirms that the policy of Russia is taking a new direction," Talleyrand reported. "The discontent of Russia with Austria and England seems to be at its highest point."[47] A bulletin from St. Petersburg reported that Paul had openly rejoiced over Bonaparte's victory at Marengo, saying: "See what a drubbing they give the Austrians in Italy now that the Russians are no longer there."[48] After he had returned to Paris, Bonaparte gave news from Russia his closest attention: "I see in the *Hamburg Gazette*, Citizen Minister [Talleyrand], the ukase of Paul I," which curtails English trade. Why, he asked, had the French chargé d'affaires in Hamburg failed to report it? "I beg you to express to him my dissatisfaction and to tell him that measures of this kind that are taken in Russia must be communicated to you by special couriers."[49]

As the evidence accumulated, it was matched by minute observation and fervent hope. The quarrels of his enemies were Bonaparte's opportunity. And, in his own words, "the First Consul neglected nothing to make these seeds of discontent germinate."[50]

3

THE STRATAGEM

A strange fact of this epoch is the incredible accord in the acts of Paul and those of the first consul in one single sense, in one single end, although the state of war continued to exist between Russia and France.—Louis Pierre Bignon, *Histoire de France*

To ENTER INTO direct negotiations with St. Petersburg, as Talleyrand proposed to do, was by no means easy. There were no diplomatic relations between the nations, and they remained technically at war. As Prussia maintained a timorous neutrality throughout these years, Berlin was the one capital of Europe where all the belligerents kept diplomatic representatives. Hence it served as a kind of diplomatic clearing house, and it was natural that Talleyrand should first consider approaching the Russians through the medium of the Prussians.

On March 2, Talleyrand appealed to the Prussian ambassador, Sandoz-Rollin: "We ask neither an army nor an alliance of the King of Prussia; we only ask of him that he employ his good offices to reconcile us with Russia. . . . But time presses, and I cannot repeat it to you enough. . . . Military operations will in fact begin in Germany the 15th or 20th of this month." A few days later, Bonaparte made the same kind of appeal to Sandoz-Rollin, and the Russian negotiation became a common topic of conversation between the two powers that spring.[1]

The Prussians informed the Russians. The Russian response was cryptic and ambivalent. The process of communication was slow, and the Prussians did not expedite it or encourage the reconciliation. So the Marengo campaign intervened and interrupted the negotiations.[2]

By the end of May the French knew that the approach through Berlin had failed, and Bonaparte was growing impatient. In June he urged Talleyrand to consider other, less conventional measures: "It is necessary to give Paul some proof of our esteem, to let him know that we want to negotiate with him. . . . I leave it to your discretion whether or not it would be suitable for our chargé d'affaires in Hamburg or some other town to make general and flattering overtures to Paul." More specifically, Bonaparte suggested: "It [is] important to have someone in Russia. The Ottoman Empire has not long to live, and if Paul I sees it this way, then our interests become common." Finally, Talleyrand was ordered "to get hold of a party and to have an agent at Petersburg," something that Bonaparte considered to be absolutely necessary. Talleyrand responded that he would do everything possible with respect to Russia.[3]

Talleyrand then undertook several of the kind of gestures that diplomats customarily call overtures. The presence of the Russian prisoners in France provided an excellent opportunity, and on July 19, Talleyrand wrote to Count Nikita P. Panin, Russia's vice-chancellor, in his best bombast:

> Monsieur le comte, the First Consul of the French Republic has taken note of all the circumstances of the campaign which preceded his return to Europe [from Egypt, in October 1799]. He knows that it is to the cooperation of the Russian troops that the English and Austrians owed their success, and as he holds nothing dearer than to express his esteem for brave soldiers, he had been eager to propose to the commissars charged by England and Austria with the exchange of prisoners that the Russians who were in France might be included in this exchange and might also receive some preference by reason of their being less acclimated to this country, the habitation being perhaps more injurious to them.
>
> This proposition, however, although so natural and several times repeated, has expired without effect. The English in particular, who cannot conceal from themselves that it is to the Russians that they owe their first successes in Batavia, as well as the fruits of them, which they alone have enjoyed, and the security of their retreat (because without the Russians, not an Englishman would have been able to reembark), though having in their possession at this moment eight thousand French prisoners, have not shown themselves disposed to effect this exchange of the Russians.
>
> Struck by this injustice and not wanting to leave in long detention such brave troops, whom perfidious allies have first compromised and then abandoned, the First Consul has ordered that all the Russian prisoners in France, about six thousand in number, be returned to Russia without exchange and with all the honors of war. To this end they will be reclothed and rearmed, and their standards will be returned to them.
>
> The intention of the First Consul is only to show in this

fashion, above all, his esteem for the Russian armies and his desire to do something which may be agreeable to His Imperial Russian Majesty.[4]

One copy of the letter was sent through the diplomats of the two countries in Hamburg. Another was carried by one of the Russian prisoners to the Russian ambassador in Berlin.

Next, Talleyrand, at Bonaparte's suggestion, offered to surrender the island of Malta to Paul.[5] The offer was cheap enough, since the French garrison was on the point of capitulating to the English siege. According to the memoirs of both Bonaparte and Talleyrand, they "found the means"—Bonaparte's phrase—of sending Paul the sword of La Valette, the most distinguished of the grand masters of the Knights of Malta.[6] Finally, Bonaparte invited several Russian officers to visit him, paraded his generosity to them, and when two of them wrote to thank him, published their letter in the government newspaper, *Le Moniteur*.[7]

In the meantime, Talleyrand began a frantic search for spies at the Russian court. As early as January or February he had written to his old friend the count de Choiseul-Gouffier to see if he would use his alleged influence at St. Petersburg in favor of France. By April, Talleyrand was corresponding with the Spanish about sending a Swedish agent to Russia. In June he had disappointing news from Choiseul-Gouffier, who, although he was glad to serve France, had fallen into disgrace. But the reprisals of the Revolution had chased plenty of impecunious French émigrés to St. Petersburg; and since Talleyrand had said that only émigrés could be employed in this regard, he did not give up after his initial failure.[8]

It was rumored that a French agent had been found in the person of the Jesuit Father Gruber, a favorite of Paul's. This story is credited in Jesuit accounts. Paul's popish sympathies are beyond doubt, as is the favor that Father Gruber enjoyed. Even Gustavus Adolphus of Sweden was careful to flatter Gruber. But the evidence for Gruber's French connection is not conclusive.[9]

At about this time the French chargé d'affaires in Hamburg, Jean-François de Bourgoing, began to provide essential information. During the Revolution, Hamburg had served as the major entrepôt between eastern and western Europe, in regard both to commerce and to espionage. Guttin had recommended that the French connive at Russian contacts there.[10] Bourgoing's first dispatch from Hamburg suggested the hidden nature of his mission: "It is generally believed that I am here to reconcile this 'petite République' with ours. I have not said anything to confirm or destroy this presumption" (26 March). He was assisted by the cooperation of the French ambassador in Berlin, General Beurnonville. Beurnonville wrote that he had been visited by Bellegarde, a French émigré in the Russian service, who came to see him at night in order to escape the notice of the Russian ambassador (10 May). Bellegarde, who had been on a diplomatic mission in Italy, was then on his way back to St. Petersburg. He had good contacts at the Russian court, including the Chancellor Rostopchin and Grand Duke Constantine, and he was willing to serve the Republic upon the promise of permission to return to France. He was referred to Bourgoing and went to see him. After examining the proposition prudently, Bourgoing reported to Talleyrand: "I have not found anything objectionable in his proposal. He will write me . . . at an address that I have given to him in a cipher that we have agreed on. As I will limit myself to receiving his letters, the correspondence can compromise only him" (15 May). Talleyrand sent his approval on the same day that he received Bourgoing's dispatch (8 June). Bellegarde left for St. Petersburg and soon proved his worth. "One can reach Paul I," Bourgoing informed Talleyrand, "by means of his favorite, formerly his barber, Kutaisov, who is enamored of a French actress, Madame Chevalier. She has spent some time at Hamburg, where she has left very pleasant memories. . . . She is very greedy, they say, but her lover satisfies all her whims, and she would undoubtedly employ her political services for a high price. I think she can be sounded out by the Frenchman mentioned in my dispatches nos. 15, 16, 17, and 18 [Bellegarde]. I have the means of corresponding with him, and I am going to try it without delay" (27 June). A month later, Bourgoing reported: "I have the strongest reasons to believe that M. de Panine will not represent us favorably to Paul I [*ne nous sera favorable auprès de Paul I*]; that this minister is too devoted to the English; and that if he were able, he would renew Russian connections with them. He is not [able]."

The chancellor, Count Rostopchin, was a better bet. "Much more moderate [*sic*] than M. de Panin, he has as much influence over the emperor, and he alone can temper the effects of the ill will of this minister. . . . You have been obliged to use official channels. It is perhaps possible for me to use more effective means yet in reaching Prince Rastapchin by this correspondent whom I have had the honor to introduce to you in my dispatches nos. 15 and 16. This is what I am going to try [to do]" (30 July).

According to Bourgoing, Bellegarde had claimed that it might be possible to persuade Paul I of the necessity of reconciling himself with the French Government and that he, Bellegarde, proposed to do so. "In order to help him," Bourgoing wrote, "it is possible that money, placed properly, would not be useless."[11]

Bourgoing's information proved to be correct. Panin was an ardent Anglophile, who freely spoke his feelings about the prospect of reconciliation with France at the first mention of it: "I have already declared that my hand will never sign a treaty with France except after the reestablishment of the monarchy or for a general peace settlement in which all our allies will be included."[12] On September 21, Panin drew up a review of Russian foreign policy. He called Paul's attention to the sad state of affairs in Austria, the weakness of the armies, their low morale, and their general discontent. He said that if hostilities were resumed, Austria would have to face a shameful peace or the collapse of the political structure of Germany. In either case, Russia would be directly threatened by the Revolution. Austria's evident need presented the opportunities for Russia to secure now the restoration in Italy that the Austrians had been unwilling to grant during the previous year and, at the same time, to resume the struggle against the Revolution.[13]

Rostopchin's politics were less definite than Panin's, more fluid, even volatile. During the summer of 1800 the two ministers were engaged in a rivalry that was certainly personal and to some extent—especially for Panin, who was something of an ideologue—political. Connection with hostile foreign parties was part of the struggle, and Rostopchin countered Panin's clique with one of his own.

Madame Chevalier, Bourgoing discovered, was no small sensation in St. Petersburg. Born in Lyons, she had entered the theater there as a young girl. She moved to Paris in 1792 and to Hamburg in 1795, where her great beauty attracted quite a following. Her unscrupulous husband, a former associate of Collot d'Herbois's during the Terror in Lyons, sought to exploit her acclaim.[14] She presided over a gambling house and dabbled in prostitution. In 1798 they moved to St. Petersburg, where she repeated her success. At the Russian capital she maintained high connections and trafficked in her influence. By the time that Bourgoing was making his reports, she had formed a well-known liaison with Count Kutaisov, a former Turkish barber who had become Paul's chamberlain and favorite. Kutaisov reputedly had an extraordinary facility for influencing Paul, and contemporary accounts agree that the two lovers made a regular enterprise of selling their persuasiveness. According to the Abbé de Georgel, Chevalier gave to Kutaisov lists of donations that had been made to her, and Kutaisov procured favors for the donors at court. According to the most cautious and sober foreign account of the

Russian court during Paul's reign (by the Bavarian diplomat de Bray), Kutaisov visited Chevalier every night, then returned to the Winter Palace, where he occupied the apartment that had formerly been reserved for Catherine's favorite and that, of course, connected directly with the imperial apartments.[15]

Did they succeed in reaching Rostopchin? Rostopchin himself acknowledged to a friend that he was "allied with . . . Count Kutaisov, who is led by a Frenchwoman named Chevalier, whose husband is considered a mad Jacobin."[16] This makes it all the more interesting to compare Rostopchin's views of European politics with those that were emanating from Paris.

Around the second week of October, Rostopchin submitted to Paul a policy paper that was very different from Panin's. He began by reviewing Russia's relations with the different powers. Sweden and Denmark, he said, were too weak to act independently and therefore were, out of necessity, deferential to Russia. Spain and Holland were pawns of France. Portugal was not important. The Italian states—Sardinia, Naples, and the Vatican—had fallen into such a state of impotence that only Russia's protection could restore them. The Ottoman Empire was in the same condition. "All measures taken by it now are nothing more than medicine given to a hopelessly sick man."

Rostopchin claimed that France was a special case:

> Ten years without law and order, through incomprehensible events produced by barbarism, madness, and heroism, leading not only herself but two-thirds of Europe into complete chaos, rising up against the monarchical government of her own native rulers, [France] has ultimately committed herself to the autocracy of the foreigner Bonaparte and, in her utter prostration, boasts of her image of conqueror and law-giver to the far-flung lands of Europe. The present governor of this power is too egotistical and happy with his undertakings and unlimited fame not to want peace. By obtaining peace he will confirm himself in power, acquiring the recognition of the exhausted French people and of all of Europe, and will use the respite for military preparations against England. . . . He has exhausted the forces of Austria, and Prussia is dependent [on him]; thus Bonaparte need fear only Russia. The truth of this is demonstrated by his conduct toward Your Imperial Highness: [his] attempts . . . to enter into negotiations and, having produced a rapprochement, to change the hostile disposition of Russia toward France into a friendly one, for which reason, Bonaparte, in contrast with the other powers, supported the

Russian prisoners and offered to return Malta to Your Imperial Highness as grand master of the order.

Austria, Rostopchin continued, had been intent, since the beginning of the French Revolutionary Wars, on partitioning France. Blinded by pride, strengthened by the subsidies of Pitt, betraying her friends, forgetting everything but chimerical conquests, Austria now awaited Bonaparte's pronouncement of her fate.

Prussia, Rostopchin said, was wise to withdraw from the war after one shameful campaign. Then he turned to England:

> England, with her universal maritime exploits, [has excited] the envy of all the cabinets by her greed and insolent behavior on the seas, the dominion of which she wants exclusively for herself. . . . still she needs peace . . . ; and she is now, or soon will be, in such a situation that, except for the Turkish and Portuguese ports, she cannot enter any others in Europe. . . . But in whatever situation she may be, the constant aim of the English ministry, and the sincere wish of every Englishman, is for the downfall of France. From the very beginning of the century this general wish of the English people was turned into a political system, for which purpose all classes in England aspired to appropriate for themselves alone the benefits of world trade.

To this end, England had excited all the powers of Europe against France and still maintained the right to inspect the ships of all nations. Rostopchin continued:

> Though all the powers outwardly place their trust in the friendship and protection of Your Imperial Majesty, almost all of them nevertheless secretly nourish envy and malice. Russia, by her position as well as by her inexhaustible strength, is and should be the first power of the world, and for this reason she keeps a constant watch over all the movements and liaisons of the powerful sovereigns of Europe in order that they, either by themselves or with the collaboration of client states, may not undertake anything prejudicial to the greatness of Russia. . . .
>
> Bonaparte is trying in every possible way to win your favor for better advantage in the conclusion of peace with England. Prussia courts you for the satisfaction of her aspirations at the general peace. Austria crawls before you in order to stand before France. England, supposing . . . a Russian rapprochement with France to be impossible, wants . . . to spread her flag over the Baltic.

But England's fleet did not have a single harbor in the Baltic, and it could be damaged more easily than it could damage other fleets. At the general peace, England and France would retain their conquests, and Prussia would be aggrandized by France as a reward for her benevolent neutrality. With the exception of Austria, the powers would

finish the war with significant benefits. Russia will not [end up with sufficient benefits], having lost 23,000 men only to assure herself [*uverit' sebia*] of the treachery of Pitt and Thugut and [to assure] Europe of the immortality of Prince Suvorov [the campaign of 1799].

. . . I conclude with a proposal of suitable means for obtaining advantages for Russia.

These advantages, procuring her new riches, seas, and glory, will place her for all time over all powers, and your name over all sovereigns . . . , and therefore I propose the partition of Turkey. . . .

Russia will take Romania, Bulgaria, and Moldavia [*sic*]; Austria—Bosnia, Serbia, and Wallachia. Prussia . . . , the electorate of Hanover and the bishoprics of Paderborn and Münster. France—Egypt, Greece with all the islands of the Archipelago. . . .

The success of this important but easily accomplished undertaking depends only upon secrecy and dispatch. The court of Vienna will be delighted with such an unexpected proposition. Prussia will find in it great advantages; but the heart of this plan must be Bonaparte. He will find in the proposed partition the surest means to the abasement of Great Britain and to confirmation, by means of a general peace, of all the conquests of France.

Not proceeding at once to reveal the real nature of the rapprochement with France, it is necessary . . . in order to keep England occupied so that she cannot oppose the partition of Turkey, to propose to Denmark and Sweden the renewal of the Northern Neutrality. . . . Bonaparte will find in it a forceful means of damaging England and of forcing her either to surrender her illegal claims on the seas or, [if she] declares war on all of Europe, to be without ports in all the seas. . . .

With this, I conclude my presentation, and if the Creator of the world, who from ancient times has preserved under his protection the Russian Empire and its glory, will bless this undertaking, then Russia and the nineteenth century will worthily pride themselves on the reign of Your Imperial Majesty, uniting the thrones of Peter and Constantine [the Great], . . . the founders of the most illustrious empires in the world.

Paul allegedly approved the plan and ordered Rostopchin to proceed with the execution of it.[17]

Rostopchin did not write about an expedition to India, as Guttin had, though he made several references to the position of the English in the Indies; and he said nothing of the restoration of Poland under Constantine, Paul's son. Guttin's plans about naval affairs and maritime commerce in the Baltic were not quite as well developed as Rostopchin's (the Northern Neutrality). There were other variations with regard to the distribution of territory and "advantages," but what is more striking is the fundamental similarity of the two plans.

Rostopchin had definite ideas about how the plan was to be executed. He proposed

> to send to Paris a trusted person to negotiate with Bonaparte. . . . because of the secrecy and importance of this mission. I am bound to propose myself . . . , and here is how.
>
> Preparing in secret—that is, by myself—all the papers constituting the project of alliance and partition of Turkey, the letters of Your Imperial Majesty to Bonaparte and to the . . . [German] Emperor, the full powers and passport, for several days before my departure I will disseminate rumors that I have fallen into disgrace, I will write to Your Imperial Majesty a letter requesting permission to go take the waters. . . . I travel to Frankfurt-on-the-Oder, Leipzig, and farther. In some little town, possibly Memel, I will have taken another name. I cannot arouse any suspicion, having a modest carriage and not being able to speak any language other than Russian. Arriving in Paris . . . , I will demand through Berthier [the minister of war] a secret meeting . . . and declare to the First Consul the plan and the full powers for the conclusion of peace if Bonaparte agrees to your proposal.[18]

Then he would hurry to Vienna, where there could be no doubt about his success.

Point 13 of Peter's "Testament" contains the same thought: "Begin by offering separately, very secretly, and with the greatest circumspection, first to the court of Versailles, then to that of Vienna, to share with one of them the empire of the universe." A different version of the "Testament" seems to have contained another idea that had been proposed by Rostopchin: "Here it was written in the margin, in a different and very difficult hand to read, it seems that it is by Catherine I: 'It is not necessary to confide oneself to any minister on this point, but to send a confidential messenger to communicate orally [*parler de bouche*], or what would perhaps be better, to arrange an interview so as to put nothing in writing.' "[19]

Did Rostopchin's policy really embody, partly through the prompting of the French, the "Testament" of Peter I? We cannot know this for sure. What we do know beyond a shadow of a doubt is that the French Foreign Ministry tried to buy Rostopchin, that he produced a policy paper similar to theirs, and that he admitted to complicity with the French party at the Russian court who had been designated to buy him. This is all the information that the documents supply. And it is not surprising. Affairs of this kind rarely leave clear accounts of themselves in public records, and ministers of state have especially good reasons for seeing that they do not. But we are not left alone with our imaginations at this point. There is more evidence on this question in the story that followed.

AT ABOUT THE TIME when Rostopchin wrote his memorandum, the French overtures to St. Petersburg began to elicit an encouraging response. The Russian ambassador in Berlin, Baron Kriudener, informed the French ambassador, General Beurnonville, that Paul would accept the return of the Russian prisoners with pleasure. As to a rapprochement or alliance between the two countries, Paul demanded first the restoration of Malta and a guarantee of the territorial integrity of Naples, Sardinia, Bavaria, and Württemberg.[20]

Paul sent General Georg Magnus Sprengporten, a Swede in the Russian service, to France to receive the prisoners formally and then to escort them to Malta, where they should serve as its garrison and he, Sprengporten, as its governor.[21] When Sprengporten reached Berlin, he had a conversation with the French ambassador, Beurnonville, who told him that the two powers of France and Russia, "situated at [*touchant aux*] the extremities of the globe [*sic*—"continent"?]," were destined to dominate it.[22] Sprengporten then proceeded to Brussels, near the camp of the prisoners, where he met with Bonaparte's representative, General Clarke. Sprengporten was wined and dined in high style. He read to Clarke from his instructions—which had been written, he said, by Paul himself—an explanation of Paul's policy:

> Although His Majesty was, at the beginning of this war, unable to avoid, for the sake of the security of his own dominions, taking a part in a quarrel which seemed to threaten the tranquillity of all of Europe, he did not, however, hesitate for a moment to withdraw his troops from the coalition as soon as it appeared that the designs of the powers were leading to

aggrandizements which his loyalty and disinterestedness would not permit; and as the two states of France and the Russian Empire can never, due to the distance separating them, find themselves in a situation that is mutually damaging, they can, if they unite and maintain constant accord, block any aggrandizement by other powers which would prejudice their own interests.[23]

The French must have been delighted to hear from the mouths of Russians the phrases that they themselves had connived so conscientiously to put there.

Sprengporten continued on to Paris. He found that some of the Russian officers, who had been invited there by Bonaparte, were applauded wherever they went. At the opera, a song was sung celebrating Peter the Great, and toasts were drunk in honor of Paul. On December 20, Sprengporten dined with Talleyrand; on December 21, with Bonaparte himself. The First Consul explained how only France and Russia could pacify the Continent. Geography made them natural allies. Geography called them to hold the other powers of Europe in check.[24]

At about this time in Berlin, Kriudener was explaining to Beurnonville that Paul had taken up arms against the excessive ambitions of the Directory: "He has seen with pleasure the fortunate changes that have taken place in France, and especially the prudent and measured conduct of the Consular government. . . . seeing all the steps that it took marked with the stamp of wisdom and moderation, he did not hesitate to respond to our overtures."[25] Talleyrand signified formally that Paul's conditions for cooperation (the restoration of Malta and the guarantee of Bavaria, Württemberg, Naples, and Sardinia) had been accepted.[26] Now the autocrat of all the Russias and the Corsican usurper astonished Europe by engaging in a personal correspondence. Bonaparte wrote first:

> I saw yesterday, with great pleasure, General Sprengporten. I charged him to inform Your Majesty that both for political considerations as well as for considerations of esteem for You, I want to see the two strongest nations in the world promptly and irrevocably united. I have tried in vain for the past twelve months to bring peace and tranquillity to Europe; I have not succeeded, and the fighting continues without cause and, so it would seem, at the sole instigation of English policy. Twenty-four hours after Your Majesty will have charged someone enjoying his confidence and privy to His desires with special and full powers, the Continent and the seas will be at peace. For when England, the Emperor of Germany, and all the other powers are convinced that the wills as well as the forces of

our two great nations reach for the same end, their armaments will fall from their hands, and the current generation will bless Your Imperial Majesty for having arrested the horrors of war and the discords of the factions. If these sentiments are shared by Your Imperial Majesty, as the loyalty and the largesse of His character lead me to think, I believe that it would be suitable . . . that Europe discover simultaneously the ordering of the borders of the states, that peace be signed between France and Russia and the reciprocal engagements that they have contracted for pacifying all the states. This strong, frank, and loyal guidance will offend certain cabinets, but it will unite the approbation of all the peoples and that of posterity.[27]

Eight days later—that is, before he had had time to receive this letter, since a fast trip between the two capitals took from fourteen to eighteen days—Paul wrote to Bonaparte:

Monsieur le Premier Consul.

It is the duty of those to whom God has given the power of governing peoples to occupy themselves with their welfare. To this end, I propose to You that we concert between ourselves the means of putting an end to the ills which have desolated all of Europe these past eleven years. I do not speak about, nor do I want to discuss, either the rights of man or the principles of different governments that each country has adopted [but] about restoring to the world the peace and calm which it so much needs. . . . I am ready to listen and to treat with you. . . . I invite you to join me in reestablishing the general peace, which, if we want it, can scarcely elude us.[28]

Upon receiving this letter, Bonaparte was ecstatic. He wrote to his brother Joseph: "There arrived here yesterday from Russia a courier who . . . brought me an extremely friendly letter from the Emperor's own hand." To Talleyrand he exulted: "The influence of Russia and France will be decisive in Prussia, and then England will be without any communication with the Continent."[29] He ordered the French fleet, even though France was still technically at war with Russia, to lend all possible assistance to Russian ships.[30] Talleyrand asked both the Spanish and the Dutch governments to follow the French example, and he carefully informed the Russians.[31] Paul responded by ordering the resumption of trade relations with France, "in consequence of the measures taken by France toward the security and preservation of Russian ships."[32]

The poor couriers who carried the frantic correspondence between the two distant capitals during the most severe months of the winter must have been driven nearly to desperation. One of them spent just four hours in St. Petersburg before leaving again with new dispatches for Paris.[33]

Paul wrote to Bonaparte a second time on January 14, a short note containing an important commitment:

> I have received Your letter and the report of my General Sprengporten. . . . My plenipotentiary Kolychev will leave tomorrow, bearing instructions which will demonstrate my sentiments and will respond to the different points of Your letter. I desire, on my part, the peace of Europe, which we can certainly achieve. . . . It is certain that two great powers which are in agreement will have a positive influence upon the rest of Europe. And I am ready to do it. To this end, I pray God, Monsieur le Premier Consul, to keep You in His Holy and worthy Care.[34]

Stepan A. Kolychev was an experienced diplomat, but not merely a diplomat, for he had just been appointed vice-chancellor of the Russian Empire. As Kolychev started for Paris, Louis Bonaparte turned up in Berlin, then Königsberg, then Danzig; and the Danish court was asked by the French to arrange to have him received in St. Petersburg.[35] Monsieur Guttin had suddenly, after all his previous trials, received some kind of mysterious commission from the French Ministry of Foreign Affairs, and not even his wife knew his whereabouts. She inquired of Talleyrand. She had not seen her husband for a month, she said, and though she had been three times to the ministry, she had not been able to find out anything. There is no indication that her letter got a response, but it soon turned out that her husband was in Berlin with Louis Bonaparte, on his way to Warsaw.[36]

In St. Petersburg, Vice-Chancellor Panin, an Anglophile and Francophobe, was dismissed from his post in November.

Louis XVIII also served as a victim and symptom of the rapprochement. In 1798, Paul had offered the hapless pretender to the French throne an asylum and a pension. It was apparently not much to Louis's taste, but it was the best offer he had received, so he accepted it. He took up residence in a chateau at Mittau in Courland. Although he chafed a bit under what he felt was the excessive observation of the Russian police, on the whole, he was, for a prince in his circumstances, fortunate. But Paul's generosity proved capricious. On 10 January 1801, Paul sent a message to Louis, asking "His Majesty Louis XVIII to join his spouse," who was in Germany. On January 22 Paul issued summary orders "to have the King of France and all his suite depart as quickly as possible without permitting anyone to depart from the main route or to stop on the way." No reason was given. The order was issued, ironically, a day after the anniversary of the execution of Louis XVI. The king and his suite were short of money; so the local nobility contributed toward the expenses of the trip, and Louis left for Warsaw.[37]

IN THE MEANTIME, Bonaparte's controlled press was tutoring Europe in how to interpret these portentous developments. In November 1800 there appeared in Paris an anonymous book, *The Situation of France at the End of the Year VIII* (September 1800, republican calendar). It was an excellent piece of Napoleonic propaganda, for both foreign and domestic consumption. It was written by Alexandre d'Hauterive, and Bonaparte was so pleased with it that he presented the author an award of 25,000 francs.[38] Hauterive attributed the continuation of the ruinous war almost entirely to England. The English, not content with the limited sovereignty that other countries enjoyed, were trying to extend their dominion over all the seas of the world. He explained how the English had subsidized coalitions for the conquest of colonies, how they had exploited colonies to finance more coalitions to acquire more colonies, and so forth. English possessions in the Orient were larger than many of the states of Europe. For the English, war was a more far-flung and sophisticated variety of mercantilism; it was an enormously profitable enterprise. The neutrals of Europe suffered from English maritime practices directly, but the powers who accepted English subsidies for fighting the French also suffered. Did they not understand that they were simply delivering the commerce of the world exclusively into the hands of the English? "It is for the governments that limit themselves still to the role of spectators in the bloody struggle . . . or that continue to take an active part in it, to judge if their hopes have not been deceived when they attach themselves to the cause of a government that founds its dominion on the destruction of their commerce and on the ruin of their power." Here was an invitation for the neutrals and the belligerents alike to recognize their interests in a Continental coalition against the most dangerous power in the world. Hauterive implied that the Russians might find advantages other than commercial ones in such a coalition; and the next topic he took up was an old favorite.

The passage on Turkey was a model of delicate but provocative and studiedly ambiguous allusions. If Turkey

is too near the abyss that has opened up to swallow her; and if her fall only awaits . . . the execution of arrangements anticipated for her dismemberment; let each of the governments that have speculated upon this event consider the consequences [either] of the opposition of France, if France judges that her opposition is capable of preventing it, or of relying on her support, if she is persuaded that the dismemberment of Turkey has become inevitable. . . .

In either case, Russia cannot regard France as being indifferent to her views. Whether Turkey becomes a prey whom it pleases Russia to partition, or whether Russia considers the Turkish Empire a neighbor whose friendship ought to be cultivated and whose old age ought to be respected, it is up to Russia to decide if the dispositions of France to oppose the partition or to swing the balance of the advantages in favor of this or that power should not be counted for something . . . , it is up to Russia to decide . . . whether [in this matter] the cooperation of France is not preferable to that of any other European power.

Russia, though large and powerful, was not, Hauterive maintained, absolutely secure. The states on her border feared her and treated her with great caution, but not a single state of Europe had ever formed a sincere alliance with her:

France is perhaps the only state that has no reason to fear Russia, no interest in desiring her decline, no motive for obstructing the progress of her prosperity. . . . In Europe there is generally a high regard for the power of this empire: but the nature of that power and the exercise of it are much abused. . . . This empire is truly powerful; but the progress of its grandeur depends henceforth more on its sovereigns' moderation and prudence than on the rash development of their forces. . . . The Russian Empire today exercises an influence that it owes chiefly to the state of confusion and disorder into which the current war has thrown . . . all the nations of Europe. But with all the sources of riches and of power that it contains, why has it not set forth any pretensions of a positive and permanent preponderance? . . . If the prince that governs it aspires to lasting honor and to attach to his empire and to his name the basis of this preeminence that he owes to accidental circumstances and that cannot last long, then he will undertake to moderate the practice of expansion that has until now governed his predecessors. . . . Henceforth, the forces of this empire will serve not to conquer but to govern. *With such principles, he will see accomplished within a few years all the dreams that the genius of Peter the Great dared conceive, and the success of which previous reigns have only imperfectly realized.* And then, not only will the Russian Empire be one of the greatest empires of the world, but it will be the only one of which it can be said that the progress of its power, far from being a subject of anxiety and jealousy, has served the principles of independence in general, in promising support to the weak nations, and in offering an example to states bent upon aggrandizement.

To borrow a phrase from Frederick the Great, this was the work of an excellent charlatan. In Europe, Paul had a certain reputation: that of being devoted to old chivalric notions of honor, generous but exacting, volatile and impetuous. Hauterive apparently allowed for any mood, any disposition. Magnanimous conquest, humble grandeur—there was a sentiment for all seasons, and all reeked of pious purpose. To rescue the poor Turk or to slaughter him, it could all be reconciled somehow in the sturdy hypocrisy of the Enlightenment.

For a hundred years, Hauterive continued, Russia had been, because of her harassment of Sweden and Turkey, the partitions of Poland, her favoritism for English commerce, and her meddling in Germany, a standing threat to the interests of France:

> The means for changing completely the nature of the relations between France and Russia . . . are extremely simple . . . all that [France] desires is in the interests of Russia as well as her own . . . that Russia should open her ports to all the nations of Europe. . . . The richer and more powerful she is, the less she will be tempted to accept subsidies and to become involved, without benefits for herself, in the ambitions of a greedy ally. . . . Then the Russian Empire . . . will not look upon France with antipathy . . . she will maintain the equilibrium of the North while France will guarantee that of the South; and their accord will assure the political equilibrium of the universe.[39]

The book made its intended impact on London. The British ambassador in Berlin reported it to Grenville at the Foreign Office:

> I must observe that there is a book lately published under the patronage of Government at Paris, called "*Etat de la France*," where the nature and extent of the scheme which, at the bidding of our inveterate enemy, these northern powers have undertaken for our destruction, are so clearly unfolded, that it could not fail to make a deep impression if published in England. . . . It is a most elaborate and able performance, and the sophisms are so ingeniously woven together that they cannot well be exposed as they ought without answering the whole book.[40]

It was translated and published in London within a few months,[41] and the English then commissioned an able German publicist, Friedrich von Gentz, to prepare a rebuttal, which they hastened to translate and publish in London the next year.[42]

Meanwhile the government newspaper, Le Moniteur, had been constantly informing the public about the successes of the French and about the difficulties of their enemies. Thus Paris learned in April 1800 that the mission of a British diplomat to St. Petersburg to repair the breach in Anglo-Russian relations had failed; in June, that the Russian ambassador had left Vienna with his entire staff; in August, that an army of Russians was assembling on the border in order to attack Austrian Galicia; and in September, that Paul had sequestered all British property in St. Petersburg. In October there was a long polemic by an economist about the vulnerability of the English to a renewal of the Armed Neutrality and about the advantage of such an arrangement to the northern powers. In November it was announced that Sprengporten was coming to Paris: "He has a special mission from the Emperor of Russia for the First Consul, . . . a response to the overtures made by the French government to the Emperor Paul I." In December the whole story of the Russian prisoners was told, how the English and Austrians had refused to accept them in exchange for French prisoners in their possession. The flattering contrast with the French treatment of them was obvious. Finally, it was reported that Paul's plenipotentiary Kolychev was on his way to Paris.[43]

Bonaparte's police made regular reports to him on the state of public opinion in Paris, and the public reaction to the Russian developments that was recorded in Le Moniteur must have pleased him. Thus, he learned on November 28: "Stock Exchange.—Confidence is reestablished. . . . The principal cause of this improvement is the reassessment of the intentions of Russia." Similarly, two days later he read: "The arrival of the Russian officer sent by Paul I was announced at the Stock Exchange. Prices advanced at once. . . . The arrival of the Russian general is the subject of all conversations and increased the hope for peace."[44]

By this time, the evidence for a French rapprochement with Russia was conspicuous enough, and a long Moniteur article of February 20, "On England," conjured up all the ugly specters that lay in store for France's most stubborn enemy.

Repeating many of Hauterive's points, it explained how England had conquered the richest lands of the world in order to pay the cabinets of Europe to fight her rival, France. One of them, however, had discovered the British game and was refusing to play it: "Russia cannot see with indifference the outrage of the friendly flags on seas confided to her protection. . . . Russia is made to fulfill in the North the place that France will occupy in the South. . . . Paul I is the only sovereign who . . . has always followed the movements of a magnanimous and disinterested policy." When Paul had fought against France, France was being ruled by an oppressive and unreliable government. Honor had been the constant motive of his policy, and this was the most striking difference between his conduct and that of England. The British had tried to blame their defeat in the Dutch campaign on the Russians. "Such is the policy of a merchant people," wrote the *Moniteur's* reporter; "to military ignorance, the English join ingratitude." He repeated the story of their refusal to exchange the Russian prisoners. England's abuse of neutral shipping was described. If the powers of Europe wanted to protect themselves against such abuse, "Europe has not a moment to lose. She must consult the two great masters of nations. . . . They will tell her that she must unite . . . to defend the rest of her commerce and her maritime independence. . . . It is necessary at last to fix limits to the growth of this usurper power that has for tributaries the sovereigns of India and that counts the sovereigns of Europe among the number of her pensionaries." The best means of making the English amenable to reason was "to close . . . the markets [of the Continent] to the people who want to sell everything themselves."[45]

By this time, obviously, it was no secret to the enemies of France what plans were being laid for their destruction. And foreign opinion, like French opinion, found the specters conjured by Bonaparte's diplomacy and propaganda wonderfully credible. The grand plan concocted in Paris had somehow leaked out and was making the rounds of the diplomatic rumor mill. The British ambassador in Berlin wrote home about a mysterious plan of alliance between the two powers that had been transmitted by William Wickham, a British agent on the Continent. "It is too much in conformity with Russian views not to have made a lasting impression," the ambassador wrote; "I must own the memorial you have received from Wickham about the project of an alliance between the French and the Russians strikes me more and more as deserving serious reflection. It is calculated to make a great impression upon Russia."[46] A British spy in Paris reported that a plan of alliance between France and Russia provided for Prussian annexation of Hanover, French annexation of the Rhineland, Poland reconstituted under a son of Paul I, and a union of all the powers of the north and, in general, all the maritime forces of Europe. The spy's report continued: "Then add that

48

Russia presses the execution eagerly and that she does not dissimulate her ardent desire to be revenged on England, who has tricked her, as well as on the emperor of Germany, who has repayed her services with the blackest ingratitude."[47] Windham wrote to Lord Keith on 2 March 1801: "It appears certain that Russia is engaged with France to attack the Turk, and that the double object is to gain for Russia the Turkish Empire and for France Egypt and our East Indian possessions."[48] The British ambassador in Constantinople asked a Near Eastern expert in Baghdad about the feasibility of a Russian attack on India.[49] And a popular travelogue published in London explained the crisis in English foreign affairs: "The favourite object of the emperor Paul is the possession of Malta; the favourite object of Buonaparte is the colonization of Egypt; and it is generally understood, that they have, mutually, guaranteed to each other their respective domination. . . . The Turkish monarchy seems to be tottering on the verge of dissolution, and that obstacle removed, Russia and France united, may, possibly, in the end, shake the stability of our Indian empire."[50]

From Paris the Danish ambassador informed his court: "I am almost certain that in the project of alliance between France and Russia there is a question of the destruction of the Ottoman Porte, or at least of driving them [*sic*] out of Europe. Paul I will thus satisfy his desire to reign in Constantinople and Bonaparte his desire to possess Egypt and to open the way to the East Indies to the French."[51]

In Berlin an astute American, John Quincy Adams, minister plenipotentiary to the court of Prussia, observed Kolychev's journey to Paris with some astonishment. Kolychev, Adams wrote, was everywhere received like a sovereign prince. His embassy was "in the highest degree splendid; with . . . an allowance of sixty thousand roubles for the expenses of his journey, and 100,000 roubles salary.—The poor Turk is to pay for it all."[52]

From Madrid, Lucien Bonaparte, who had recently been sent there on a diplomatic assignment, reported to his brother: "You are regarded here since the Russian rapprochement as the Master of Europe."[53]

Everyone was convinced, and the First Consul himself must have concurred. For the French were now in possession of a recent note from Paul to Sprengporten: "After the news that you give me of the sentiment of the First Consul, I do not see anything that could obstruct the accomplishment of our mutual projects."[54]

4

THE RESULTS: AUSTRIA

The break with Russia is the source of all the misfortunes of Austria.
—Louis de Cobenzl

THE AUSTRIANS were the first to feel the power of Bonaparte's approaches to the Russians. The Austrians were much better acquainted with the Russians than the French were, having discovered them late in the fifteenth century, when a traveling German knight reported that there was a Slavic kingdom east of Poland. The Habsburgs, involved at that point in a conflict with Poland, lost no time in proposing to Moscow an alliance. One of their distinguished diplomats, Sigismund von Herberstein, left a travelogue of his visits, *Notes on Russia* (1549), that for generations served as a kind of statesman's handbook to the land. The proposed alliance foundered, but the issue arose again, in a familiarly modern form, during the reign of Ivan IV, who proposed a partition of their common neighbor. This, too, failed. The latter part of the sixteenth century and much of the seventeenth century were characterized by Habsburg and papal appeals to Moscow to join the Christians of Europe against the Turks. The Russians, however, were for a long time more concerned with the threat of Poland.

Peter I shifted the emphasis of Russian diplomacy. He managed the Polish problem satisfactorily by means of internal manipulation of the country, and he was at last ready to accept the proffered alliance against the Turks. But the Habsburgs were then embroiled in the War of the Spanish Succession (1700–13), and Peter had to content himself with a league of northern European powers against Sweden and a unilateral attack on Turkey, which turned out disastrously.

When the French spurned Peter's 1717 offer, he turned, in his search for a powerful ally, to Vienna. The alliance that resulted formed the cornerstone of Russian diplomacy throughout most of the eighteenth century: it settled the War of the Polish Succession (1733–35) in favor of the Russian candidate, and it made a minor contribution in the miserable Turkish war of 1735–39. Various complex intrigues paralyzed Russian policy during the War of the Austrian Succession (1740–48). Only the vagaries of dynastic succession at the Russian court deprived it of the rich rewards of its great victories over Frederick II in the Seven Years' War (1756–63).

At this point the new Russian sovereign, Catherine II (1762–96), chose to form an alliance with Prussia. She was more concerned with Polish than with Turkish affairs at the time, and such an alliance seemed logical. It interrupted Austro-Russian amity for eighteen years, 1762 to 1780, at which point, Catherine, shifting her attention, proposed to the new sovereign of Austria, Joseph II, the destruction of the Turks. Their scheme, the notorious "Greek Project," called for the partition of European Turkey and for the placing of a Russian prince, Catherine's grandson Constantine, on the throne of a restored Byzantine Empire at Constantinople. But the French Revolution, by diverting the attention of Austria to western Europe, helped to spare the Turks the fate that was plotted for them.

There is no evidence that the Austrians knew anything about the "Testament" of Peter I. They were, however, Russia's nearest neighbors in southeastern Europe, they were thoroughly familiar with Russian ambitions in the Balkans, and they were accomplices in those ambitions.[1]

During the summer and fall of 1799 the Austrians refused to restore the legitimate princes in the liberated states of northern Italy. At the end of September they withdrew support from a Russian army that was facing a superior French army near Zurich, leaving the Russians to sustain a serious defeat. Back in Italy in November, when the French surrendered the town of Ancona to a joint besieging force of Austrians and Russians, the Austrian commander refused to raise the Russian flag over the fortress or to admit Russian forces within it, and he stubbornly ignored the protests of the Russians. Whereas the refusal to restore the Italian princes was merely self-seeking and suspicious and was subversive of harmony in the alliance, the desertion of the Russians at Zurich was both politically and militarily unwise, and the affair at Ancona was entirely intolerable. This kind of conduct would have offended allies who were far less sensitive than Paul.

The Austrian ambassador in St. Petersburg, Count Louis de Cobenzl, had for years reported that Paul was unstable, petty, volatile, capricious, tyrannical, and, above all, vindictive. It was this vindictiveness, which, after Austrian policy had offended Paul in the fall of 1799, was most dreaded in Vienna. Before his expulsion from St. Petersburg, Cobenzl was himself treated to Paul's offensive conduct: he was under virtual house arrest, and spies were placed all around him to inquire into the secrets of his household and his correspondence.[2]

When Bonaparte, then, began to conjure up visions of a Russian alliance against Austria and a partition of Turkey, the Austrians readily received his message.

THE VICTORY at Marengo (14 June 1800), crucial as it was for Bonaparte's career, was not militarily decisive. It was followed by an armistice during which Bonaparte hoped to find the Austrians willing to negotiate seriously. He was soon disappointed. Their light-headed emissary, the Count St. Julien, came to Paris in July and signed a peace for which he was not only repudiated but jailed. Vienna turned to a much more formidable personality to negotiate with the French, the ambassador who had just been expelled from St. Petersburg, Count Cobenzl. He, being an old hand at European diplomacy, was especially fitted for this assignment by his having dealt with Bonaparte in Italy in 1797. Bonaparte appointed his brother Joseph as plenipotentiary, and when Cobenzl arrived in France, the two of them opened negotiations at Lunéville in October.

The Franco-Austrian settlement which preceded the outbreak of the War of the Second Coalition was the peace of Campo Formio of October 1797. The Austrians' dissatisfaction with the terms of this treaty was partially responsible for their joining a new coalition. Campo Formio provided for the French annexation of the left bank of the Rhine and the Austrian Netherlands (Belgium) and for the cession by Austria of Lombardy in north-central Italy. In compensation, Austria received the formerly independent state of Venice, which was no trivial acquisition. But the settlement was by no means as neat and definite as a mere statement of its terms suggests, for it had to be ratified, not by the government of Austria alone—that is, by her Habsburg sovereigns— but also by the hoary apparatus of the German Imperial Constitution.

Since the time of Charlemagne, upwards of three hundred separate and more or less sovereign states of the Germanies had pretended to govern themselves by this body of now-ancient precedent, which was complicated in the extreme. What Campo Formio required this body to do was to ratify the cession of a part of its territory, that part on the left bank of the Rhine, and to find some way of compensating within the Germanic Empire the princes who were dispossessed there. The connection between Austria and the empire was intimate but tenuous. The Habsburg archduke of Austria had been regularly elected as emperor of Germany since 1438 (with two exceptions). But he could

TERRITORIAL CESSIONS AT
CAMPO FORMIO 1797

▤ To France

▨ To Austria

① Austria renounces claim to
Lombardy and other parts
of the Cisalpine Republic.

② Ionian Islands (Corfu, etc.)
ceded to France.

L.R. Ligurian Republic
L. Lucca

0 ———————————— 500
miles

Adapted from William R. Shepherd's *Historical Atlas*, 8th ed. (New York: Barnes & Noble, 1956),
p. 150, and Paul Marie Joseph Vidal de la Blache's *Atlas historique et géographique* (Paris:
Colin, 1951), p. 40.

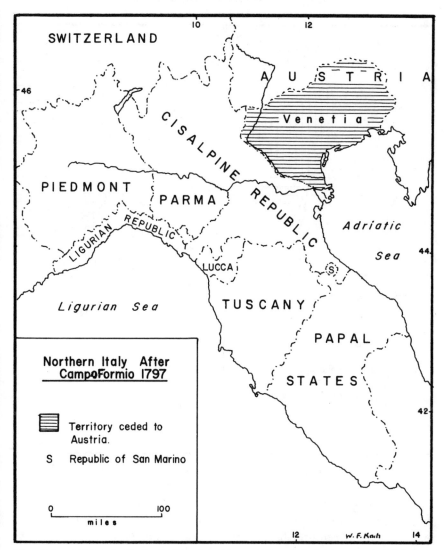

SWITZERLAND

A U S T R I A

Venetia

PIEDMONT

PARMA

CISALPINE REPUBLIC

LIGURIAN REPUBLIC

LUCCA

Adriatic

Sea

Ligurian Sea

TUSCANY

PAPAL

STATES

Northern Italy After
CampoFormio 1797

▤ Territory ceded to
Austria.

S Republic of San Marino

0 ————————— 100
miles

Adapted from William R. Shepherd's *Historical Atlas,* p. 150, and Paul Marie Joseph Vidal de la Blache's *Atlas historique et géographique,* p. 40.

govern the empire—unlike his own hereditary dominions, where he enjoyed full sovereignty—only by the consent of the representatives of its separate states sitting in the Imperial Diet. Moreover, the Peace of Westphalia of 1648, the real foundation of the international law of modern Europe, had damaged his prerogative beyond repair by granting the individual states the right to conduct their own independent foreign policies.

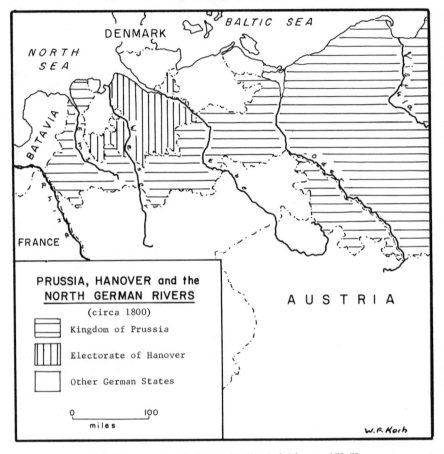

NORTH
SEA

DENMARK

BALTIC SEA

BATAVIA

FRANCE

PRUSSIA, HANOVER and the
NORTH GERMAN RIVERS
(circa 1800)

Kingdom of Prussia

Electorate of Hanover

Other German States

0   100
miles

AUSTRIA

W. R. Korb

Adapted from William R. Shepherd's *Historical Atlas*, pp. 150–51.

One of the more novel subversions of Habsburg power which Campo Formio entailed was known as secularization. In the still feudal structure of the German Empire there were two categories of the emperor's vassals: secular and ecclesiastical. The secular ones were of the kind that is commonly envisaged: they ruled large states such as Prussia and small ones such as Baden or Hesse-Darmstadt. The ecclesiastical vassals were clerics who also participated in the political hierarchy. Their fiefs were bishoprics, monasteries, and the like. According to the terms of the feudal contract, the lord, in this case the emperor, was bound to renew contracts with his vassals' heirs unless he found sufficient legal grounds for a breach of contract. This practice, reinforced by the diplomatic autonomy which the German princes obtained from the Peace of West-

56

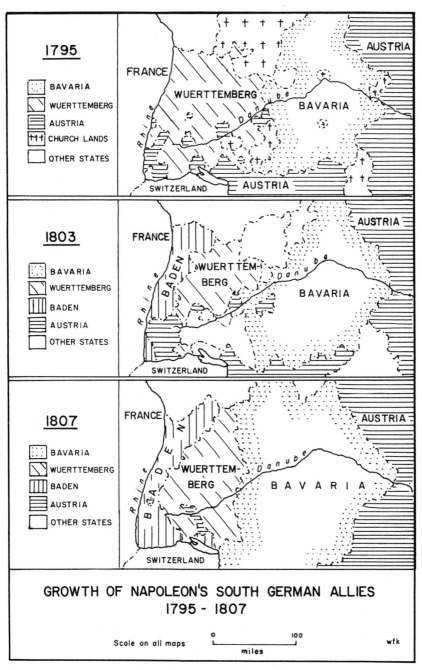

**GROWTH OF NAPOLEON'S SOUTH GERMAN ALLIES
1795 - 1807**

Scale on all maps

0   100

miles

wfk

Adapted from William R. Shepherd's *Historical Atlas*, p. 150, and Paul Marie Joseph Vidal de la
Blache's *Atlas historique et géographique*, p. 40.

phalia, enabled his secular vassals to achieve an independence that left his authority over them almost entirely theoretical.

It was for this reason that the ecclesiastical vassals were so important. They did not have heirs, or if they did, they could not afford to recognize them. Consequently, the emperor was able to invest a new vassal in his ecclesiastical fiefs every generation. And vassals who were so invested tended to support the emperor in the Diet more loyally than did his secular vassals.

In an anticlerical age, however, the Church was virtually defenseless against the caustic effects of revolution—Bonaparte might well have asked, as Stalin did, "How many divisions has the pope?" The ecclesiastical fiefs were the easier ones to appropriate for the purpose of indemnifying the secular princes who had been dispossessed by French annexations.

At Campo Formio, Francis II, archduke of Austria and emperor of Germany, signed for Austria only. Thus, the ceding of the left bank of the Rhine and the secularizations for indemnifying the injured princes had to be approved by the Imperial Diet. In effect, Francis resorted to the vagaries of the German Constitution to cheat the French of what he had ostensibly promised them. It was like giving a check on which he intended to stop payment. When, much to Francis's surprise, the Diet of Rastadt sanctioned the terms of the Treaty of Campo Formio, he did not hesitate to refuse to ratify its decision. Before the Diet broke up, the French had consummated their territorial aggrandizements in Switzerland, Rome, Naples, and Egypt, and the French representatives at Rastadt were assassinated. It was these events that had provoked the War of the Second Coalition.

CHANCELLOR THUGUT had exulted at the victories of 1799, but by the summer of 1800 he was in despair. When the court could hold out no longer and the decision to negotiate was made, Thugut resigned. He nevertheless continued to direct affairs from behind the scenes for some time; in fact, his resignation was symbolic and nominal.

At Lunéville in October 1800, Cobenzl was instructed that the Treaty of Campo Formio was too adverse to serve even as a basis for negotiations.[3] The Austrians hoped to do much better this time. But they reckoned without the resourcefulness of Bonaparte's diplomacy. The deterioration of their position at Lunéville derived from three things. One was simply military defeat in the field. Another was the preoccupation of their English ally with the Franco-Russian challenge in the

Baltic (the subject of the next chapter). The last was the growing threat of hostile Russian intervention.

THE NEGOTIATIONS at Lunéville can be divided conveniently into three rather distinct phases. The first and longest phase was also the least productive. It extended from the middle of October to the beginning of December, and its features were comparatively simple: Austria used dilatory tactics, attempted to avoid further fighting, and yet realized that she was not in a strong negotiating position. The French, on the other hand, were in a hurry, anxious to exploit their successes. Cobenzl drew on all his immense personal resources in order to obfuscate and procrastinate, but he received little help from the Austrian army.

The French plenipotentiary at Lunéville was the First Consul's

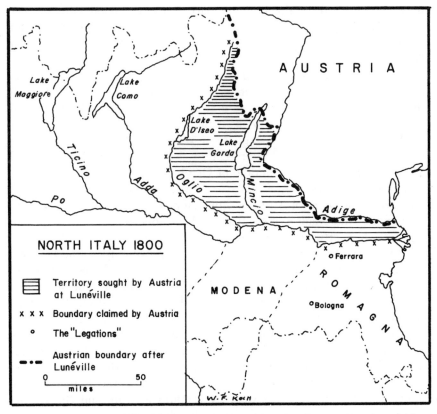

Adapted by W. F. Koch from William R. Shepherd's *Historical Atlas,* p. 150, and Paul Marie Joseph Vidal de la Blache's *Atlas historique et géographique,* p. 40.

brother, Joseph Bonaparte. Joseph, who had none of the distinguishing abilities of Napoleon, was supplied with the most detailed instructions, from which he was forbidden to deviate. Questions on which he had no instructions were referred to Paris. His first assignment was to insist that Austria negotiate separately—that is, without the participation of her ally, Britain.[4] When Joseph and Cobenzl exchanged credentials on November 9, Joseph discovered that Cobenzl was empowered to negotiate only in collaboration with an English plenipotentiary.[5] But since the First Consul would not admit an English negotiator, they were deadlocked from the outset.

Cobenzl took the position that if French professions of peaceful intent were sincere, the French must consent to negotiate with the allies together. He remained at Lunéville, proclaiming the rectitude of the Austrian position. He engaged Joseph in the most frivolous and academic debates. They discussed the history of Franco-Austrian relations since the outbreak of the Revolutionary Wars, the good faith of their respective governments, various alleged violations of the armistice, and the Declaration of Pillnitz (1791). Then, after Cobenzl had been confined to his sickbed for three days, the debates were resumed.[6]

This vexing process had for some time been trying the thin patience of the First Consul. On November 12 he issued the ten days' warning that was necessary in order to terminate the armistice.[7] The first phase of the negotiations thus ended as it began: in a deadlock.

Already during this first phase it was evident that the possibility of Russian intervention was present in the minds of both the French and the Austrians. In the middle of October, Thugut expressed the fear that any intervention by Prussia or Russia or both would completely undermine the bases of Austrian diplomacy. If the northern courts were to meddle, "the whole system that we have followed until now [would be] entirely overturned, because we have adopted the principle that we would be able to arrive at a barely tolerable peace only by the exclusion of foreign intrigues." The Austrian foreign minister, Colloredo, expressed the same apprehensions to Cobenzl: "The courts of Petersburg and Berlin seem determined to use all possible means to procure for themselves a marked influence on . . . the peace."[8]

At Lunéville, Joseph was making capital of the Russian menace. He warned Cobenzl that if the English were permitted to negotiate at Lunéville, it would also be necessary to invite the Russians.[9] Obviously, the Austrians were already discomfited by the Franco-Russian amity, but that partnership was not yet firm enough, and the Russian threat not yet tangible enough, to render them desperate.

The second phase of the negotiations extended from the beginning of December to the middle of January, and it was characterized by Cobenzl's tenacious courage in the face of the aggravation caused by the Austrian political and military crisis. This phase opened on December 3 with the Battle of Hohenlinden, in which General Jean Victor Moreau administered a sound defeat to the Austrians. News of Hohenlinden reached Lunéville on December 7.[10] Talleyrand imagined that this news would change Cobenzl's stubborn disposition. Quite the contrary: Joseph reported that Cobenzl was unmoved. He reiterated his former declaration that he would not negotiate unless an English representative were present. Again he threatened to leave Lunéville.[11] Cobenzl displayed the most amazing fortitude. Talleyrand was not only perplexed, he was furious. Joseph repeatedly remarked upon the growing disparity between the strengths of the two armies. Cobenzl had the arrogant courage to respond, "Eh, bien! You will force us . . . , if we are driven further, to make a new treaty with England."[12]

THE SITUATION of the Austrian army was undoubtedly bad,[13] but why it should have been so is a mystery. Its prospects in the spring had been brilliant. The Marengo campaign had been short, and its results, ephemeral. The preparations during the fall had been vigorous, and the winter campaign, brief. Between the Battle of Marengo (June 14) and the Treaty of Lunéville (February 9)—almost eight months—a condition of hostilities had prevailed in Italy for only eight weeks (from November 22 to January 16) and in Germany, for only nine weeks (from June 14 to July 15 and from November 22 to December 25). The Battle of Hohenlinden was admittedly a grave defeat, costing the Austrian and Imperial armies 13,727 casualties and prisoners of war while costing the French less than a quarter of that number; but the Germans had brought more troops (129,500) into the field and still enjoyed a parity in numbers and a superiority in guns and cavalry. Thus, although Austrian resources were far from exhausted and although the demands of the French would have been extremely subversive of Habsburg power and prestige, the war and its leading advocate, Baron Thugut, were very unpopular. Furthermore, both the court and the army were discouraged. Even though the army possessed equal strength or better, it repeatedly requested armistices and accepted morale-crippling terms—such as the surrender of its most defensible strong points—which were tantamount to a battle lost.[14] Yet, as late as December 18, a week before the last armistice was signed in Germany, the emperor was urging energetic measures and preparing for a stout defense of Vienna.[15] And Moreau and his chief of staff, Desolles, agreed that they could not safely advance on Vienna until Brune's army, which was still heavily engaged in Italy, had taken Carinthia, a province northeast of Venice.[16] Moreau's letters from the battlefield suggest anything but a confident ascendancy. He decided to halt his advance because, as he explained, "My front was so long, the success of the other armies so uncertain, since they needed a month of regrouping . . . , that I thought myself obliged to stop, as the season was extremely severe, and our soldiers were beginning to fatigue."[17]

The Austrian military crisis was not, then, decisive, but the Austrian predicament did not derive from French military pressure alone. In November, Paul instructed General Kutuzov to be ready to march at a moment's notice.[18] Late in December, Paul stationed Kutuzov's army at Vladimir-Volynskii, seven miles from the Austrian border, moved General Pahlen's Lithuanian army south to Brest-Litovsk, two miles from the border, and backed them up with a third army at Vitebsk.[19]

At about this time, General Sprengporten arrived in Paris. Of course, neither Bonaparte and Talleyrand, on the one hand, nor Cobenzl on the other could have known the strictly limited nature of Sprengporten's mission until he presented his credentials. This information was naturally withheld from Cobenzl for as long as possible, because Sprengporten had been charged with nothing more momentous than the formal acceptance of the Russian prisoners. The effect that the French had expected to derive from the Russian alliance now became clear, however. Talleyrand's letters to Joseph were full of warnings to Cobenzl about the proximity of Russian action against Austria. Talleyrand sought to draw full advantage from the ugly phantom of Russian intervention. On December 13 Talleyrand wrote to Joseph that Sprengporten had arrived in Brussels and was on the way to Paris: "It would seem to me that the presence of General Sprengporten ought to give some warning to M. de Cobenzl."[20]

In Lunéville, Joseph lost no opportunity to speak of the arrival of Sprengporten and its possible consequences. For the first time, Joseph thought, Cobenzl seemed to be impressed with Austria's predicament.[21] In fact, Cobenzl was impressed. He clearly saw the source of the high and rising price of peace with France: "The cajoleries between Paul I and Bonaparte render the latter all the more recalcitrant to accord us good conditions."[22] A few days later, Cobenzl confided to his court that his disposition was relenting: "I confess that as things now stand . . . I do not believe myself obligated to refuse entirely the idea of signing a definitive treaty [without the English]."[23] On December 31 Cobenzl finally yielded and informed Joseph that he was ready to negotiate separately.[24] The protocol of the negotiations was formally opened during the first week in January.[25]

NATURALLY, Austria's territorial claims suffered as much as her principles of negotiation. On December 7 Talleyrand had sent to Joseph the terms on which France would sign peace. On her northeastern frontier, France demanded the boundary of the Rhine, and Joseph was to insist that Francis II sign in the name of the empire, thereby making the emperor responsible for the indemnification of the imperial princes dispossessed by the French annexation of the left bank of the Rhine. In Italy, France was willing to restore the Kingdom of Sardinia and to concede the expansion of the Austrian province of Venice from the Adige River to the Mincio, farther west. In the remainder of northern Italy the First Consul required the recognition of the Cisalpine Republic in Lombardy, enlarged by the annexation of Parma and Modena, and the cession of the Grand Duchy of Tuscany, augmented by the Romagna and the Legations (to the south and west), to the former duke of Parma.[26]

Cobenzl was amenable to some of these terms but was opposed to others. Austria was prepared to see France annex the left bank of the Rhine, but the emperor was not willing to accept the liability for indemnifying the dispossessed princes. Austria would recognize the Cisalpine Republic but would seek the Oglio, far west of the Mincio, as the boundary of Austrian Venice. Cobenzl insisted on the restoration of the grand duke of Tuscany.[27] Austria also wanted to incorporate the Legations into Venice and to leave the Romagna to the pope.[28]

Their objectives thus conflicting, the two negotiators worked out a compromise. Joseph told Cobenzl that if the emperor would relinquish his claims to Italy west of the Adige, France would consent to the restoration of the grand duke.[29] Cobenzl accepted this proposition, and he also persuaded Joseph to renounce the principle of secularization as a means of indemnifying the injured secular princes.[30] At this point, Cobenzl decided that he had done the best he could under the adverse circumstances, and he advised Vienna that it would be well to sign the treaty immediately. He warned that procrastination would only incur further sacrifices: "There is everything to lose and nothing to gain by delaying longer."[31] The two diplomats had finally reached an agreement. But a rude surprise awaited the persecuted Cobenzl in the third phase of the negotiations—a surprise that is attributable to Paul I.

The new period was opened by Bonaparte's receipt of Paul's first letter, which arrived on January 20. This had occasioned the note to Joseph about the "extremely friendly letter from the Emperor's own hand." Bonaparte wrote: "I expect, in four or five days, a Russian plenipotentiary. Russia's disposition toward England is most hostile. You can understand why we must not do anything abruptly, because peace with the Emperor [of Germany] is nothing compared with an alliance that would subdue England and save Egypt for us." Joseph was instructed to cause delays, to raise continual complaints about the situation in Italy, to continue discussions, but to sign nothing during the next six days, "by which time we shall have reached an accord with Paul."[32]

Talleyrand now felt that he could afford to raise the French terms, and he repudiated the agreement that had been reached by Joseph and Cobenzl on January 15. He instructed Joseph to insist that the duke of Parma receive Tuscany, that Francis sign in the name of the empire, and that Austria accept as the boundary of Venice, not the Oglio, which Cobenzl had demanded, nor the Mincio, which France had previously been prepared to grant, but the Adige, a much more restricted boundary than either of the other two. Joseph was urged to exploit the imminent arrival of the Russian plenipotentiary, Stepan A. Kolychev, in support of these terms.[33]

Poor Cobenzl now had to complain that the delays were coming from the French instead of from himself. Joseph referred all Austrian proposals to Paris, and the answers never came back. Cobenzl asked in vain for a draft treaty.[34] Joseph then proceeded to use the ominous threat of Kolychev's visit to Paris in order to gain Cobenzl's consent to new terms, which finally arrived, as he had used Sprengporten to prod Cobenzl on the old ones. Talleyrand coached him as before: Austria was without a Continental ally; England was preoccupied elsewhere; despair prevailed in the Austrian army; and the Russian threat was abundantly tangible now.

So Cobenzl yielded, and the treaty was signed on February 9. Tuscany was given to the duke of Parma. The emperor agreed to indemnify the injured princes by secularizations. Austria recognized all the French satellite republics. The Adige was established as the boundary of Austrian Italy.[35] Bonaparte wrote to Paul: "In the treaty of peace that has been concluded between France and Austria, Your Majesty will see that all has been calculated to fulfill His wishes."[36]

In Vienna there seems to have been more concern with the military crisis than with the meddling of the Russians. But Cobenzl, who was far from Vienna and was armed with full powers to use his own discretion in concluding the peace,[37] was much more impressed with the danger from St. Petersburg, with whose vagaries and power he was better acquainted than was anyone in Vienna, for he had been Austria's most recent ambassador at that court. He was well aware of the serious military setbacks, and he complained of "the weakness of our army" and the "progress of the enemy," which "pass all belief,"[38] but his references to Russian interference were more frequent.[39] On January 27 he heard about Kolychev's mission. On January 30 he learned that Kolychev was no ordinary emissary but the vice-chancellor of the Russian Empire.[40] Cobenzl was extremely sensitive to pressure from that quarter. Even after the signing of the treaty and the measure of relief which that afforded him, he continued to feel the disadvantage to Austria of Russia's ill will. He hoped that Paul I would be satisfied with Austrian conduct.[41] When Kolychev arrived in Paris, Cobenzl established with him a secret line of communication, whose nature he reported to his court: "I do not fail . . . to seek means of enlightening at least Kalitschef on French policy. . . . Paul I will see more and more . . . what kind of people he has to deal with."[42] In a conversation with Kolychev, Cobenzl declared that "the break with Russia is the source of all the misfortunes of Austria."[43]

In March, Baron Thugut had his last audience with the emperor and then withdrew from the court.

5

THE RESULTS: ENGLAND

In those days . . . it was a matter of life and death for England that no Power, whether Denmark or Sweden or Russia, should acquire the power of shutting the Baltic. On this principle our Baltic policy almost exclusively rested.—John Robert Seeley, *The Growth of British Policy*

Now, it was England's turn. The English, like the Austrians, had discovered Russia much earlier than the French had. In 1553 Richard Chancellor had gone to the court of Ivan IV to search for a northeastern passage to China and to explore whatever possibilities for trade the prince of Moscow could offer. Ivan granted trading concessions to England in 1555, and the English Muscovy Company soon enjoyed a favored place in the Russian market. For the remainder of the century the contacts between the two nations multiplied. Ivan brought English craftsmen to Moscow, and English merchants probed the commercial routes to India and Persia. Ivan proposed an alliance with England, and he sought and received assurance from Queen Elizabeth of an asylum in England in the event that his enemies drove him into exile.

Evidently the new-found land excited elements of romance and fantasy among the English. Shakespeare referred to the Russians, not unflatteringly. Thus *Love's Labour's Lost* (5. 2. 363–64): "KING: 'How madam? Russians?' PRINCESS: 'Ay, in truth my lord; trim gallants, full of courtship and of state.'" The realities of the intercourse of the two nations did not match this image. The Russians resented the privileges that Ivan accorded to Englishmen, and Englishmen who traveled and traded there reported, in spite of their favored situation, that this was a land of despotic tyrants, crooked merchants, strong drink, and barbarous curiosities. George Turberville, an English ambassador to Ivan IV, wrote descriptive letters to his friends in verse:

I left my native soile, full like a retchlesse man,
And unacquainted of the coast, among the Russes ran:

A people passing rude, to vices vile inclinde,
Folke fit to be of Bacchus traine, so quaffing is their kinde.
Drinke is their whole desire, the pot is all their pride,
The sobrest head doth once a day stand needfull of a guide.

The cold is rare, the people rude, the prince so full of pride,
The Realme so stored with Monks and nunnes, and priests on
    every side:
The maners are so Turkie like, the men so full of guile,
The women wanton, Temples stuft with idols that defile
The Seats that sacred ought to be, the customes are so quaint,
As if I would describe the whole, I feare my pen would faint.
In summe, I say I never saw a prince that so did raigne,
Nor people so beset with Saints, yet all but vile and vaine. . . .
If thou be wise, as wise thou art, and wilt be ruld by me,
Live still at home, and covet not those barbarous coasts to see.

Loe thus I make an ende: none other newes to thee,
But that the countrey is too colde, the people beastly bee.[1]

The similar, but somewhat less amusing, observations in Giles Fletcher's *Of the Russe Commonwealth* (1591) are well known, as are reports of others.

When Ivan IV died, in 1584, there was a general reaction against the English, who lost their privileged position in Moscow. Throughout the seventeenth century the most active traders of western Europe on the Russian scene were the Dutch. But the travels and descriptions of Englishmen had by this time provided a great deal of information about the country. Some time around 1650, John Milton used these accounts to write *A Brief History of Muscovia*. He was interested in part in natural history. He reported that the Russian Sea "breeds a certain Beast which they call a Morse; who seeks his Food on the Rocks, climing up with help of his Teeth; whereof they make as great account, as we of the Elephant's Tooth." Walrus (*morzh*) ivory was evidently unknown in England. The Russian army, according to Milton, was 300,000 strong, a great exaggeration, and "6 great Cannon they have, whose Bullet is a yard high, so that a man may see it flying." This is undoubtedly a reference to the epic Tsar-*pushka* (or Tsar cannon), on display in the Kremlin, which was cast in 1586 and had a barrel calibre of 35 inches; it, however, never fired a shot. Milton's comments on the people and their customs not only reflected observations that were common among early travelers, but they portended the fundamental attitudes of Westerners who were to discover Russia for a long time to come. On the Church, he observed: "They hold the Ten Commandments not to concern them, saying that God gave them under Law, which *Christ* by his death on the Cross hath abrogated. . . . for Whordom, Drunkenness and Extortion none [are] worse than the Clergy." On the relations of the sexes: "When there is love between two, the Man among other trifling Gifts, sends to the Woman a Whip, to signify, if she offend, what she must expect; and it is a Rule among them, that if the Wife be not beaten once a week, she thinks her self not belov'd." And on the people's culture: "They have no Learning, nor will suffer [it] to be among them; their greatest friendship is in drinking; they are great Talkers, Lyars, Flatterers and Dissemblers."[2]

By the time of Peter I the commercial supremacy of the Dutch had been supplanted by that of the English in most parts of the world. The English were initially alarmed by Peter's conquest of the Baltic coastline. They sent expeditions to the Baltic ten times during the fourteen years following the Peace of Utrecht (1713). But calmer counsels prevailed. The account of Peter's work published in London in 1716 by an English engineer who had worked for him, John Perry's *The State of Russia under the Present Czar*—and others like it—portrayed Peter as an enlightened and progressive reformer.

England and Russia were soon drawn together by two factors. One was their common enmity for France. Russian expansion at the expense of France's eastern European allies was not regretted in England. The second was commerce. The two nations, it appeared, were ideal trading partners in a number of respects. Peter coveted European commerce but had no merchant marine; whereas the English, anxious to expand their carrying trade, were glad to provide it. England was also eager to continue her importation of naval products from the Baltic, much of the trade now being in Russian hands. As for the nature of the commercial exchange, the Russians supplied raw materials in general and sought the finished products which British ships brought from their own and other western European industries. The first commercial treaty between Russia and England, which was signed in 1734, established the enduring dominance of the English in Russian foreign trade, a situation that was to continue well into the nineteenth century. Both nations benefited from it. The balance of trade favored the Russians by more than two to one. Their trade was, however, more vital to England than to Russia for two important reasons: the naval supplies that the English imported were strategically essential; and foreign trade itself was more vital to the advanced English economy than to the backward Russian economy. The English lived with a lively awareness of their dependence on commerce. In Russia, commerce provided a significant portion—about 10 percent—of annual state revenues, in the form of tariffs, as well as luxuries for the landowners. The Russians could live without commerce; the English could not.[3]

On the basis of these two factors, then, the English and the Russians in the eighteenth century came to think of themselves, and were thought of by others, as natural allies. The significance of their relationship was clear for all to see in 1770, when, during Catherine's first Turkish war, the British helped the Russians both to fit out and to man a fleet that sailed from the Baltic to the eastern Mediterranean to annihilate the Turkish fleet in the great Battle of Chesme.

Before this decade had passed, the first signs of trouble in the alliance appeared. The Russians helped to carve up Poland, and some of the more sensitive Englishmen thought that that was not an altogether admirable thing to do. More seriously, Catherine refused to assist the English during the War of American Independence. Worse yet, before that war was over, in order to protract the conflict in western Europe and thus give herself more freedom to maneuver against the Turks, as well as simply to play a game of prestigious posturing, Catherine formed the League of Armed Neutrality.[4]

By the middle of Catherine's second war against Turkey (1787–92), the English government was alarmed about Russian designs in the eastern Mediterranean. Pitt, in this respect ahead of his time, was more alarmed than anyone else. He rather abruptly and quite prematurely sent Catherine an ultimatum in 1791, demanding that she end the war without making any annexations. Pitt had overreached himself. Catherine was both stubborn and artful when she developed an appetite for territory—it was her best talent, or at least her best political talent. She conducted an extensive public-relations campaign in the English press, giving her ambassador S. R. Vorontsov—an old English hand who was well versed in the ways of the land—plenty of money with which to do the job. In the end, the Commons, by not making any military preparations, refused to back Pitt, so he had to back down.

This was the situation in Anglo-Russian relations when the French Revolution occurred. In retrospect, it seems fairly obvious that the problems that were to bedevil these relations throughout the nineteenth century were maturing rapidly. There is no sign that the English knew anything about the "Testament" of Peter I, but it is clear that they were showing increasing concern for the fate of the empire that the "Testament" promised to destroy as the basis for all the rest of its schemes.

The outbreak of the French Revolution interrupted and postponed the natural deterioration of Anglo-Russian relations for some time. These two powers perceived the Revolution as far more threatening to both of them than either power was to the other.

Catherine had first encouraged all the other powers to involve themselves in the affairs of the Revolution, as she had encouraged them in 1780 in the affair of neutral trade, while she took the opportunity provided by their entanglement in western Europe to subjugate the Poles and the Turks in the east. That done, she prepared, in 1796, to join the coalition against France. But she died before doing so. Paul, as we have seen, first withdrew the commitment that Catherine had made to the coalition. He proclaimed his intention of remaining at peace. Then he joined the coalition in a rush of antirevolutionary fervor, after which he withdrew again. The statesmen of western Europe could find no constancy in his policy. As an English cartoon put it, playing on Paul's notorious favoritism for the Maltese Order, the orders of St. Petersburg were three: order, counterorder, and disorder.[5]

This thought was not confined to the English; but they, like the Austrians, were increasingly convinced of it. Just before taking leave of representing his government to Paul in the spring of 1800, Ambassador Whitworth wrote: "The fact is, and I speak it with regret, that the Emperor is litterally [*sic*] not in his senses. . . . This truth has been for many years known to those nearest to Him, and I have myself had frequent opportunity of observing it. But since He has come to the Throne, his disorder has gradually increased, and now manifests itself in such a manner as to fill everyone with the most serious alarm. The Emperor's actions are guided by no fixed rules or principle; Everything is the effect of Caprice and of a disordered fancy; consequently nothing is, or can be, stable."[6]

For Bonaparte, Britain was a more formidable adversary than was Austria. Austria, a land power, was vulnerable to the conventional pressure of French and Russian armies; whereas England, a sea power, was not: England was out of reach. Thus, at two critical times in Bonaparte's career, when his armies had forced the entire Continent to accept peace on his terms, the most viable weapon that he could turn against the English was commercial war. As England was the leading commercial power in the world, he needed, in this kind of war, as many allies as he could get.

Commercial war was by no means novel in the Napoleonic era. A natural accompaniment of Anglo-French wars for generations, it had been standard procedure in every war since Louis XIV at least. Therefore, the two powers lost no time after the outbreak of the Revolutionary

Wars in resorting to it. Since England controlled the sea and France did not, their strategic and economic objectives necessarily differed. The objective of the English, ostensibly at least, was to lay down a conventional blockade, the simple purpose of which was to deny France the materials that were essential to her war machine—in other words, to interrupt imports to France. The French retaliated in the only way that they had the power to retaliate: they established a land-based blockade of English exports to the Continent, at least along as much of the Continental coast as they and their allies controlled. The English hoped, figuratively, to starve the French into submission. The French hoped to impoverish England, and thus render England unable to finance the coalitions, by destroying the lucrative English export trade. The English tried to interdict imports to France; the French tried to interdict exports from England. In this struggle, the French were at a decided disadvantage, since England's control of the sea was practically unlimited; whereas French control of the land was limited to southern Europe, and the English could normally divert their exports elsewhere.

International trade in Europe was primarily seaborne. The imposition of a blockade therefore brought England into conflict with neutral trade. As the war continued, constant disputes defined three general issues of continuous discord between the mighty English navy and the smaller but commercially active powers of Denmark, Sweden, and the United States. One of these concerned the nature of contraband. The neutrals defined contraband narrowly, limiting it to materials that were of use primarily in combat. The English, on the other hand, interpreted it much more generally, including naval supplies such as sailcloth, lumber, tar and pitch, and sometimes even food and provisions.

Another issue was the definition of a blockade. The British frequently proclaimed blockades along much longer stretches of the southern European coast than they had the ships to invest effectively. The neutrals repudiated such notions of a "paper blockade," claiming that a blockade was binding on a given port only if it was so invested as to make entry into it a clear and evident danger. But when neutrals sailed ships for ports that were under an English paper blockade, British warships did not hesitate to overtake them anywhere on the high seas, examine their papers for destination, and then haul them into a British port for the purpose of confiscation.

Another issue was the neutrals' favorite principle, "free ships, free goods," by which they meant that neutral ships could trade with belligerents without any restrictions so long as they did not carry actual contraband or enemy cargoes. The crucial nature of this apparently bland proposition derived from the mercantilist practice of excluding foreigners from the trade between colonies and their mother country, to the profit of the latter. But the English navy made it impossible for the French to continue to trade with their colonies in time of war. Both the French and the neutrals were anxious to have the neutrals step into the breach—the neutrals for their own profit; the French because it was the only way for them to supply themselves from the colonies. In other words, the French and the neutrals wished to exploit the presumed immunity of the neutral flag in order to do, for different reasons, what the French were helpless to do for themselves: to supply France. The English, for obvious reasons, maintained, according to the famous "Rule of 1756," that a trade which was illegal in peace was illegal in war, on the ground that "a neutral has no right to deliver a belligerent from the pressure of his enemy's hostilities."[7]

Lastly, in order to enforce the paper blockade, the English exercised the right to "visit and search" neutral vessels in order to determine their port of embarkation, their destination, and the nature of their cargoes. The neutrals objected, arguing that a belligerent had no right to stop a neutral ship unless it had a good reason to suspect that the ship was carrying contraband. To be stopped and searched—especially if, as often happened, it was necessary to take the merchant ship into a British port in order to examine the cargo carefully—cost time and money. But merchant ships that were faced with British warships simply had to submit to search. In about 1798 the neutrals adopted the practice of convoying, that is, of giving a fleet of merchant ships a warship as escort. They ordered the captain of the warship not to allow any vessels under his escort to be stopped and searched, and to resist by force if necessary. The neutrals maintained that the presence of a warship represented the official pledge of the neutral government that the cargo under its convoy was legitimate. The English responded that the neutral governments lacked the capacity, even if they had the will, to examine all the cargoes that were carried by their ships from ports all over the world. Moreover, "from the moment that examination cannot take place, fraud no longer fears discovery."[8]

From the point of view of abstract principles of justice on the part of a power which is engaged in blockading an enemy, there is much to be said for the English position on these issues—more than there is to be said for the way in which they in fact applied them. For, with the belligerents, as with the neutrals, the principles of maritime neutrality were more a question of interest than of principle.

The neutrals' grievances stemmed primarily from the fact that the English position on these issues damaged their trade. The English could not take neutral protests very seriously, for, as they pointed out, in spite of English practices, the neutrals were benefiting enormously from the war because of the new commercial opportunities that it offered to them. After all, though the insecurity of shipping increased greatly and the cost of insurance and freight rates rose because of this, the blockade was highly imperfect, and many ships got through it—or were allowed by the British to get through, for a price. For those that did, the scarcity that the blockade caused in France bid the price of the cargoes up more than enough to make the additional risks worth while. The neutrals' complaints, then, really came down to three things. First, not that the British commercial war damaged their trade—far from it, for their trade flourished—but that British commercial practice prevented that trade from being as profitable as it potentially might have been! Second, the rights of neutral trade were not a matter for genuine compromise between two conflicting views; rather, they were largely whatever the superior navy had the power to enforce. Thus, international maritime law was, in effect, a thoroughly British and national law. Third, and most irritating of all, the British violated and abused their own system. They sailed through their own blockade, trading with the French when they found it advantageous, while denying these privileges to the neutrals except on British terms—that is, by the purchase of a special license. The British violated their own Rule of 1756 when they seized American ships trading between French colonies and the United States, a trade that the French had permitted in peacetime. In addition, the British practice of visit and search was frequently as abrupt and as arbitrary as it could well afford to be. In sum, though the British system was not necessarily disingenuous in its initial objective of forming a strategic blockade, the practices required to enforce it, plus the uneven balance of naval forces, gave the English a power that approximated invulnerability. Inevitably this tempted them to abuse their impunity, by converting the strategic blockade into a commercial blockade—a device for profiteering—to damage their competition, and to engage by violent means in commercial aggrandizement, partly for its own sake and partly to obtain the profits necessary to finance the war. The public expression of this purpose by some English statesmen might well have been attributed to them by the most caustic creations of French propaganda.

Perceval, the chancellor of the exchequer, explained it thus: "The object of the Orders in Council was not to destroy the trade of the continent, but to force the continent to trade with us." Grenville said, in 1808: "This principle of forcing trade into our markets would have disgraced the darkest ages of monopoly." Sir John Nicholls was more explicit: "If we shut the door upon neutral commerce, we must also shut it in a great degree, upon our own. If the commerce of the neutrals with the continent was stopped, we must be totally debarred from all access to the continental market. If neutrals are deprived of the continental market for their colonial produce, they will not have the means of purchasing from us. . . . The commerce of neutrals with our enemies was also necessary to us in another view. We wanted some of the produce of the enemy's country for our manufactures."[9] The foreign secretary, the marquis of Wellesley, explained to the new British minister in Washington in 1811: "You will perceive that the object of our system was not to crush the trade with the Continent. . . . we have endeavoured to permit the Continent to receive as large a portion of commerce as might be practicable through Great Britain."[10] Thus, as the war progressed, commercial blockade overwhelmed strategic blockade, and as Britain's enemies argued, Britain attempted to establish her dominion in such a way as to monopolize the trade of the whole world; as Perceval put it, "to subordinate the trade of the whole world to the development of the navy and the shipping of Great Britain."[11]

It was this policy of turning the war into an instrument of unfair competition that the neutrals found infuriating in spite of their profits.[12] In this situation it made sense for France, which was at the mercy of England on the seas, to court the neutrals and to exploit, if possible, their resentment against England. Though the Directory had made the mistake of not doing that, Bonaparte was not so foolish. Within a month of taking power, he began to parade his government as the protector of the neutrals, the disinterested advocate of "freedom of the seas."

As HAS BEEN OBSERVED, three regions of Europe were crucial to English interests. One, the Low Countries, had been in French hands since the period 1793 to 1795. Another, the Mediterranean, was hotly contested. And now, for the first time, with Russian assistance, Bonaparte prepared to strike at the third—the Baltic.

The idea for the League of Armed Neutrality was apparently French in origin. The French foreign minister, the Abbé de Bernis, conceived the project in 1758 and communicated it to his ambassador in St. Petersburg. The following year, the Russians and Swedes concluded an agreement for the protection of neutral trade against the English fleet in the Baltic, and France adhered to that pact.[13] At the time, France was not neutral, but was at war with England. Russia was at war, too, but not with England.

The League of 1780 was more formidable. Consisting of Russia, Denmark, Sweden, Prussia, and Holland and sponsored by Russia, it hurt England critically and was an important factor in England's capitulating to the American colonies. The situation in Europe at the beginning of 1800 was much like that which led to the League of 1780. But there was one important difference: early in 1800, Russia was not yet sympathetic. The French had encouraged the Swedes and Danes to form such a league in 1794, but they found that they could not sustain such pretensions without Russian support. The Russian vice-chancellor explained his government's attitude to the Danish ambassador: Russia had chosen to ignore the principles of neutral trade during the recent war simply because France would have derived too much advantage from it.[14]

By late spring of 1800 the new state of Russian relations with England augured a change in maritime policy. As soon as the new opportunity was recognized, French diplomats in northern Europe were ordered to encourage a renewal of the league.[15] Rumors of the league in the north, which circulated in late May and early June, were faithfully reported to Paris by French agents in Copenhagen and Hamburg.[16] Bonaparte told the Americans who had been sent to negotiate on neutral rights in July that the league was being formed again.[17]

The incident that precipitated the developing crisis occurred on July 25. The Danish frigate *Freja,* which was convoying Danish merchantmen, was summoned by a British squadron in the Channel to undergo search. Captain Krabbe of the *Freja* refused. In the battle that followed, the Danes had to submit to superior force. They were then taken into an English port, whereupon the Danish ministry protested to London. A long dispute ensued, followed by a convention in which the English agreed to release the convoy, and the Danes agreed to suspend convoys temporarily. However, the settlement of the principle at issue —namely, the right to search vessels under convoy—was deferred to a future negotiation.[18] The convention obviously represented simply a truce. In the meantime, even before it was signed, several things occurred which deeply aggravated the crisis.

First, the Danes proposed to London that Paul be invited to mediate the dispute, and the English, naturally, refused.[19] Simultaneously, both Denmark and Sweden appealed to Paul to support neutral rights.[20] Finally, the English sent a fleet to the vicinity of Copenhagen.

Paul responded to the appeals of the Swedes and Danes by inviting them to join him and the court of Prussia in reestablishing the Armed Neutrality of 1780.[21] He responded to the news of an English fleet in the Baltic by laying an embargo on all English ships and goods in the ports of Russia. The embargo was lifted when news of the Anglo-Danish convention reached St. Petersburg six days later,[22] but plans for the armed league proceeded. The Swedes and Danes accepted Paul's invitation at once, with great satisfaction, and the Prussians acquiesced to it in October.[23]

About this time, on September 5, the French garrison on Malta surrendered to the English siege. According to the Anglo-Russian agreement of December 1798, the island was, upon its surrender, to be occupied jointly by the English, the Russians, and the Neapolitans.[24] During the spring and summer of 1800 the British complained bitterly that the Russians had done nothing to assist in the siege. The Russian commander in the Mediterranean, Admiral Ushakov, had orders to assist the English at Malta, but he was delayed by serious supply difficulties. As he was provisioning his force in Naples in June, he received orders to return to the Black Sea.[25] In spite of the vexing lack of Russian aid, the English ambassador at Naples, Sir Arthur Paget, gave the most positive assurances that his government intended to stand by the agreement of 1798. Thus, he was quite embarrassed to learn in August that General Pigot, the new commander of English forces at Malta, had instructions to exclude Russians from the island.[26] As an honorable English diplomat, he expressed his shock and considered resigning. Foreign Minister Grenville explained to him the sudden change in policy: "Since the date of the Instructions which were given to you, the conduct of the Emperor of Russia has been repugnant. . . . The Emperor's forces have in no degree contributed to the reduction of the Island of Malta. . . . He has recently adopted measures hostile to the interests of this Court. . . . He has taken steps as must leave it doubtful whether his occupation of the whole, or any part of the Island of Malta, might not, under the influence of his present disposition, be converted to purposes essentially injurious to this Country. The former agreement was by these circumstances wholly annulled."[27] Much later, Grenville made the happy discovery, as he told his ambassador in Berlin, that the convention in question "was never signed; if it had been signed and ten times ratified, the Emperor's conduct has released us from it; but signed it never was."[28] This viewpoint was totally specious, for the Admiralty had long since informed naval commanders in the Mediterranean of the convention and had ordered them to abide by it.[29]

In any event, the English refused to admit the Russians. Paul, of course, was furious. He immediately laid down another embargo (on 30 October), and this one was accompanied by other vindictive measures. The captains and the crews of English vessels in Russia were arrested and shipped off under guard to different towns in the interior, some of them as remote from the Baltic as Voronezh. All payments to Englishmen were stopped, and a guard was posted at the door of the residence of every English merchant in the capital.[30] Finally, orders were issued to prepare all the Baltic ports against attack, to ready a fleet of forty warships, and, if units of the British fleet appeared off Russian shores, to burn all English ships and goods in reprisal.[31]

Meantime, Bonaparte left no stone unturned in encouraging the small powers of the north to take a similarly strong stand. He offered, if the league should provoke England to hostile acts against Denmark, to provide several battalions of French troops to defend that kingdom.[32] He negotiated a liberal agreement on neutral trade with the Americans, which he published in Le Moniteur.[33] He instructed Talleyrand to inform the diplomatic corps that France would not make peace with England until the sacred principles of the Armed Neutrality were recognized.[34] His Spanish ally also intervened to try to stiffen the neutrals' attitude.[35] But Bonaparte was too far away to have much direct influence on the Baltic. He had to rely chiefly on the initiative of Paul, who was determined to play the role of Baltic big brother.

It is not true, as historians have often said, that the northern neutrals were reluctant to form the League of 1800. They were actually anxious to do so, and both Sweden and Denmark responded with alacrity to Paul's proposal, which they had done so much to encourage. But it is quite true that they were reluctant to convert a league for the defense of neutral rights into a device for a despot's revenge. This was especially true of Denmark, whose situation at the very entrance of the Baltic would expose her to the first English retaliation. Bourgoing quite accurately informed Talleyrand of this state of affairs;[36] the Danes insinuated it unmistakably to the English.[37] But once these powers had asked Paul to take up their cause, thereby provoking the English, he was all the protection they had. They were at his mercy, and they dared not provoke his temper by refusing to do his bidding. The Danish chancellor, Bernstorff, voiced the dilemma thus: "We do not deceive ourselves . . . that the general object of the union that this Sovereign proposes to the powers of the North may lead us beyond the limits of our particular interests, and that we must, like the Court of Sweden, use some circumspection in this regard, but we can promise ourselves from this union advantages so important, and the Emperor has acquired such a right to our confidence . . . , that we do not think that we should rebuff him by [raising] difficulties . . . that would only serve to change his good dispositions and weaken the favorable impression that he seems to have conceived for us."[38] In September, Bernstorff was more optimistic about this dilemma than he was in December. The degree to which the situation forced him to surrender his foreign policy to St. Petersburg was pathetic. In negotiating the new league, each power had dealt exclusively with St. Petersburg: not one official communication on the subject had passed between Copenhagen and Stockholm. As the British minister in Berlin put it, the conduct of the neutrals was to be ascribed in great part to their dread of Russia. Prussia was in a similar situation: "Her interest indeed should lead her a different way, but her only political motive is fear, and the fear of Russia is perhaps the one which now preponderates."[39]

So, on December 16 and 18, Denmark, Sweden, and Prussia signed, in St. Petersburg, treaties renewing the League of 1780. Separate and secret articles in the Russo-Danish treaty required Russia to prepare fifteen ships of the line and five frigates and Denmark to prepare eight ships of the line and two frigates in order to enforce their claims.[40]

John Quincy Adams, in Berlin, was a little astonished at these proceedings. He thought that "the question whether free ships shall make free goods is to the empire of Russia, in point of interests, of the same importance that the question whether the seventh commandment is conformable to the law of Nature, would be to the guardian of a Turkish Haram." He clearly recognized, however, the chief beneficiary of the arrangement. "From the moment when the convention of armed neutrality was signed the northern league must be considered as in effectual alliance with France."[41] This reflected Bonaparte's view as well. He even offered to join the league, belligerent though he was. He wrote to Paul about cooperating with the league and about vast expeditions against the English in Ireland, India, and the New World.[42] He made arrangements with the Spanish navy to combine their movements, if possible, with a Russian squadron.[43] Not by formal coalition but by virtue of the partial coincidence of aims of the French and their allies, on the one hand, and of the Northern League on the other, the English faced the prospect of hostilities with the navies of France, Spain, the Low Countries, Russia, Denmark, and Sweden at once. In addition, they were afraid that if the American election were won by Jefferson—"the life and soul of the French faction in America"—the United States would also adhere to the league.[44]

On 27 January, Paul wrote to Bonaparte, asking him to do something to reinforce the Northern League: "I cannot but propose, if it would be at all possible, that you undertake something against the coasts of England, which, though it may seem isolated at the moment, might produce an effect to make her repent of her despotism and her arrogance."[45] Bonaparte prepared to do just that, and by summer he had assembled a threatening force in Boulogne.[46]

Among other joint projects, Guttin had proposed an expedition to India. There is some vague evidence of communication between the powers on this subject, but it is neither clear nor satisfactory. It is certain, however, that Bonaparte considered such a scheme at the time.[47] The Danish ambassador in Paris reported the First Consul's thoughts:

> While talking the other day with the First Consul about the probability of a war between Russia and England, he expressed the opinion that the Emperor of Russia could not attack England more damagingly [*essentiellement*] or with more advantage than by sending from the Caucasus an army of 100,000 men across Persia to fall on the English in India. . . . It is certain that the execution of this project has very seductive charms for the Court of Petersburg, and like a good Dane, I prefer that the Russians turn their attention toward the Orient rather than toward the West, [so] I strongly urged Bonaparte to recommend to Paul the expedition against the English in India. There are many reasons for preferring to see the English attack the Russians in the Black Sea rather than in the Baltic without molesting us.[48]

Eight days later, Paul issued orders for such an expedition.[49] It would take a long time to reach India, of course, and it may have been chimerical to try. In any case, the English were not long in learning about it: it was reported to them by their minister in Hamburg.[50]

ON FEBRUARY 27 Bonaparte sketched out for Paul the next step in the grand plan. Bonaparte would undertake to close the ports of Naples and Portugal to English trade. Paul could do the same with respect to the northern powers. Could he not also do something about the coast of Hanover? If so, England would be entirely cut off from the Continent.[51]

Paul was thinking along similar lines. Having crushed English trade in his own land, he next banned Russian exports to Prussia on the ground that they would be reexported to England. Then he forbade Russian merchants abroad to trade with Englishmen. Finally, he forbade any Russian exports at all without his express approval.[52]

In southern and western Europe, France's allies—Spain and Holland—had followed French commercial policy for years. After the Peace of Lunéville, Naples remained at war with the French. Thus the Italian coastline was the only part of southern Europe from which trading could still be carried on with England. A Russian diplomat, Levashev, who had just arrived in Naples, was received in grand style by Bonaparte's commander, Murat. Murat presented him, to make his travels safer, with a pair of pistols "de la manufacture de Versailles." Levashev and Murat were seen at the theater together. Murat informed Bonaparte: "Costume ball, grand illumination, spectacles, banquet, guard of honor, visits of all the authorities, this is how I have received M. Levachoff."[53]

Immediately thereafter, Murat, on Bonaparte's orders, informed the Neapolitans that Paul had interceded for them and that the French were thus disposed to be merciful, but that the Neapolitans must first close their ports to the English. General Acton, the English adventurer and prime minister of Naples, reported to Paget that there was some secret understanding between the French and the commander of the Russian troops at Naples, General Borozdin.[54] A French diplomat was dispatched hurriedly to Florence, where he signed a peace with Naples on March 28, stipulating that trade with the English be stopped.[55]

Farther north, off the port of Leghorn, the American consul reported that the English warships that had been patrolling the shore had suddenly disappeared.[56]

Northern Europe, however, remained beyond Bonaparte's reach. On January 20 he ordered Talleyrand to write to the Senate in Hamburg, suggesting that "the time has come when the maritime powers must take sides." He made similar hints to Prussia. When the Prussians demurred, he threatened them. But, as he put it, "the Prussians always talk of marching [to the ports], but they don't budge."[57]

The position of the Prussians was peculiar. They alone of the confederated northern powers had no navy; thus, they risked little or nothing through English retaliation. But however insignificant Prussia was as a naval power, she was, from the commercial point of view, at the heart of the whole grand scheme. The course of the French Revolutionary Wars, especially the conquest of the Low Countries and the commercial policy of the French governments, had caused a major reorientation of English trade from southern to northern Europe. During the eight years preceding this crisis, English exports to Germany had multiplied by more than six times. Of the five great river systems that bore the bulk of English trade with the Continent in 1801, three—the Vistula, the Oder, and the Ems—emptied on the coasts of Prussia; and the other two—the Weser and the Elbe—could be controlled merely by occupying the neighboring, helpless little state of Hanover. As John Quincy Adams explained, "Almost the only commerce of England with the continent of Europe is at the mercy of this [Prussian] Government. . . . In this contest not one of the powers engaged will have a part so little hazardous and so certainly advantageous to perform as Prussia." But the Prussians, less than a generation after the death of Frederick the Great, had already acquired a reputation for being cravenly cautious. Thus, Prussia was excepted from the retaliation of the British against the shipping of the other powers in the league in the hope that she would take a passive role in it. And the Prussians were genuinely torn between their profound timidity and their commitment to neutrality, on the one hand, and the prospect of cheap aggrandizement in Hanover on the other.[58]

Bonaparte was not in a position to do more than threaten. Here, especially, his ambitions required the services of a stout ally. In the words of Le Moniteur (20 February 1801): "Russia was created to take the part in the North which France has taken in the South." It was up to Paul to help the northern powers decide what they should do.

Paul had already stationed a large army on the border of Prussian Poland in December. On March 7 A. B. Kurakin, vice-president of the College of Foreign Affairs, had an official conversation with the Danish ambassador, which the ambassador, apparently in a high state of excitement, reported as follows. Kurakin had come to see him to ask him "to transmit to His Highness the [Danish] Prince Royal [Paul's] views of friendship for our court and its projects, and finally His Ultimatum in the present circumstances, Ultimatum already known to His Majesty the King of Prussia, to the Great Consul Bonaparte, and also has the approval and consent of these two governments." The ultimatum demanded the immediate occupation of Hamburg by Denmark and of Hanover by Prussia.[59] Presumably, a similar notice was given the Prussians at the same time. If so, they did not heed it soon enough, for a more severe warning soon followed. On March 23 Paul wrote to his ambassador in Berlin: "Declare, Monsieur, to the King that if he does not decide to occupy Hanover you are to quit the court within twenty-four hours."[60]

The Danish minister in Berlin began to clear arrangements for the occupation with the Prussian government at once. He reported to Copenhagen that Kriudener, the Russian ambassador, had just received a packet from St. Petersburg and had then hurried to the court. He explained that it was the twenty-four hour ultimatum, and that the Prussians were very *pleased* about it.[61] On March 29 the Danes occupied Hamburg, embargoed English trade throughout their dominions (for the first time), removed the sea buoys from the Elbe, and extinguished the beaconlight on Heligoland. On April 5 they occupied Lübeck on the Trave. On March 30 the Prussians occupied Hanover and closed the Elbe, the Weser, and the Ems.[62]

Thus, Bonaparte and Paul severed English intercourse with the Continent from the Adriatic to the Arctic with the single exception of Portugal, and Portugal succumbed to a Franco-Spanish invasion during May and June.[63]

TWICE DURING HIS CAREER, Bonaparte succeeded in this trick of closing the Continent to English trade. Unhappily, the first occasion has been nearly ignored by historians. The second blockade lasted much longer, and it has been remembered, wrongly, as having been much more dramatic. The purpose of the rather carefully worked out Continental System of 1806–12 was twofold. The most obvious object of it was to ruin the English economy and, hence, England's ability to finance coalitions and to make war. As such, it did not aim at starving England into submission; for even when France controlled all the Continent, she did not control the seas. Hence, the blockade was designed primarily, not to keep England from importing goods from Europe, but to keep England from exporting goods to Europe, her most important market. The theory was that if England, the most highly developed industrial and commercial nation of the day, could not export, her sophisticated industry, commerce, and finance alike would collapse. A second feature of the system was traditionally mercantilist and protectionist. With England excluded from the Continent, France could make all of Europe a captive market. France could, and did, force most of the Continent to substitute France for England as a purveyor of finished goods, and she traded with the other nations of the Continent on terms that were profitable for France and ruinous to them. Bonaparte was therefore willing to sell to England from the Continent, but only through France on a regular basis. At times, when he found it advantageous, as, for example, when he needed uniforms for the Russian campaign, he was even willing to issue licenses to buy from England, though he never allowed his satellites to do so. His own system of commercial blockade, then, once he had acquired control of the entire Continent, was much like the English system: it was both a strategic and a commercial blockade, whose different aims sometimes were but sometimes were not compatible.

The most informed opinion on the effects of the Continental System on the English economy from 1806 to 1812 is that of François Crouzet. Crouzet thinks that it hurt the English badly, that it caused them to have an adverse balance of trade consistently, and that it interrupted the growth of English industry, inflicted serious hardships on the working class, and stimulated inflation. The English responded by seeking new markets, especially in Latin America, and by bribing and smuggling in order to beat the blockade. Through such means they succeeded in maintaining their exports at a remarkably high level. The system ultimately failed to bring England to her knees, which Crouzet blames on Bonaparte himself. First, he cheated on his own system. Second, his foreign policy drove the three nations that made up the system to go to war against him, and therefore to have to trade with England: Spain in 1808, Austria in 1809, and Russia in 1812. Crouzet says flatly that the system *was* working from the Treaty of Tilsit (July 1807) to the Spanish insurrection (July 1808) and from the spring of 1810 to the campaign of 1812.[64]

The situation of the British economy in the spring of 1801 was not like that of 1807. It was more precarious in a number of ways. First, the English, in 1807, warned by their previous experience, were carrying on more trade with the United States and Canada than they had in 1801. Second, the Spanish insurrection of 1808 had provoked a revolt of the Spanish colonies in Latin America and thus, during the second blockade, had provided the English with an important market that had not been available to them in 1801. Third, Sweden remained outside the Continental System during the second blockade throughout 1808 and 1809, during which period English trade with Sweden increased by three and one-half times.[65]

Finally—and from the point of view of short-term effects, most significantly—the earlier blockade had fallen more heavily on England's imports than on her exports for two reasons: it had been hastily improvised; and it was not—as the second blockade was—a sophisticated plan designed to subvert English credit, but was simply an embargo on trade. And for completely fortuitous reasons—the accidents of geography and of nature—it was precisely in the area of imports that England was peculiarly vulnerable in 1801. The Baltic countries supplied the two things that were most essential to England if she were to persevere in the war: naval supplies and grain.

More than any other nation in Europe, England needed a good supply of forest products, and perhaps this made England the most deforested nation in Europe.[66] Eight years of war had worked a serious strain on the navy, and now the navy was cut off from its most essential foreign source of supply.

Ambassador Whitworth had foreseen the consequences of the blockade as early as April 1800: "The unfriendly and irritable state of the Emperor's disposition towards the English makes it absolutely necessary that every means should be employed to prevent his knowing that the Navy board is in want of Stores. The Board should be cautious in writing by the Post as every Letter is opened and His Imperial Majesty may be induced to stop the exportation [from Russia] which is now allowed, and that only for the spars and timber cut down." Whitworth was trying to have an Englishman ship timber out of Russia under a pseudonym. He hoped that Grenville would "have the goodness to communicate this to Sir Andrew Hammond [English consul on the Baltic] as [diplomats in the capital have] no safe mode of doing so."[67]

For hemp, pitch, tar, and turpentine, England was almost entirely dependent on imports. The United States supplied most of the turpentine, but pitch and tar came from Sweden and Russia as well as from the United States; and Russia supplied almost all the hemp.[68]

Though the sources of English timber were somewhat more generally distributed and though timber from non-British (and colonial) sources amounted to only one-fifth of the total needs of the navy, in certain specialized categories— large oak planks, bending boards, heavy ship timbers, and, especially, masts, spars, and yards—the situation was more critical. Almost all the great masts and the majority of spars and yards came from the Baltic area. The most important supplier was Prussia, which sent most of the oak, especially the famous "crown planks" of Danzig, four-fifths of the fir and pine, and many of the masts. Russia's only important contribution was masts, but she supplied two-thirds of these. Norway (Denmark) and Sweden were of somewhat lesser importance. These four countries furnished England with virtually all the timber supplies that she got in Europe, especially masts and oak.[69] England got over four hundred loads of heavy oak timber annually from Danzig, one thousand masts a year from Memel, and eleven thousand loads of oak planking from Prussia.[70] In the spring of 1801 this supply was cut off absolutely.

The naval-supply situation was serious, and it could be expected to affect the combat stature of the navy within a matter of months. But it was not so mortal a threat as the grain crisis.

During the first half of the eighteenth century, English agriculture had flourished, but during the second half, there had frequently been bad harvests. Unfortunately, at about the same time, a rapid growth in population began. The English populace approximately doubled during the reign of George III (1760–1820). Around 1770 to 1775, therefore, the English began to import more grain than they exported.[71] Three-fourths of these imports, during the Napoleonic era, were supplied by the Baltic countries. Though reformers and the government made strenuous efforts to expand production in England during the Napoleonic Wars, and with considerable success, the situation remained precarious. With a normal or good harvest, the English, if they practiced economies and imported from the United States or Ireland, could feed themselves; otherwise they had to import from the Continent.[72]

In the winter of 1799/1800 there were heavy rains and frosts. In the summer of 1800 there was intense heat and a prolonged drought. The grain crop, which normally was harvested in August and September, reached the market in October and November. Hence, the price of grain was usually highest in September, when the previous harvest was nearly depleted. The harvest of 1799 had been quite bad, and by late summer of 1800, food riots and civil disturbances occurred in many parts of the kingdom. The *Morning Chronicle* reported such events on August 19 and September 3, 5, 11, 14 (Birmingham), 17, 18, 19 (London), and 23. The *Times* began to devote a regular column to such riots. This news was conscientiously reprinted in *Le Moniteur*. Arthur Young, the famous journalist and agronomist, felt compelled to publish a pamphlet, "The Question of Scarcity Plainly Stated, and Remedies Considered," to disprove rumors that there was a conspiratorial grain monopoly:

> The Author of these papers has but one motive in printing, which is that of convincing the people, that the evil they suffer at present, is to be attributed only to the unfavourable seasons; and consequently that there is every reason for submitting with patience to the will of Heaven. The kingdom in general was well impressed with this idea, till certain persons attempted to prove that the scarcity was not real; that the deficiency was small; and the stock in hand last harvest large; manifestly, though perhaps not intentionally, implying that the high price was unjust, and therefore might be easily remedied.

Young, who had investigated carefully by corresponding with friends, found a shortfall in the harvest that varied from one-fourth to one-half throughout the kingdom. "The least sign of discontent or disturbance, can only increase the evil; while patience, quiet, and tranquillity, will second and give effect to every measure that is had recourse to."[73] Nevertheless, seditious slogans circulated, such as "Peace and Large Bread or a King without a Head."[74] In fact, the harvests of 1799 and 1800 were the two worst during the whole Napoleonic era.

In November of 1800, Bonaparte gave strict orders to prohibit the export of grain from the Low Countries "under any pretext whatsoever." About the same time, Paul's embargo caught one hundred and fifty English ships in Russian ports; these were laden chiefly with timber and grain.[75]

On November 11 the king called a special session of Parliament, where he explained:

> My lords and gentlemen;
> My tender concern for the welfare of my subjects, and the sense of the difficulties with which the poorer classes particularly have to struggle, from the present high price of provisions,

have induced me to call you together at an earlier period than I had otherwise intended. [Parliament must] alleviate this severe pressure. . . .

For the object of immediate relief, your attention will naturally be directed, in the first instance, to the best mode of affording the earliest and the most ample encouragement for the importation of all descriptions of grain from abroad.[76]

Parliament responded promptly. Commons established the Special Committee on the High Price of Provisions; placed bounties on the importation of fish, wheat, barley, rye, oats, flour, and rice; gave special poor relief to certain towns; prohibited the use of grain for distilling; established public soup kitchens; forbade the exporting of grain; and incidentally, suspended the writ of habeas corpus.[77]

Both the Special Provisions Committee and the Board of Trade interviewed Claude Scott, the largest grain merchant in the kingdom. Scott estimated that only one-eighth of the grain that was then being sold in the kingdom was home-grown. Asked about likely sources for additional foreign grain, Scott replied: "Our principal source . . . may be looked for this year from the Baltic, and chiefly from Poland [Danzig, i.e., Prussia]."[78] In fact, the Baltic usually supplied about three-fourths of Britain's grain imports; the New World, about one-fourth. The importation of all varieties of grain into England in 1800 had been about twice the annual average, and even more than that was required for 1801.[79]

British apprehension was reflected in the press. On January 19 the *Times* nervously explained the rising prices of grain: "The pretence for these advances is, a report circulated with great industry, but destitute of all truth, that the Prussian ports will be shut against us, and all further importation stopped." There was a similar rumor two days later, "and our Funds again fell in consequence of it." But the Prussians did join the Continental league in spite of the blandishments of British policy.

The Sound Dues toll book, the ledger that records the tariff assessed by the Danes since ancient times on cargoes passing through the narrow strait between Elsinore and Helsingborg going to and from the Baltic, accurately reflects the impact of Bonaparte's diplomatic successes on English supply. In the first four months of 1801, not a single English ship was recorded in the Sound, and only one was recorded in May. Admittedly, this was not the busy season in the Baltic, but during the same four-month period, 1,176 other ships were recorded; and in the corresponding months of 1800 and 1802, there were 745 and 1,071 English ships respectively.[80] This critical part of the blockade was airtight.

Merchants in the New World, who hurried to take advantage of this lucrative situation, supplied during 1801 about four times their usual average. Still, the 3.5 million bushels of all kinds of grain that were provided by the United States and Canada did not approach the more than 16 million bushels that were needed.[81] The net supply of the most important categories (barley, oats, wheat, and wheat flour) fell from a weekly average of 408,000 bushels in the last six weeks during which the Baltic was open (from mid November to 1 January) to an average of 136,000 bushels in March.[82]

Prices, of course, reflected the crisis. In March, when Parker and Nelson sailed for the Baltic, the general price index reached its highest level of the Napoleonic period, and the price of wheat reached the highest level since grain prices had first been recorded during the fourteenth century.[83] In the words of an old classic: "The prices of provisions, which, at the beginning of 1799 were as low as they had been on an average of some years anterior to 1793, advanced, in common with other articles of European produce, to an unprecedented height, as a necessary consequence of the two very deficient harvests of 1799 and 1800, combined with actual and apprehended obstructions to importation."[84] The suffering in the kingdom was such that the birth rate (as reflected by baptisms) fell by 8.4 percent (258,685 in 1799 to 237,029 in 1801) and the death rate rose by 11.5 percent (183.267 in 1799 to 204,434 in 1801).[85] And this was still seven months from the next harvest and six months from the seasonal price peak in September.

As IF THIS were not trial and tribulation enough for merry old England, there was more. The Irish rebellion of 1798 had been put down with great ferocity. Martial law was still being maintained there, amid much political tension. The prime minister, William Pitt, was concerned about pacifying the land with concessions. Otherwise, it represented a standing invitation to a French invasion, which actually materialized, but was bungled, in 1798. The governments of England and Ireland were at this time united only in the person of the king. Self-government for Ireland was a nasty problem. Since the Restoration Settlement of Charles II's Clarendon Code (1661–65), Catholics had had no political rights. In 1793 they were given the right to vote, but they still did not have the right to hold political office. Therefore, the Irish Parliament consisted entirely of Protestants who were elected by a populace that was three-fourths Catholic. This situation led Pitt to consider the prospect of emancipation, which would grant Catholics the right to hold office. But he thought that a Catholic Parliament would make the land a hell for Protestants. So he hit upon a clever solution, a combination of emancipation and a union of the English and Irish parliaments. This arrangement would satisfy the demand for representation but would provide for protection of the Irish Protestant minority by the English Protestant majority. In March 1800 the Irish Parliament was persuaded to pass a bill that provided for parliamentary union.[86] Emancipation was a clearly implied concomitant. But here Pitt hit a snag: George III flatly refused to go along with emancipation; the cabinet was divided. When Cornwallis's son was asked who would succeed his father as viceroy of Ireland if emancipation were refused, he answered, logically enough, "Bonaparte."

In the meantime, to add to England's difficulties, George III went mad.[87]

At the end of March, Prince Adolphus Frederick, George's seventh son, went to Potsdam to confer with the King of Prussia.[88] From December a sense of the desperateness of England's situation and an inclination to make peace became more and more evident. The American ambassador reported: "I am not unmindful that the present is a favourable moment for the discussion of the Questions of disagreement between us and this Government, and in one or two conferences with Lord Grenville I have thought I perceived a temper which promised rather more than I have been accustomed to expect." Somewhat later, he recounted the embarrassment that the Northern League caused George III personally because of his dual role as elector of Hanover and king of England. "Among the surmises which circulate in the present moment of uncertainty, one which is not the least curious, nor most improbable, states a division of opinion in the cabinet respecting Hanover, to preserve which against the King of Prussia it is said to have been proposed that the Elector should join the northern League at the risque of a misunderstanding with the King of Great Britain."[89]

A Commons deputy named Jones moved, in December, that "an humble address be presented to his Majesty, earnestly imploring his Majesty, that, taking it into his royal consideration, the sufferings of his loyal and affectionate people, he will be graciously pleased no longer to listen to the counsels of his present Ministers, who, by their profusion and extravagance, have brought their country to the brink of famine and ruin, and who, by their incapacity, have shewn themselves unequal to conduct the war with effect, or enter into negotiations of peace with honour." The motion failed. But by March the situation was more alarming. Another deputy, named Grey, said on March 25:

270 millions have been added to our national debt, exclu-

sive of imperial and other loans, and of the reduction effected by the sinking fund; and yet we are told . . . that . . . the country [is] in a flourishing situation. I ask any man, whether, from diminished comforts, or from positive distress, he does not feel this declaration an insult. Ask the ruined manufacturers of Yorkshire, Manchester and Birmingham; ask the starving inhabitants of London and Westminster. In some parts of Yorkshire, formerly the most flourishing, it appears from an authentic paper, which I hold in my hand, that the poor-rates have increased from 522*l.* to 6000*l.* a year; . . . In Birmingham, I know, from undoubted authority, there are near 11,000 who receive parochial relief, though the whole number of the inhabitants cannot exceed 80,000—and this of a town reckoned one of the most prosperous in England. . . . It is said, that though one half our property is gone, it is well sacrificed, as it has saved the remainder. Sir, I deny the assertion. One half of our property is gone, but the remainder is in greater danger than before.[90]

Even six months earlier, Grenville's brother foresaw the only way out: "The scarcity of bread and the consequent distress of the poor, if it continues, will I believe, force you whether you will or not to make your peace with France."[91]

And so it was. The cabinet of Pitt and Grenville resigned, giving way to Addington (prime minister) and Hawkesbury (foreign minister) on March 14. This completed Bonaparte's rout of his enemies. It is astonishing what changes he worked in the politics of Europe in the eighteen months after 18 Brumaire. One cabinet after another was restructured with men who either were sympathetic to Bonaparte or were less hostile to him than their predecessors: Rostopchin supplanted Panin in Russia; Godoy took the place of Urquijo in Spain; Thugut was forced out in Austria; and finally, Pitt fell.

Six days after taking office, Hawkesbury invited M. Otto, the resident French commissioner for the exchange of prisoners, to call on him. On the following day, March 21, he gave to Otto a note which declared "His Majesty's Disposition to enter into immediate Negotiations for the Restoration of Peace. . . . His Majesty is ready to send a proper Person to Paris."[92] In January 1800 the English had contemptuously refused to negotiate with France until the Bourbons had been restored. Fifteen months later, they offered to send an Englishman to Paris.

Simultaneously, on March 24, Hawkesbury sought a reconciliation with Russia on Russia's terms through Carysfort in Berlin:

You will endeavour, in the first Instance, to negotiate a

Treaty on Maritime Law . . . similar to that which Mr. Vansittart is instructed to negotiate with the Government of Copenhagen, but if you should find the Russian Government unwilling to enter into Engagements of this nature, His Majesty will be satisfied with a formal Renunciation of the Convention signed at Petersburgh on the 16th of December, and will, on this Condition, and on that of the Embargo being immediately taken off, consent to the Terms which have been proposed respecting Malta [i.e., restoration].[93]

6

BLOOD, SWEAT, AND TEARS

At a time, when the convulsions, the efforts, and the malignity of France, have shaken, more or less, every government in Europe but our own; at a time, when every other country is nearly exhausted, both in treasure and population, by the expences and ravages of this cruel and unparalleled war, with what satisfaction, notwithstanding all our reverses, ought we to look around, from the proud eminence on which we are placed. Whilst other nations, breathless and terrified, are shrinking from the contest; imploring peace, or suing for protection; deserting their old friends, and leaguing with their late enemies; Britain, reposing on her resources, the virtue and patriotism of her inhabitants, the extensive range of her commerce, the vigour and firmness of her government, the distinguished bravery of her troops, and the unconquerable spirit of her navy, surveys the scene with interest but calmness, with solicitude but without dismay.

Deserted by every friend, surrounded by a host of foes, she stands alone, to try her strength against the united efforts of Europe. But, neither the disgraceful secession of her allies, nor the unexpected increase of her enemies, can startle her from her purpose, which is the conservation of her independence and her rights. As she has been moderate in prosperity, so she can be firm in adversity. Fear will not accomplish, what force can never extort.

. . . The disjointed politics, the follies, and dissensions of our allies, have, in regular succession, severed them from their interests, and applied the seal of ruin to their fate. . . . Let us profit by their example. . . . Against a free, an unanimous, a brave and loyal people, nothing can prevail.
—William Hunter, *A Short View of the Political Situation of the Northern Powers . . . in 1800*

WITH HIS PLANS probably developing better than he had dared to hope, Bonaparte prepared after the Peace of Lunéville to undertake the last two parts of his Franco-Russian project. In late February or early March he approached Cobenzl in Paris about partitioning the Ottoman Empire. Emperor Francis wrote to Cobenzl that though Austria did not wish to see the Ottoman Empire partitioned, it would be impossible for her to stop the French and Russians if they were determined to do so. In that case, he said, Austria would, of course, participate.[1]

Next came the so-called pacification of the Continent, or what Guttin had called "giving the law" to Europe. Because of the French annexation of the left bank of the Rhine, the princes who had lost territory there had to be compensated in other parts of the empire. In Guttin's view, the German Empire would have to be dissolved, and the German powers would have to look to France and Russia to mediate their claims.[2] When Sprengporten arrived in Paris in December, Talleyrand appealed to Paul, as we have seen, to "send a plenipotentiary armed with full powers to make definitive arrangements of affairs in Europe." Talleyrand invited Paul not only to take part in the negotiations at Lunéville, which Kolychev was too late to do, but to join in settling the question of the German indemnities—that is, the reorganization of the empire.

The Prussian ambassador in St. Petersburg actively sought to have Russia intervene in favor of Prussian gains in Germany. A special Prussian emissary, M. Lucchesini, was sent to Paris to intercede for Prussian interests there. Lucchesini was led to believe that Talleyrand intended to settle the question during the course of tripartite negotiations carried on by a French, a Prussian, and a Russian plenipotentiary. In February, however, Lucchesini reported with some alarm: "All the information which I have received since my last dispatch and all the inferences which I draw from the dispositions of the First Consul and of his minister confirm me in my . . . conviction of the preponderance which they want to accord to Russia in the final arrangement of the affairs of Germany."[3]

Every facet of the grand plan, it seemed, was proceeding toward a smooth consummation.

IT WAS NOW TIME, if there was ever to be such a time, for the English to defend themselves. They had been pushed to the last extremity, and though they had committed themselves to negotiations in March, they could not negotiate a decent settlement unless there were a material improvement in their circumstances.

In January they retaliated. They captured the Danish colonies in the New World—the Virgin Islands; laid an embargo on Danish, Swedish, and Russian shipping in the British Isles; forbade the payment of British debts to nationals of these three powers; and took measures to get British shipping out of range of reprisals.[4]

Meantime, in a plan so secret that it was called simply "a particular service," Admiral Sir Hyde Parker was directed to go to Yarmouth and await orders. His mission turned out to be an expedition to the Baltic. The First Lord of the Admiralty said that it was "necessary more than ever to expedite the preparation of the [Baltic fleet], as the season is advancing, and the Dane seems by the latest accounts likely to fight stout."[5]

Admiral Parker, however, was in no mood to expedite his departure. For he, at the age of sixty-two, had "recently married to an ample young creature known to the irreverent as 'batter pudding.' "[6] Lady Parker, "the fair Fanny," as the First Lord called her, had arranged a farewell ball for March 13. Parker delayed his departure in order to attend the ball, thus risking the success of his crucial mission. Lord Nelson, his second in command, chafed, impatient as always. Even the market women gossiped, "Consider how nice it must be laying in bed with a young wife, compared to a damned cold raw wind!"[7]

Someone apparently informed the Admiralty. It has been suggested that it was Nelson, through private channels; and this would not be unlikely. In any case, the First Lord wrote to Parker to say that, having heard that the fleet might delay for several days more "for some trifling circumstances," he had "sent down a messenger purposely to convey to you my opinion, as a private friend, that any delay in your sailing would do you irreparable injury."[8]

So, the ball was canceled, and the fleet sailed on March 12. As it departed, Nelson wrote to a friend that "the ball for Friday night is knocked up by your and the earl's un-politeness to send gentlemen to sea instead of dancing with nice white gloves."[9] But to Parker he wrote: "Never did our Country depend so much on the success of any Fleet as on this. . . . I am of the opinion that the boldest measures are the safest."[10] He was to have the opportunity at Copenhagen to vindicate his principle.

The combination of Nelson and Parker was not a happy choice of commanders. Nelson, who had just been promoted to vice-admiral on 1 January, did not have enough rank to be placed in command. He was, true to his reputation, headstrong and impetuous, and he had not always been scrupulously and willingly obedient. Parker apparently did not feel comfortable with Nelson, so he snubbed and neglected him and did not keep him informed of plans. This pattern of behavior was noticed by the other officers. When a junior officer boasted of having previously caught a fine turbot—a European variety of flounder, which was considered a delicacy—off the Dogger Bank, Nelson conceived a plan for breaking the ice between them. Remarking that Parker showed a taste for fine living, he ordered a line to be cast, and a turbot was duly caught and sent to the admiral. Though the incident did not altogether thaw the old man, he did respond with a note of thanks, and it thus prompted somewhat better communications between the two.

But there were differences of strategy as well as of temperament. Nelson had no patience with the diplomatic niceties of protocol. As he expressed it, British warships were the best negotiators in Europe. Hence, he wished to sail into the Baltic with guns ablaze. Moreover, during the Mediterranean campaign of 1799, he had already developed a distaste for Russians, especially for Paul; and his attitude was much like the one expressed to Grenville by the marquis of Buckingham: "Denmark will pay the piper; but I wish I could see the prospect of shaking the *bear* by the *beard*."[11] He wanted to leave a few frigates in front of Copenhagen, ignore the Swedes, and sail straight for Russian waters. There he would find half the Russian fleet at Kronstadt and the other half frozen in at Revel, and he could destroy it piecemeal. He was sure that, once the Russians had been humbled, the other powers would be reasonable.

Parker saw it quite otherwise. He had no intention of barbarously attacking anyone without negotiating first, and he would not consider anything so daring as to sail deep into the Baltic with the Swedish and Danish fleets left intact in his rear. Hence, Parker anchored the fleet outside the Sound and sent a diplomat, Nicholas Vansittart, to Copenhagen with an ultimatum: The Danes must consent within forty-eight hours to withdraw from the Northern Coalition. Vansittart returned on the twenty-third with Denmark's refusal. Moreover, he brought his personal observations regarding the defenses that the Danes were building at Copenhagen. He said they had made much progress and that it would be futile for the British to attack the city. In addition, the Danes had removed the buoys and markers from one of the more treacherous channels in Europe, or they had deliberately placed them wrongly. This brought on much discussion, to which the hired pilots contributed the customary pilots' advice: do not try to navigate in such a channel without the markers.

On the twenty-fifth the wind was bad. On the twenty-sixth the fleet weighed anchor and sailed for several hours to the west, with the intention of reaching Copenhagen by the Great Belt, that is by sailing all the way around the western coast of Zealand (Danish: Sjaelland) and approaching the city from the south. But on the way, Captain Otway, one of Parker's officers who lacked enough rank to attend the councils of war, found out this intention and, as he was acquainted with those waters, told Parker that the channel was intricate and more dangerous to the fleet than were the guns that guarded the Sound. So they sailed back. From the evening of the twenty-sixth the fleet was

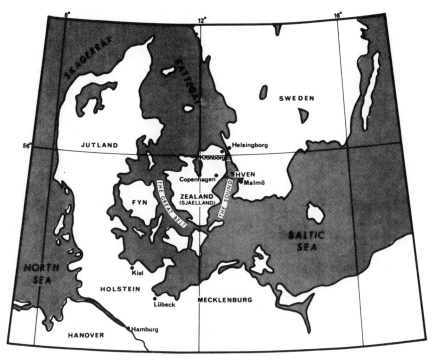

THE APPROACHES TO COPENHAGEN
Map by Pat Tamarin.

detained for three days by head winds and calms. In the meantime, on the twenty-eighth, Parker had sent a message to the commander of the fortress of Kronborg, which is adjacent to Elsinore, "Hamlet's castle," to inquire whether the fleet would be fired upon if it attempted to pass the Sound. The commander replied that it would be. Parker warned that he would consider such an act to be declaration of war. On the thirtieth the wind changed, and the fleet sailed.

The entrance to the Sound is less than three miles wide. In plain view from Kronborg, on the Danish side, is the Swedish fortress of Helsingborg, on the other. Kronborg mounted nearly a hundred fine cannon, and the British assumed that there was a like force in Helsingborg. They did not expect to get through without serious damage. As they proceeded south, the Danish guns opened fire, and the English responded. But the Swedish guns were silent. Much to the surprise of the English and the disgust of the Danes, the Swedes had not adequately prepared Helsingborg, which had not been fought for a long time, and because it contained only eight small guns, the Swedes did not contest the passage, not firing a single shot. The English moved over to the Swedish side of the channel and sailed through without taking a single hit. That evening the fleet anchored near the island of Hven, about fifteen miles from Copenhagen Roads, and Nelson and Parker went to reconnoiter the Danish line of defense.

As a consequence of their convention, Sweden, Denmark, and Russia had been preparing their fleets for some time. But in northern waters, such preparations proceed slowly in the winter months. The three fleets were to rendezvous off Copenhagen in the spring. Though hostilities with the English were not unanticipated, the Swedes and Danes were anxious to exhaust the diplomatic leverage of the Northern Neutrality before resorting to open combat, and the Russians were, as always, slow. What all three powers were unprepared for were the early arrival of the English and the size of the fleet that they sent. To support their negotiator, Whitworth, in the August convention of 1800, the English had sent a fleet of fifteen warships (including seven battleships). The fleet that now arrived was an armada by comparison: twenty-three battleships, seven frigates, and twenty-three smaller ships. The Danes reacted by suspending work on their own fleet, concentrating instead on the defenses of the city of Copenhagen. These defenses were what Nelson and Parker observed on the evening of March 30th: thirty-seven ships of varying strength, drawn up before the city and supported by shore batteries. It was, in Parker's words, "far more formidable than we had reason to expect," and it occasioned another council of war.

Nelson offered to lead a strong force to attack the Danes from the south. Parker accepted his offer and assigned to him twelve battleships and their complement. Parker was to join the attack from the north as soon as Nelson's force was engaged. Only Nelson proceeded with any degree of optimism. On the thirty-first the unmarked waters had to be explored. It was general knowledge that the waterway before the city was divided into two channels by a large shoal in the middle. Nelson personally supervised the sounding of the channel that was nearer the city and satisfied himself that his plan of attack was feasible. On the first of April a northerly breeze sprang up, and he took advantage of it by sailing south and anchoring just east of the southern tip of the shoal. At eight o'clock that night he sent a Captain Hardy in a rowboat to sound the bottom that lay between the two opposing forces. Hardy performed this task by using a pole, to avoid making the splashing sound that would have accompanied throwing a rope with a weight attached, and succeeded in plumbing the water under the very noses of the Danes. He reported that Nelson's plan of attack was perfectly feasible, since the water got deeper the nearer one approached the Danes. Nelson finished issuing the orders for an attack upon the first favorable wind during daylight, and then went to bed, though he was too agitated to sleep. The east wind that he needed developed obligingly about 8:00 the next morning, April 2, and at 9:30 the fleet weighed anchor.

As the English force sailed into battle, three of the big battleships ran aground almost immediately. The other ships took up stations opposite the Danes and opened fire. The channel, which was narrow, left little room for tactical maneuvering. The battle simply became a question of a cannonade. The last of Nelson's ships reached their battle stations about 11:30. A murderous fire commenced, inflicting heavy damage on both sides. What followed then has been the subject of considerable controversy. These facts, however, seem to be beyond doubt. Late in the morning, Parker sailed south to join Nelson. As he got close enough to sight the battle, at about 1:00 P.M., he did not like what he saw. The direst warnings he had been given seemed to have been borne out. The Danish fire was formidable; three English ships were out of action and were flying signals of distress. Parker apparently panicked. Four of the logbooks of the ships under Nelson's command agree that sometime between 1:15 and 1:30, Parker signaled "Discontinue the action." Nelson's frigates, which were hotly engaged by superior Danish ships, obeyed at once and joined Parker out of the field of fire. Naval historians agree that this action probably saved them from destruction. Nelson, however, demurred. England's condition was such that she simply could not afford a defeat at Copenhagen. Rear-Admiral Thomas Graves, captain of the battleship *Defiance,* thought that obeying this order would have been fatal to the larger ships: "If we had discontinued the action before the enemy struck [colors], we should have all got aground and have been destroyed." Several of these ships did run aground later. In any case, Nelson had no intention of quitting. What he did was later described by an eyewitness, Colonel Stewart: " 'Why, to leave off action.' 'Leave off action!' he repeated, and then added, with a shrug, 'Now damn me if I do.' He also observed, I believe, to Captain Foley, 'You know, Foley, I have only one eye—I have a right to be blind sometimes'; and then with an archness peculiar to his character, putting the glass to his blind eye, he exclaimed, 'I really do not see the signal.' "[12]

The commander of the ship directly behind Nelson's in the line of battle was Captain William Bligh, who has been remembered since 1789 because of a mutiny on the *Bounty.* Bligh was on a relatively small ship of fifty-six guns, which came to anchor abreast of the flagship of the Danish fleet, the *Dannebrog.* He overcame it, and it exploded with all hands. After all, "no one ever impugned Bligh's conduct as seaman or fighting officer, for his professional capabilities were exceptional."[13]

99

Before long, the tide turned in favor of the English. Parker's signal must have come at the climax of the battle. By two o'clock, Nelson had gained the upper hand. He sent a negotiator ashore with a white flag of truce and a note for the crown prince:

> To the Brothers of Englishmen, the Brave Danes: Vice-Admiral Lord Nelson has been commanded to spare Denmark, when she no longer resists. The line of defence which covered her shores has struck to the British flag. Let the firing cease, then, that he may take possession of his prizes, or he will blow them into the air along with their crews who have so nobly defended them. The brave Danes are the brothers, and should never be the enemies, of the English.

Nelson had been especially irritated by the fact that the Danish ships that had struck their colors in surrender were still being defended and their guns were still being fired by cadets who apparently did not know the meaning of such signals.

By this time, most of the Danish ships were out of action, but the shore fortifications were still intact. They were brimfull of troops and probably could not have been taken by assault. The crown prince, however, accepted Nelson's proposed truce, and the firing ceased just after three o'clock. Nelson immediately began to remove his ships out of range of the shore batteries. This maneuver proved to be quite awkward, as several of the ships grounded in the process. Both sides had suffered heavily; however, the English had lost no ships. Still, Nelson confessed that though he had "been in a hundred and five engagements, . . . that of today is the most terrible of them all."[14]

Each side prepared for the resumption of hostilities, but the truce was renewed each day until April 9, when a fourteen-week armistice was signed. It required the Danes to withdraw from the league for the duration of the armistice, and it allowed the English the freedom to provision their fleet in Denmark.

The armistice having been duly ratified, the English sailed on April 12 for Russian waters. One day, in a fit of impatience over the lack of wind, Nelson jumped into a rowboat and began to row the fleet to Kronstadt. Events in St. Petersburg had, by this time, however, transformed the political situation.[15]

In St. Petersburg, Paul's conduct of policy had generated a dangerous amount of discontent. His nobility of purpose was often obscured by fiery capriciousness. Whatever his objectives, he always pursued them with fanatical passion. Because he was suspicious, he attributed many of his ordinary frustrations to the malice of others. Once someone disappointed him, he was relentlessly vindictive. All who worked near him, and all without exception in the military regiments, which it was his obsession to drill daily to a peak of perfection, came to dread his whimsical tyranny. Neither civil nor military servants enjoyed any security either of position or of person. Under such circumstances, it was impossible to establish any mutual confidence between the emperor and the government. Various persons became persuaded, probably through good motives and bad, that the continuation of his reign threatened to undo the well-being of the Russian state. They therefore decided to take steps to put his reign to an end. The story of what followed this decision is both an intricate and uncertain one, which has been told in ever so many fanciful ways. In any such situation, there are two sides, but only one of them lives to tell the tale. The eyewitness accounts of the plot in this case are highly partisan and undoubtedly highly embroidered. While they must be read with skepticism, especially insofar as anecdotes and details are concerned, they are probably reliable in the fundamentals. In any case, they are all we have.

The most significant characteristic that was shared by the leading conspirators was the fact that almost all of them were Anglophiles. As early as the spring of 1800 a court cabal developed around the English ambassador Whitworth, and his mistress, Olga Zherebtsova, a sister of the Zubov brothers, whom Catherine had favored so much during the last years of her reign. Catherine's last lover, Platon Zubov, may have felt obliged, as he claimed, to carry out the intention that Catherine had contemplated but had not had the chance or the resolution to carry out: namely, the dispossession of Paul. In any case, the English sympathies of the group were unmistakable, and so was the distress that they felt because of recent developments in Russian foreign policy. Nikita Panin was perhaps the instigator of the plot. His opposition to Paul's flirtation with Bonaparte was well known. Russia's pro-Austrian ambassador in Vienna, Count Andrei Razumovsky, had been relieved of that post and exiled to Siberia. He, therefore, had no role in the conspiracy. The ambassador in London, however, Count S. R. Vorontsov, did as much as he could from afar to encourage it. His correspondence was full of provocative hints and alarums, one of which is extremely plain. On 5 February 1801 he wrote to Grand Duke Alexander's close friend Nicholas Novosiltsev:

> It is as if we . . . were on a vessel. . . . I am seasick and cannot leave my bed. You come and announce to me that the

storm is violent and the vessel will perish, for the captain has gone mad, thrashing the crew of more than thirty persons who do not dare to oppose his extravagances, since he has already thrown one sailor into the sea and killed another.[16] I believe then that the vessel will perish, but you tell me that there is yet hope of being saved, as the second in command is an affable and reasonable young man who has the crew's confidence. I pray you to return to the deck and persuade the young man and the sailors that they must save the ship, a part of which, together with the cargo, belongs to the young man; that they are thirty against one, and that it is ridiculous to fear being killed by this fool of a captain, when in a little time all will be drowned by him.[17]

Panin, who had been exiled from the capital in November, was not in a position to lead the plot. Moreover, in view of the nature of the Russian police regime, it was not feasible to make the necessary preparations without the complicity of somebody in the office of the police. Panin therefore took into his confidence the chief of the capital's police, Count Peter Pahlen, the military governor of the city. Pahlen, owing both to his position and to his temperament, was a formidable addition to the conspiracy. He arranged a meeting between Panin and Grand Duke Alexander in a public bathhouse, and they had a conversation, allegedly vague and guarded, during the course of which Alexander quite obviously gave his support to a coup of some sort. Most accounts say that he carefully stipulated the personal inviolability of his father, and most agree that if he did, he was either naïve or deliberately deceiving himself. There is in Alexander's life, including his own later dealings with Napoleon, little evidence of naïvete. There was one other principal in the plot whose contribution was crucial, General Bennigsen, a Hanoverian whose country was being occupied by the Prussians at Paul's instigation.

According to Pahlen's own account, he saw Paul during the last few days before the coup, and Paul confronted him with the rumor of a plot in which he, Pahlen, was implicated. He allegedly responded that Paul was quite right: there was a plot, and he was involved in it, because as police chief it was his duty to be; and when he had all the information that he needed, he would dispose of plot and plotters alike. Paul is reported to have been satisfied, and the plans continued. It makes a good story, and it may have happened.

In any case, the conspirators convened on the evening of March 23 and liquored up their nerve and resolve. They then summoned two bodies of soldiers to march to the royal palace to secure the guard. One of these units was led by Platon Zubov and Bennigsen, the other by Pahlen. Pahlen arrived a little late—in time, as it was reported about him, to support the coup, if that was the way things were going when he arrived, or to arrest the conspirators, if the plan had been foiled. In fact, when he arrived, the crisis had passed. Though it is impossible to sort out from the accounts of Bennigsen's and Zubov's men—most of whom were drunk—exactly what happened in Paul's bedroom, Paul did not survive.

When the deed was done, Alexander was summoned, and, though it required Pahlen's best efforts to restore Alexander's lost nerve, he was proclaimed tsar, and the troops took an oath of allegiance.[18]

Paul died about midnight of March 23/24. The news of his death did not reach Copenhagen in time to forestall the battle on April 2, which it might have done. Lucchesini tells what effect it had in Paris: "The news of the death of the Emperor was for Bonaparte a veritable thunderclap. In receiving it from Talleyrand, he uttered a cry of despair and gave himself up at once to the idea that his death was not natural and that England was a party to the coup. He believes that he has lost his strongest support against [England]."[19] *Le Moniteur* proclaimed Bonaparte's suspicions: "Paul I died in the night of 24-25 March!!! The English squadron passed the Sound on the 30th!!! History will teach us the connections between these two events!!!"[20]

The interest of the English in disposing of Paul is obvious. There was as much rejoicing in London as there was despairing in Paris. Already on 21 January, the *Times* had printed a remark that can hardly be taken as other than a hint of what actually happened: "We have so long been teazed and tormented with the name of Paul *the First,* that we congratulate ourselves upon the prospect of calling him shortly Paul *the Last.*" In fact, recent findings show that during the last days of his unhappy ministry in St. Petersburg, in the spring of 1800, Ambassador Whitworth had received a large appropriation from a secret-service fund for a purpose about which he was subsequently stubbornly vague.[21] More than this we do not know.

In any case, Paul's death did not solve all of England's problems; for the ramifications of Bonaparte's plan were not yet played out.

THE NEW ENGLISH CABINET, which had yet to arrange peace with France and Russia, hoped to find Alexander more amenable to English interests than Paul had been.

Alexander's first diplomatic act was encouraging: on the first day of his reign he recalled the expedition to India. The next day, he instructed S. R. Vorontsov to seek a reconciliation with Great Britain. He did not, however, turn his back on the treaty obligations that Paul had assumed toward the northern powers. He invited the British to reestablish diplomatic relations with Russia and to recognize the just principles of neutral trade as embodied in the recent maritime convention.[22]

In the meantime, Parker was informed through Copenhagen that Russia wished to negotiate a reconciliation. She would not, however, do so under the threat of an English fleet in Russian waters; she would meet force by force.[23] Parker accordingly removed his squadron to the western Baltic. The British sent Lord St. Helens to St. Petersburg, and a treaty of peace was signed there, to which Denmark and Sweden later acceded. It was for the British quite a compromise of their commercial principles. Favoring the neutrals, it rejected paper blockades; gave a very narrow definition of contraband, including only items exclusively useful in combat and listing all of these; and accepted the principle of "free ships, free goods." On the other hand, the right of visit and search was recognized as extending to ships under convoy, and the "Rule of 1756" was maintained. In addition, the British agreed to remove their fleet from the Baltic, and the Russians consented to lift the embargo on British goods.[24]

The Battle of Copenhagen and the death of Paul provided critical relief for the British, but their depressed circumstances were clearly reflected in their negotiations with the French. The new government apparently regarded peace, even a sacrificial peace, as essential. The man sent to negotiate it, Lord Cornwallis, was not the best choice available. He was a distinguished man in his own way, and he had had much experience in both military and civil service. He had recently commanded the English defenses on the Channel coast, and he had previously served as viceroy of Ireland, a post of extraordinary difficulty. Nevertheless, he was best remembered for a battle lost at Yorktown, and he had had no diplomatic experience whatever. He showed the most conspicuous sense of insecurity in his dealings with Talleyrand, who overawed him completely. The state of his morale during the negotiations made him unfit for his task. In February 1802 he wrote to a friend:

> God defend me from ever being again a negotiator. . . .
> I have had as serious difficulties, and have suffered as much painful anxiety of mind, as you have ever known me to experience, and you have been witness to some severe trials. The apprehension that an unguarded expression, or an error in judgment on my part, might be the cause of renewing a bloody

and, in my opinion, *a hopeless war,* or, what would be still more dreadful, might dishonour and degrade my country, has constantly preyed upon me, and I have often wished myself . . . in the backwoods of America.[25]

In the course of the war, Britain had lost no territory of her own and had preyed upon and captured the colonies of France and France's allies with impunity. In the Mediterranean, Malta fell, and Egypt followed in September 1801. Once the neutral league was dissolved, it was impossible for the French to threaten the British militarily. While the negotiations were in progress, Bonaparte proceeded unabashedly to revolutionize and conquer on the Continent whatever he would. He took measures to coordinate the affairs of France's "sister republics," or satellites. In the fall of 1801 the Batavian Republic in Holland was asked to approve a new constitution modeled on the one that Bonaparte had designed for France. The Dutch voted 16,000 yes, 52,000 no. Bonaparte declared that the new constitution had carried by a large majority, the 350,000 citizens not voting having been discovered to have voted yes. A few months later, Talleyrand convoked an assembly of north-Italian notables at Lyons, where they were persuaded in January 1802 to offer Bonaparte the presidency of the "Italian Republic." If the British protested, they were to be told that the Continent was none of their business. And they did not protest very much. Hawkesbury wrote to Cornwallis: "The Government here are very desirous of avoiding to take notice of these proceedings."[26]

The Peace of Amiens virtually recognized the Continent as Bonaparte's imperial playground. He soon reorganized the Helvetian Republic in Switzerland to his taste, and he was overturning Germany entirely, in consultation with the Russians. The most graphic contrast between the gains by war and those by peace for the two powers was cited by a contemporary British newspaper (see accompanying chart). It was by far the most disadvantageous peace the British have made in modern times and the only one in which they have surrendered the Low Countries into the control of a nation that was both a major power and a sea power. Even so, when in October 1801 the French General Lauriston arrived in London with the ratification of the preliminary treaty, he was met by an enthusiastic crowd which detached the horses from his carriage and pulled it through the streets. Celebrations were carried on all night in spite of rain and thunderstorms.

THE GAINS BY WAR AND BY PEACE
FOR ENGLAND AND FRANCE

===

BY WAR:

England	France
Ceylon	Belgium and the boundary of the Rhine
The Cape	Savoy
All French and Dutch possessions in the East Indies except the Ile de France and Batavia	Piedmont
	Milan
	Genoa
Martinique	Tuscany
Santa Lucia	Control of northern Italy
Tabago	The Spanish part of St.-Domingo
Saint-Pierre and Miquelon	The Helvetian Republic
Surinam	The Batavian Republic
Demerary	The Cisalpine Republic
Curaçao	The Ligurian Republic
Minorca	
Malta	
Egypt	

BY PEACE:

England	France
Ceylon	Belgium and boundary of the Rhine
Trinidad	Savoy.
	Control of Italy
	Spanish St.-Domingo
	Restoration of all British conquests in the New World
	Pondichery and Raiapurka in India
	Martinique
	Santa Lucia
	Tabago
	St.-Pierre and Miquelon
	The various republics
	Restoration of all British conquests to the Dutch except Ceylon
	Restoration to Spain except Trinidad.[27]

7

THE DENOUEMENT

The Emperor Paul covets nothing but the general welfare; honor is his only guide. . . . The Emperor does not lose from sight the general well-being; and when the time comes, he is ready to take up arms again.—Paul I, Manifesto on withdrawing from the Second Coalition

KOLYCHEV ARRIVED in Paris before Paul's death. Presumably, he had come to sign a treaty of alliance to consummate the increasingly obvious accord of the two powers. He was received with a conspicuous display of pomp and ceremony, as expected, but he lost no time in getting down to business.

Talleyrand invited him first to sign a peace with France, after which he offered to discuss the details of the general European settlement. Kolychev demurred; he proposed to work out the terms of the general settlement in careful conformity with Paul's stipulations and then to crown the process with a treaty of alliance. He offered Russia's alliance in exchange for France's agreement to Russian terms in a European peace settlement. Talleyrand found this position very inconvenient and frustrating. What France required of Russia was enthusiasm and support, not caution and criticism.

The particulars of the general peace which Kolychev proposed were more objectionable yet. He demanded the restoration of Egypt to the Turks. This was a rude surprise for the French. It had obviously been their understanding all along that the Russian connection would serve to secure Egypt for them, in exchange for hypothetical Russian acquisitions in other parts of the Ottoman dominions. Talleyrand refused even to discuss the matter.

Kolychev objected to Bonaparte's unilateral intervention in Italy in a spirit contrary to Paul's stipulations and Talleyrand's promises. The French had sent troops into Naples, Russia's ally, and they proposed to occupy the Neapolitan ports in order to reinforce their army in Egypt.

One of the conditions of Paul's cooperation had been the integrity of the Kingdom of Naples, and Bonaparte had agreed to it. Another condition had been the restoration of the king of Sardinia, an issue that Talleyrand would now give no assurances about.[1]

Kolychev reported to his court conscientiously. He had been in Paris only a few days before he assessed the prospects of his assignment thus:

> I am generally dubious about the success of my mission. There is here a measureless ambition since the abasement of Austria and our rupture with England. . . . I strongly doubt that we have anything good to expect from France; . . . they seek to embroil us with all the world. . . . I beg you, M. le comte [Rostopchin], to withdraw me from here as soon as possible; I see everything in the blackest colors, and I am sick of it. . . . I would never become accustomed to the kind of people who govern here; I would never trust them. . . . Their intention is to embarrass us and to subjugate Europe; finally, they know that they can accomplish this only by encumbering us.[2]

Kolychev was convinced that Bonaparte was deceiving Russia, using her entirely for his own ends. He made no effort to compromise conflicts, and he behaved in a most disagreeable fashion.

Bonaparte and Talleyrand, though they had infringed Paul's stipulations in Italy, were nevertheless shocked at Kolychev's truculence. They had especially not anticipated his position on Egypt. They accused him of misrepresenting what they had understood Paul's intentions to be. They virtually accused him of attempting to thwart Paul's intentions.[3] Talleyrand wrote to Bonaparte: "It is difficult to be so impertinent and such a blockhead as M. de Kalytchef."[4]

In fact, though he was undoubtedly guilty of personal spitefulness, Kolychev's negotiating position was based squarely on Paul's instructions.[5] Paul's death did not forestall the alliance of the two powers. Rather, the political combination which seemed to have all of Europe at its feet was deadlocked by the incompatible policies of Paul and of Bonaparte before Paul died. This is confusing but true, and this hard fact introduces a considerable element of perplexity into our story. How is it to be explained?

As CONFUSING as it may seem initially, the explanation of this state of affairs is relatively simple. Paul's policy was, in fact, not what it appeared to be. It has been recorded here, as conscientiously as possible, according to the way in which it was understood in Paris, London, and Vienna. Obviously, the policies that those three capitals evolved toward Russia were based on their understanding of Russian policy. Hence, in order to be faithful to the story as it developed, it has been told here in terms of their understanding of that policy. But that understanding was a misunderstanding. To set the Russian part of the record straight, we must focus more carefully than Paul's western contemporaries did on the diplomatic chronicle of St. Petersburg. The real situation there was unsuspected by the smug statesmen of western Europe. In the end, in spite of what may appear for the moment to be a schizoid image of politics, the explanation turns out to be alarmingly simple.

IN THE FIRST PLACE, the "Testament of Peter I" was apocryphal, as all scholars today agree. The document as we know it consists entirely of French copies. No Russian original has ever been produced. There is not even, so far as is known, a Russian text of it. The various copies contain significant textual variations. Furthermore, it does not follow the protocol of Russian state papers of the period.[6]

For a long time the "Testament" was attributed to General Michel Sokolnicki (1760–1816), an officer in the Polish legions of the French army.[7] But the Quai d'Orsay possesses versions of it that are earlier than the 1797 one identified with Sokolnicki. The most recent attempt to trace the origins of the document suggests that it may date, in its most primitive forms, back to the earliest years of the eighteenth century and that it may have evolved in Hungary and the Ukraine.[8]

On the other hand, the first twelve points of the "Testament," unlike the chimerical reveries of the last two, are plausible enough. They read like the manifest history of Russia in the eighteenth century. Westernization was the dominant theme of the domestic policy not only of Peter but of his successors ("Neglect nothing in order to give the Russian nation European forms and usages"). In the judgment of Kliuchevskii, "war was the most important condition" of Peter's reign ("Maintain the state in a system of continual war in order to harden the soldier and militarize the nation").[9] Kliuchevskii calculated that only twenty-five months of the thirty-five years of Peter's reign were free of war. The primary theaters of war, from Peter I through Catherine II, were the regions around the Baltic and the Black seas ("Expand by all possible means around the Baltic and the Black seas"). The major antagonists, or victims, of the Russians were the Swedes and the Turks ("prepare Sweden for subjugation"; "Engage the cooperation of the Austrians against the Turks"). Since the commercial treaty of 1734, England had enjoyed a near monopoly of Russian trade ("Contract a close commercial alliance with the English"). Peter had married all his heirs into German princely houses, and Catherine II (1762–96) had an excellent record of meddling in German affairs ("Meddle at all cost, either by force or by ruse, in the quarrels of Europe, and especially in those of Germany"; "Contract marriage alliances in Germany in order to gain influence there"). Russian Orthodox dissent in Catholic Poland provided the standard excuse for the Russian interventions that ultimately led to the extinction of that country ("Use religious dissent to disrupt Poland and Turkey"). The triumphant Treaty of Kuchuk Kainardjhi (1774), which gave Russia what she considered to be a protectorate over Christians in the Ottoman Empire, threatened the Turks with the same fate.[10]

The last two points of the "Testament," those concerned with setting the Austrians and French at each others' throats and then destroying Europe with a swarm of barbarians, are different in quality from the preceding twelve. They are hardly credible. In spite of that, the officials of the French Foreign Ministry, including Talleyrand himself, described Russian policy in long phrases that are quite close to those used in the last two points of the "Testament." If they were not actually copied from the document, then its contents must have been extremely familiar and accepted without reservation.

Though Bonaparte and Talleyrand understood Russian policy in terms of the "Testament," they did not publish the document during Paul's lifetime, and they did not make any reference to it in their dealings with the Russians, the English, or the Austrians. Is it not logical, then, in view of the fact that the English and the Austrians were ignorant of the document, to expect them to have understood Russian policy in a fundamentally different way from that in which the French understood it?

The answer to this question is no; for, as we have observed, the bulk of the "Testament" was almost a description of Russia's foreign policy for several generations prior to the coming of Bonaparte. By the late eighteenth century the Russians had become notorious in Europe as aggressors. Frederick II had scorned their "Cossack civilization," but he had facilitated their conquest of Poland. The Austrians, too, had learned about Russian policy while collaborating in it. The English had tried, under Pitt, to stop Russian expansion, but belatedly. The notion that Russians were scarcely civilized vandals was so deeply ingrained in the western European consciousness that few contemporaries were able to conceive of them in any other way.

In fact, Paul rejected the policy of expansion and conquest abruptly and decisively, and the factors that prompted him to do so were quite compelling. One of them was the political and territorial environment. The fact is that Catherine's achievements in war and diplomacy had reached something like the natural limits of cheap aggrandizement. The great powers would not readily allow the destruction of Sweden in the north or Turkey in the south; and since Poland had already disappeared, the central sector of Russia's western frontier then abutted directly on the quite stable states of Prussia and Austria. Russian expansion in Europe had matured, and a leveling-off process was in the nature of things.

The other factor was purely personal: it was Paul's personality. His mother, Catherine II, had murdered his father, Peter III, and seized the throne. The myth sprouted among the serfs that Peter III had been about to do what seemed logical to them—namely, to emancipate the serfs from the nobility, just as he had emancipated the nobility (1762) from compulsory state service. The nobility, according to this notion, had then offered to put Catherine on the throne if she would reject the idea of emancipating the serfs—which she did, and then they did. Both Paul and the serfs suffered from this dirty deal. When the great peasant rebel Pugachev declared against the nobility and Catherine in 1773, he called himself Peter III and promised to do justice both to the serfs and to Paul. Paul was quite popular among the common people; so, naturally, he was suspect to Catherine.

During twenty years of adulthood, he had suffered his mother's usurpation. She had taken a variety of lovers into the counsels of state and had exalted them. Paul she had kept at a distance and under considerable surveillance. He occasionally tried to make policy recommendations, but she spurned them. Toward the end of her reign she threatened to disinherit him of the succession and might have done so had she lived a few months more.

For Catherine, Paul harbored a kind of cosmic sense of injury and grievance. Whatever she stood for, he fervently repudiated. She stood for aggression and conquest. Therefore he designed his own policy to be different.

UPON HIS ACCESSION, Paul had proclaimed loud and long that Russia stood in need of recuperation, reform, and prosperity—therefore of peace. He had recalled the corps of troops sent to campaign against the Persians in the Caucasus. He had withdrawn the squadron that had been operating with the British in the Channel. He had decided against sending the promised corps to join the coalition against France.

A few months later, in the summer of 1797, the Austrians appealed

CRAZY PAUL!!

A New Ballad—to the Tune of Crazy Jane.

1.

Why, fair Isle, in every Sailor
Are such signs of rage express'd
Can a moonstruck Russian ruler
Draw the fleet of France from Brest?
Do you dread my late embargoes,
Trust me soon my power will fall,
Man your vessels, ship your cargoes,
Fear no harm from Crazy Paul!

2.

Do you mock my fierce defiance,
Act like me—'tis glorious fun,
Search the globe round for alliance,
League with all—adhere to none;
Once for thee I fought courageous,
(Twas a lucid interval)
But a Gallic pest contagious
Stole the wits of Crazy Paul!

3.

Malta's Isle your fleet blockaded,
Martin's skill [?] each pass secures,
Silly I, by France persuaded,
Thought it mine—but found it yours!
Little Paul, no more Grand Master,
Mad with baby rage I bawl,
Malta fell—but how much faster
Fled the faith of Crazy Paul.

4.

Now for Gallia's course right hearty,
Fickle as the passing air,
Led about by Bonaparte,
Growling like a dancing bear.
How I shame the sons of Russia,
While intent to work my fall,
Holland, Denmark, Sweden, Prussia
Cry, Come help us, Crazy Paul!

The cartoon, by Isaac Cruikshank, and poem were originally published by W. Holland, no. 50 Oxford St., London, on 5 February 1801. From A. M. Broadley's *Napoleon in Caricature, 1795–1821*, 2 vols. (London and New York: John Lane, 1911), facing p. 140.

to him for support against Bonaparte. Paul offered, instead, to act as mediator in the conflict. He tried to persuade Prussia to join in the proposed mediation. But Bonaparte forced Vienna to sign the Treaty of Campo Formio before Paul's plan had matured. The course of French aggression in the Low Countries, Italy, and Switzerland followed; and Bonaparte himself took Malta, the Ionian Islands, and Egypt.

Paul had a well-known predilection for things chivalric, and he had long been fascinated by the Knights of Malta in particular. He prized their values: religion and duty, especially military duty. He was also undoubtedly pleased with their ritual, as he had a rather obsessive taste for ceremony. Therefore he immediately came to their defense, allied with the Turks, and soon entered the Second Coalition.

Paul's war aims at that time were to obtain the cooperation of the Prussians, to protect Naples from the French, to return France to her pre-Revolutionary borders, to prevent the aggrandizement of Austria, and to restore the king of Sardinia.

We know about the course of the Second Coalition. When Paul withdrew from it, he issued a manifesto to explain why. He had gone to war, he said, to protect the equilibrium of Europe from the threat of the French. During the course of the war he had discovered that the Austrians were using Russian troops for their own imperialistic purposes. But Paul did not intend to tolerate in Austria what he combatted in France: "The Emperor Paul covets nothing but the general welfare; honor is his only guide. . . . The Emperor does not lose from sight the general well-being; and when the time comes, he is ready to take up arms again." He assured the little powers of Europe that he had not forgotten them.[11]

In the meantime, before he broke with England, Paul again tried to associate Prussia with his policy aims. The Prussians were, as usual, noncommittal. The English remained faithful to Vienna, and Paul's break with England soon followed. It was at this point that he allegedly succumbed to the blandishments of Bonaparte.

In fact, Paul rejoiced at Bonaparte's victory over the Austrians at Marengo (14 June 1800), not because the French won, but because the Austrians lost. The perfidy of Thugut had thus gotten its due. Even before Marengo, reports circulated all over Europe that Paul admired Bonaparte. There is evidence that he counted on Bonaparte to discipline the Revolution, and this outlook was typical of him. Paul's attitude toward the First Consul remained, however, tentative and skeptical even while it was hopeful. He reserved judgment on the new government of France until he had seen more of it.

The initial qualified enthusiasm which he had shown toward the new regime was understood by contemporaries, and has subsequently been understood by historians, to be one more example of the notorious instability of his opinions. The truth is quite the contrary. His first principle in politics was good order. Legitimacy was not an important consideration. Whoever had the capacity to establish good order was, for Paul, legitimate enough.

The acid test of Paul's reaction to Bonaparte came after Marengo. His real reaction to Talleyrand's offer to return the Russian prisoners was cold and sober. He agreed to accept the prisoners, it is true. How could a chivalrous sovereign refuse the repatriation of his own soldiers? But he proudly stipulated that they would be received only in accord with the terms of military honor, that is, as the convention went, *sur parole:* they would have to take an oath never to fight the French again. The peculiarity of this response, as Rostopchin explained to the Danish ambassador Rosenkrantz, "was dictated by the Emperor's distaste for the gratuitous favors of the French government."[12] This was not—perhaps due to the work of Bonaparte's propaganda machine—what Pitt and Thugut understood Paul's response to be.

Paul's reaction to the French offer of Malta was quite similar. Rostopchin told Rosenkrantz that Paul regarded the offer as illusory, since it could not be unknown to Bonaparte that the island was on the point of surrendering.[13] The Swedish ambassador, Stedingk, reported the same reaction.[14]

The French approaches served, nevertheless, to indicate to Paul that he was being courted, and he therefore communicated to Paris, in rather abrupt and summary form, the terms of his cooperation. Rostopchin wrote that "concord with my Master can be established only by the fulfillment of his desires: 1. The return of the island of Malta . . . to the Order of St. John. . . . 2. The reestablishment of the King of Sardinia in his dominions. . . . 3. The integrity of the dominions of the King of the Two Sicilies. . . . 4. Of those of the Elector of Bavaria. . . . 5. Of those of the Duke of Württemberg. . . ."[15]

The Austrians and the English were not aware of this note, and it would have caused the scales to fall from their eyes if they had been. It hardly breathed the spirit of fiery projects and territorial holocausts; it did not mention the Ottoman Empire; it stood rigidly for the maintenance of the status quo.

What is perhaps more remarkable, in view of Paul's reputation for irrational changes of mind, is the fact that Rostopchin's note reflected precisely the objects that Paul had sought by entering the Second Coalition. The only thing that had changed, then, in the course of

Paul's alleged flip-flops in foreign affairs, was the choice of partners with whom he would cooperate in pursuit of his unchanging ends.

Rostopchin's list of conditions did not suit the French at all; and therefore they did not soon respond. In the meantime, Paul turned again, for the third time in three years, to the power that had disappointed him least recently—Prussia—and there he made a familiar proposal for a joint mediation of peace. He explained the objectives that he sought: to see that France did not abuse her preponderance in Italy, to restrain the ambitions of Austria, to preserve the political existence of the kings of Sardinia and of Naples, to save as much as possible of the political order of Germany, and thus, "to employ . . . our combined mediation for a general, stable, and permanent peace that would put an end to the plagues of humanity and would guarantee the future security of nations."[16]

In order to lend force to his proposal, he began to parade large armies on his western frontier, and this is the explanation for that series of military maneuvers which Cobenzl at Lunéville had understood to be concerted by Paul and Bonaparte against Austria alone.[17]

What Paul proposed was too daring for Frederick's heirs. He could not find an ally who shared his aims. Still he was not ready to cooperate with the French. He had not had, he said in early December 1800, a satisfactory response from Paris regarding the conditions of his cooperation. Rostopchin told Rosenkrantz on December 5: "His August Sovereign has no intention of signing any act or convention whatever with plenipotentiaries of the current chief of the French government until he fulfills . . . the conditions attached by His Imperial Majesty to the reconciliation of His Empire with France. . . . Count Rastapsin remarked to me very judiciously that until then they had nothing to offer Bonaparte."[18] A few days later, Paul's disposition was even worse, and Rostopchin reported that Paul was "persuaded that Bonaparte is not in good faith." The evident designs of France on Germany, Rostopchin told Rosenkrantz, had "reawakened in His Imperial Majesty the strong repugnance that He has not ceased to have against any measure by which He would contribute to the consolidation of the authority of the Chief of the French nation. . . . [Rostopchin] maintained that it would not accord with the dignity of the Emperor to seek the friendship of Bonaparte, who, until now has not offered any security" on those points that Paul demanded of him.[19]

Ironically, all of this adverse opinion about the French preceded by just sixteen days those enticing letters from Paul to Bonaparte which were quoted earlier. What had happened between December 13 and December 29 to change Paul's mind? Did Father Gruber, Jesuit and archfiend, turn the trick by providing Paul with his favorite French chocolates, as has been reported? Did he blend western science and Jesuit occult arts in order to cure the toothache of Mariia Fedorovna, Paul's wife, with whom Paul was not at the time on good terms? The truth is more consonant with our story.

In the first place, Rosenkrantz became alarmed about the exposed position of Denmark, situated at the entrance of the Baltic. Naturally, he wanted to see the league against England made as strong as possible, and he hoped that the league would divert English hostilities away from the Baltic. Therefore he made some suggestions to Panin:

> If the Emperor is bound to quarrel openly with England and [if] Denmark and Sweden must act in concert with Russia, His Imperial Majesty must join . . . those powers that are at war with England . . . , not in order to destroy England, but to lead her back to equitable principles. . . . Only urgent necessity could bring me to insist upon the Emperor's joining the chiefs of the French government; because without such a union—and the cooperation of Prussia, which must be persuaded to occupy Hanover and to close, together with Denmark, the Elbe and the Weser—to demand of us to risk being treated as an enemy by the English would be to destroy us to no purpose and without any hope of attaining a reasonable political objective.[20]

These are precisely the things that Paul subsequently did.

Panin—although he must have hoped that they would not—responded that circumstances might force the formation of just such a system. As he was a devoted Anglophile, it was not likely that he encouraged these views even if he reported them. In any case, he was soon dismissed from his post, and Rosenkrantz took up the same subject with a much more sympathetic listener, Rostopchin: "I showed him that by the vigorous measures that have been taken here against the navigation and the commerce of Great Britain, Russia has in fact committed acts of hostility against this power, with which Bonaparte, as head of the French government, is at war; that consequently when once Russia pulls in the same harness with France, since she acts against the same enemy, it would be only natural to cooperate together . . . against a common enemy, which England certainly is."[21]

This line of argument may have had some effect on Paul's outlook. In the meantime, he had been receiving the mindless reassurances of Sprengporten, and he was soon persuaded to undertake a more direct and intimate form of exploratory talks with Bonaparte.

A few days after Paul wrote to Bonaparte for the first time, a note arrived in St. Petersburg, fully endorsing all of the five conditions posed by Rostopchin.[22] Paul decided to send Kolychev to Paris. Paul did not surrender his skeptical sense of concern about the course of French policy; he was not yet convinced of the moderation of the French government. It had been slow, after all, perhaps reluctant, to approve his good principles. He gave his plenipotentiary Kolychev instructions that would prove to his satisfaction which way things lay in Paris. These instructions leave no doubt about the nature of Paul's own objectives. He proposed the "humbling of the house of Austria, convinced that the peace of the rest of Europe depends on it." Next he made some significant concessions: he consented to French annexation of the left bank of the Rhine, and he consented to the secularization of some of the ecclesiastical principalities of Germany. Thus, he no longer insisted on the territorial integrity of his two German client states, Bavaria and Württemberg. Rather, he asked that they be indemnified by secularizations. He demanded that the territories that might have been designated for indemnifying Austria should go to Sardinia instead,[23] and he continued to insist on maintaining the integrity of the territory of Naples. He required the restoration of Malta to himself as grand master, which, in view of the fact that Bonaparte no longer held it, meant that France must guarantee that the British would give it up. He demanded the evacuation of Egypt and the restoration of the pope in the Vatican. Bonaparte was invited, as soon as he made peace with England, to join the League of Armed Neutrality. Finally, Paul said, *when all these conditions had been formally met,* he would recognize the French Republic.[24]

It must be obvious now that Paul's antagonism to Austria and England was not a function of his collusion with Bonaparte. It derived strictly from his purely bilateral relations with each of them. Moreover, though his conflict with the Austrians was rooted in matters of some substance and would have been hard to remove, given his principles and their practices, if the English had understood the real nature of Paul's policy before mid December, they could very likely have worked out a reconciliation with him. Is it too much to suggest that such a reconciliation might have spared them the Peace of Amiens?

Now, THE HISTORIAN, as most readers understand, is part magician, part stage manager in the selection of his material and the ordering of his story. But if he is also an honest man, he must review at this point the one bit of evidence that is not consistent with the story he has thus far told. This has to do with the knotty problem of Rostopchin's memorandum of October 1800 that called for a French alliance in terms that reflected Guttin's paper.

All the histories of Paul and all the diplomatic histories of this period say that Paul approved the memorandum and directed Rostopchin to proceed with the implementation of it.[25] There is no point in citing all of them here. They would fill several pages, but they only repeat one another. They would include books both by imperial Russian and by Soviet historians who are obviously embarrassed about a document which portrays Russian policy as aggressive.

In fact, it is not likely that Paul approved the document. For on October 8, about the time that he is said to have reacted to Rostopchin's proposals, he approved something quite different, the five conditions of cooperation with France. These had been communicated to France, through one channel or another and in one form or another, during the past eight weeks. Paul's objectives in foreign policy have been shown here to be consistent, contrary to the common conception of him both among his contemporaries and among historians. Ironically, then, it would have been uncharacteristic of him to have changed his mind as often as he would have to have done had he approved not only the five conditions, which he clearly did, but also the Rostopchin memorandum.

There is no evidence that Paul ever took a single step to implement Rostopchin's proposals. His relations with the Turks in the spring of 1801 were as harmonious as ever, and the Turks would surely not have failed to register signs of alarm if the Russians had threatened them.

Moreover, what Rostopchin proposed was an enormous revolution; and revolutions were simply not Paul's style. Everything that we know about him indicates that he lived in irrational fear of upheaval and change and that the only reforms and changes that he ever countenanced were dedicated to improving and thereby maintaining the status quo.

In addition to this circumstantial evidence, there is documentary evidence. Rostopchin's project was published by the Russians in *Russkii arkhiv* in 1878 from a copy of the original, which was furnished by his son. This copy allegedly bore marginal comments in Paul's hand, which contained his approval of the project and the order to implement it. The Russian original has never been produced, and the history of this copy raises an embarrassing question about it. When have the nervous courtiers of fastidious Russian tyrants submitted copies of documents to them while withholding the originals?

In 1889 the French journal *Revue d'histoire diplomatique* published a slightly different, poorly translated version of the same document.[26] The editor of the journal, the duke de Broglie, wrote that he had published it from a copy given to him by General Fain, whose grandfather,

Baron Fain, had been with Napoleon at Moscow, and that the author and date of the project were unknown. In the same issue of the journal the Russian historian Aleksandr Trachevskii identified the document as the work of Rostopchin but pointed out some inaccuracies in translation.

In 1922 the diplomatic historian Emile Bourgeois provided more information about the mysterious document. He related that General Fain, some time after 1889, had brought the Rostopchin paper to him, that he had found something which the duke de Broglie "had not taken the care to notice," a note which read:

> Manuscript from the hand of Count Rostopchine, *found in his papers at Moscow 16 September 1812.* The entire original is in the hand of the count with marginal notes in the hand of the Emperor Paul I. It was found by me in the papers of the governor of Moscow [Rostopchin]. I reported it to the Emperor, who ordered me to have it translated at once. On September 20, I gave him this translation, which he kept on his desk four days. In returning it to me, he told me to send it to the Duke de Bassano[27] at Vilna. I had a copy of it made, which went by courier on 27 September. Moscow, 27 January 1812 [*sic!*] D'Ideville, auditor of the Council of State, private secretary of the Emperor.[28]

This provocative note raises several other questions. Paul is alleged here to have put his comments on the original and on a copy. This is very unlikely. It is not quite clear from the context of the note whether the paper that was sent to the duke de Bassano was the original or a copy. It is not clear how many copies were made, who translated them or how competently, and how the handwriting of Paul was identified and by whom. It is not clear why such an important note was entirely overlooked by the editor who published the document. This note tells us, however, not only that the history of the document in France was very complex but that the editing was very sloppy. There is no reference to these alleged events in the two memoirs which Baron Fain wrote about the campaign.[29]

An unquestioned fact is that Rostopchin wrote the memorandum, as his correspondence refers to it unmistakably several times. Paul's relation to the document is what is doubtful. When we consider, first, that the documentary record of his alleged approval of it is little short of ludicrous; second, that nothing that Paul ever did had the remotest similarity to Rostopchin's recommendations; and third, that Paul sought stability and shunned upheaval, we may conclude safely and simply that he did not approve it.

FINALLY, how is it that Pitt and Whitworth, Thugut and Cobenzl, and Bonaparte and Talleyrand—all of whom were undeniably competent and experienced statesmen—so badly misunderstood diplomatic developments of the winter of 1800/1801?

During the period when the events described here were moving toward their climax—approximately June 1800 to March 1801, the period of the supposed Franco-Russian alliance—neither England nor Austria had diplomatic representation in St. Petersburg. Paul had broken off relations with the Austrians and the English in the spring of 1800. They knew the basic facts about Russia's political behavior, of course. They could read about it in the press, especially, unfortunately for them, in Bonaparte's press. They interpreted it in terms of the well-developed eighteenth-century clichés about Russian foreign policy. They did not, because they could not, ask Paul for an explanation.

France, too, lacked diplomatic representation in St. Petersburg. Catherine II had broken off relations with France in 1793, and they were not restored until October 1801. Nevertheless, Bonaparte had more information than his enemies had. Half a dozen times during the summer and fall of 1800 France was informed about what Paul stood for. And the government received at least one intelligent analysis of Paul's policy from its man in Hamburg, Bourgoing. Bourgoing's proximity to Copenhagen and the quality of the information that was in the hands of the Danes suggest them as the likely source of his ideas. Bourgoing represented Paul's attitude toward France as follows: "[The] present Govt. [of France] does not at all inspire in me the same misgivings as the preceding one, and I sense that one may have an understanding with it . . . but I am entitled to demand of this new government some token of its good faith." Paul understood, Bourgoing reported, that the return of the prisoners simply relieved France of an onerous expense and that the offer of Malta was rendered illusory by the imminence of its capitulation: "At present [the French government] seeks to put me at ease [tranquilliser] in some other way. It can do so by guaranteeing the fate of the Kings and the States in which I take an interest."[30]

This was a very plausible analysis. It probably reflects Rosenkrantz's conversations with Rostopchin early in November, and it may well have —although there is no indication of this in the French archives—provoked Bonaparte formally to accept Paul's five conditions of cooperation.

Though the French had more information about St. Petersburg than did their rivals, they also had more misinformation, even though the misinformation was virtually of their own manufacture. Neither Rostopchin's five points nor Bourgoing's report contained anything that could not be assimilated into their view of Russian policy as the pursuit of the aims of Peter I. None of Rostopchin's points ruled out a French alliance or a partition of the Ottoman Empire. Bonaparte and Talleyrand may have thought that Paul was being greedy in presuming to make stipulations for states so much closer to the conventional French sphere of influence than to his own. But they had no reason to conclude that their grand design had aborted. Sprengporten had taken all the flattery and assurances of the French uncritically, and he sent Paul glowing reports. Paul, his misgivings evidently somewhat allayed, had responded: "After the news that you give me of the sentiments of the first consul, I do not see anything that could obstruct the accomplishment of our mutual projects."[31] Given what we know about the French assessment of Russian policy, it is not hard to imagine that in their reading of this note the French misconstrued Paul's meaning.

The first really rude shock which their expectations received was Paul's position on Egypt. That, too, however, was consonant with the "Testament" ("Conquer the Levant, in order to dispose exclusively of the commerce of the Indies"). Did Paul demand of them, they must have wondered, the whole Ottoman heritage? Would he not share with them those parts of the Turk's dominions as remote from his own frontier as Egypt?[32]

Of course, they possessed letters from Paul that set out his principles and appealed for an end to the evils of war. But principles were, to people as cynical as these, deceptions practiced on the innocent. They had appealed to the English and to the Austrians at Christmas 1799 in similarly beatific phrases. They had tried unsuccessfully to pull the same trick on Paul in Talleyrand's turgid and saccharine letter offering the prisoners. If Paul's letters to Bonaparte breathed a spirit of mission, so did Peter's "Testament," and it required more credulity than Bonaparte and Talleyrand were capable of in order to discern the difference.

In conclusion, it seems that where Russian policy was concerned, Bonaparte and Talleyrand had closed minds. Consider the efforts which they made to tutor Kolychev in Paul's *real* wishes. When this drama was all but played out, an evidently frustrated First Consul turned away from Kolychev and back to Sprengporten, a Finnish traitor, romantic, and political cretin. He invited Sprengporten to dinner and gave him a message for Paul:

> I offer to sign a peace, which no one desires more sincerely than I, in conformity with the five points established by His Majesty himself. . . . I will sign it whenever he wants; but regarding Egypt, that is a matter entirely apart. I would not cede it voluntarily. This colony is the prize of the purest blood of France, useful besides for a thousand connections to the arts,

to the commerce of the two nations, to humanity at large. It is the only possession through which France may one day be able to counterbalance the enormous maritime power of the English in the Indies. I have little to refuse your Emperor; but if he will consider these great interests, I believe that he will see that his and ours are the same. Can the Turks . . . oppose us? We shall arrange things as we like and share the reciprocal advantages of a lucrative commerce upon a sea from which the English can and must be excluded, or where they will enjoy only such privileges as we want to accord them: they enjoy enough power in the world. . . . If the English want war, we will give it to them. . . . You will not remain indifferent, I hope, to this argument. You have as much interest as we in humbling their dominion; we can, we want to, end this struggle as soon as possible.[33]

In the documents at the Quai d'Orsay that *originated in Paris* there is not so much as a hint that the light ever dawned, that they ever saw a need to rethink their assessment of Russian policy.

How MIGHT THE STATESMEN of western Europe have improved their understanding of Paul's politics? This question has two answers. First, those nations that had diplomats in Paul's capital throughout these months continued to have good information about his policy, and this account of it is based directly on their reports, especially those of the Danish ambassador. The documents from the foreign offices of the Prussians, the Swedes, and the various Italian states all agree with the reports made by Rosenkrantz.

Second, those nations which could not, for reasons already given, maintain diplomats in St. Petersburg could have applied more patience and intelligence in using whatever information they did have. After observing what were admittedly the complex and confusing particulars of Paul's conduct, they found that understanding him was a frustrating business, and the quite facile conclusion which they readily adopted was that he was mad. "Mad" meant to them, as their correspondence makes clear, essentially inexplicable and incomprehensible, capricious, inconstant, wild, and unpredictable. It was a bit of a lazy explanation, but a few of Paul's contemporaries understood him better. The best example is the Bavarian diplomat François Gabriel de Bray, who reported to his court late in 1799:

Russia has no system, the whims of its sovereign are its whole policy and these whims are dominated by passions so violent that it is impossible to take account of them.

His intentions, however, are always the same. Perhaps no prince has been more constantly occupied with the same idea, more imbued with the same sentiment; and it is a phenomenon not a little extraordinary to see this instability of actions joined so intimately to this constancy of principle.

A scrupulous probity, the sincere desire to see each one come into possession of his own legitimate rights, an innate penchant for despotism, a certain chivalrous turn of spirit, which makes him capable of the most generous resolutions, or the most rash, have constantly guided Paul in his relations with the other powers. He placed himself at the head of the Coalition by sentiment and not by interest. . . .

This Monarch wanted to make himself the restorer of Europe, the one to redress all wrongs. He believed himself capable of making all submit to his intentions; he deceived himself. He believed that in declaring that he had no designs of ambition, no interests [to pursue], he would prompt the others to do as much; he deceived himself again. . . .

The Emperor entered into the coalition with right views, with pure intentions. He declared that he wanted to overturn the impious government of France, and this was true; that he wanted nothing for himself, but everything for those to whom it belonged, which was also true. Whoever knew the dispositions of his allies could foresee the shock that has resulted from the discord of principles and of plans. . . .

If Paul I had been better acquainted with men and his century, he would not have made the strange mistake of supposing them [to be] without passions and without interests other than those of justice. He would have joined the powers, not in order to do good absolutely, but to do what good he could.

The Emperor is a poor ally for a great power; he is a very essential protector for a small one. . . .

The manner in which he is today treating the ambassador of Vienna is without examples in the annals of diplomacy, . . . and proves that no consideration stops him when he believes himself wounded in his dearest principles.[34]

What a service this intelligent man might have performed in the foreign ministry of a great power!

Paul liked peace, feared war, and lived in morbid dread of revolution and tumult. Even war was better than the latter, and the war that he did fight was intended to end the tumult of war. His father had been the victim of a palace coup—that is, a small revolution—and he had lived in fear of a similar fate at the hands of his mother during most of his adult life. To approach politics by unimpeachable principles was, for him, to advance not simply morality but his own security as well. He was not, as he has sometimes been cursorily perceived to be, a legitimist. Good government in powerful nations, he believed, required three attributes: it must be autocratic, male, and orderly. He was not, therefore, shy about dealing with Bonaparte, but he was characteristically fastidious about Bonaparte's political principles, as he had been about those of the Austrians and the English.

Fate made the effective arena of influence of the emperor of Russia quite large, and the dictates of Paul's psyche also impelled him far beyond Russia's borders. He used his army, his own personal ideology, and anyone who, for one reason or another, embraced his outlook—such as the Knights of Malta and insecure petty princes—to dispose affairs throughout Europe in such a way as to make him feel safe. He would gladly—as would his son Nicholas—have made over all of Russia and all of Europe into a society that would love predictable, preferably religious, principles, and would school itself in orderly exercises.

Of all the illusions laid bare in this study, his were the greatest of all.[35]

8

EPILOGUE AND A REFLECTION
FOR OUR TIMES

His mind was one of the most perfect that has ever been: his unflagging attention tirelessly swept in facts and ideas which his memory registered and classified; his imagination played with them freely, and being in a permanent state of concealed tension, it never wearied of inventing political and strategic motifs which manifested themselves in unexpected flashes of intuition. . . . In the splendid and terrible isolation of the will to power, measure carries no meaning.—Georges Lefebvre, Napoleon: From 18 Brumaire to Tilsit

THE RUSSIAN CAMPAIGN of 1812 is commonly recognized as the beginning of the end for Napoleon: it was an effort to restore the arrangements of 1807, which had come undone. The arrangements of 1807 represented the realization of the system that Bonaparte had attempted in 1800/1801. All of this raises the question whether Bonaparte's ultimate undoing really dated from Trafalgar and Austerlitz in 1805, as is so often maintained, or rather from his stubborn preference for the Russian alliance and his egregious misunderstanding of Russian foreign policy, an outlook which he conceived, fatally, in 1800.

There are two features of Bonaparte's grand design of alliance with Russia that are especially striking. One is the fantastic unity and coherence, the all-encompassing quality of the conception. Properly worked out, it would have satisfied all his foreign-policy needs; and according to appearances, it almost worked out properly and completely. The other is how this grand design, conceived in 1800, influenced his Russian policy, and therefore all his foreign policy, throughout the remainder of his career. Though the plan collapsed in 1801, as we have seen, we find him resurrecting it, even in detail, at the first opportunity. In 1807, as in 1800, the Russians were part of a coalition that they had grown tired of. In 1807 Napoleon tempted them, trying to seduce them again. The ports of Europe were again closed to the English. The naval balance depended both times on Denmark, and in 1807, as in 1801, the British peremptorily bombarded Copenhagen and destroyed the Danish fleet. There was again talk about a partition of the Ottoman Empire and a Franco-Russian invasion of India. When the system broke down, Napoleon marched to Moscow in 1812 in order to reconstruct it.

Napoleon seems to have regarded the Russians as his most valuable allies. They were certainly his most dangerous, because they were his least conquerable, adversaries. Battles with the Russians were among the most costly of his career: for example, Eylau in 1807 and Borodino in 1812. The vast distances and the stubborn will of the Russians proved, in 1812, to be insuperable.

Napoleon ignominiously abused the other powers of Europe. Austria was punished by territorial sacrifices after every war, in 1797, 1801, 1805, and 1809. His only peace with England, that of Amiens, was so oppressive that it lasted for only a year. In the peace of 1807, Prussia lost half of her territory. The Russians, on the other hand, were never asked to make any territorial sacrifices, but rather were allowed to aggrandize themselves—for example, in Finland in 1808—and to cooperate in the Continental System.

Such was Napoleon's passion for a Russian alliance and so relentless was his pursuit of it, it seems, that the historian is tempted to think that he has discovered, in the ideas of Guttin, the constant principles of Bonaparte's foreign policy and the unchanging aims of his diplomacy, that he has at last discovered a simple key that will decipher the mysteries of the complex Napoleonic system. Is it true?

The usefulness to France of contacts with the Russians in the spring of 1800 is obvious. Though Russia had left the coalition, the English and the French émigrés were inviting her to rejoin it. The establishment of relations between France and St. Petersburg might help to keep Russia neutral, and the development of a rapprochement between the two powers might even bring Russia to put pressure to bear on France's enemies.

But Russia did not make a clear response to Bonaparte's first efforts to interest her, so he had to fight the Marengo campaign. Afterwards, he made more serious overtures to St. Petersburg. Almost simultaneously, however, Count St. Julien, an incompetent Austrian diplomat, signed a peace treaty with Talleyrand in Paris. This relieved Bonaparte's anxiety, and he quickly lost interest in Russia. He told the Prussian ambassador that the intervention of Prussia and Russia was no longer useful. "Today I am negotiating with Vienna. . . . I would say to you [that] the delays of the court of Berlin in negotiating our peace with Petersburg, its delays in offering its mediation, and finally the delays of Russia herself in approaching France, all make one suspect that these two powers seek to prolong the war rather than to end it."[1]

Only the day before, on August 6, St. Julien had arrived in Vienna, where the cabinet repudiated his treaty and then threw him into prison for "confounding affairs in a frightful fashion." Bonaparte's remarks to the Prussian ambassador had been premature. He was soon in pursuit of the Russians again.

At this stage, in the late summer and early fall of 1800, Bonaparte was not willing to accept Paul's proposed five conditions as the basis for cooperation. Rather, he made a counterproposal, which was not acceptable to Paul.

In the meantime, Austria was very stubborn, and Bonaparte grew anxious again. By December he was sufficiently anxious to inform the Russians that he accepted their conditions fully. At that point, they sent a man to Paris to negotiate.

But the Austrians were not aware how slowly the Franco-Russian rapprochement was developing. Rather, they saw only the overt signs of it, which were overinterpreted for them by Bonaparte's press. They were in a sorry condition, so at Lunéville, they capitulated to virtually all of the French demands.

Bonaparte was exultant, and he wrote to Paul, disingenuously, that all of Paul's wishes had been fulfilled. In fact, this was not at all the case. Paul had demanded the territorial integrity of Bavaria, Württemberg, Naples, and Sardinia; but Lunéville stipulated French annexation of the left bank of the Rhine, including territories belonging to both Bavaria and Württemberg.

This raises an important question. Did Bonaparte really want to associate the Russians with Lunéville and the complex territorial compensations which the annexation of the left bank of the Rhine would imply for the German princes dispossessed there? Or did he simply engage in offering blandishments to the Russians for the sake of deceiving the Austrians and rushing them into a punitive peace?

The answer is that Lunéville included two distinctly different areas and that Bonaparte wished to involve the Russians in one of these areas but to exclude them from the other.

It was in Germany that he was not only willing to accept Russian assistance with the peace settlement but was even anxious to secure it. In December 1800 Talleyrand urged Paul to "send a plenipotentiary armed with full powers to make definitive arrangements of affairs in Europe." When Bonaparte received news that a Russian plenipotentiary was on his way, he ordered Joseph, who was at Lunéville, to do no further business until the Russian arrived. Twice he showed apprehension over the plenipotentiary's delay in reaching Paris. The Prussian ambassador reported on February 9 that the First Consul had been seriously worried over the lack of news from St. Petersburg. He was thus delighted to learn of Kolychev's departure from Berlin.[2] More time passed, Kolychev did not show up, and the apprehension reappeared. On March 2 Lucchesini reported: "The news of Kolychev's entry into France arrived here in time to stop the departure of a letter from the First Consul to the Emperor of Russia full of bitterness at the delay that had attended the trip of the Vice-Chancellor. Gen. Sprengporten had done all he could to stop this letter."[3]

What advantage did Bonaparte find in inviting the Russians to assist in this business? The Russians had had pretensions since the Treaty of Teschen in 1779 to be coguarantors of the German Constitution. It was really an excuse to meddle in German politics. They had offered in 1797 to mediate a peace settlement in Germany. At that time the French explicitly denied Russia constitutional rights in the German Empire. But the French had proved unable, on their own, to force the annexation of the left bank of the Rhine, provided in the Treaty of Campo Formio (October 1797) with Austria, through the complicated apparatus of the German Constitution. The impasse reached over this issue at the Diet of Rastadt was one of the causes of the Second Coalition. Bonaparte probably thought it was impossible to resolve this issue except by forming an association with another great power. In any case, this aspect of his policy reflects perfectly Guttin's phrase about France's and Russia's giving the law to Europe. In his own words, "This alliance [having been] realized, how would Prussia and Austria disturb it; then the [business of the] Congress of Rastadt would soon be terminated."[4]

In Germany, Bonaparte sought Russia's cooperation because he needed it. Even so, he promised things that he was not willing to make good on.

In Italy, on the other hand, he wanted to exclude Russian influence entirely, and he showed himself the very soul of deceitfulness. Paul had intervened in the interests of two states there, Sardinia and Naples; and Bonaparte had promised to respect his wishes. In October, Bonaparte ordered the commander of the French army in Sardinia to hold everything in abeyance, in deference to Paul's protection of the kingdom. In the meantime he invited a Sardinian diplomat to Paris to negotiate. King Charles Emmanuel sent Saint-Marsan, but he sent him via Berlin, where the latter held conversations with Russian diplomats. When he arrived in Paris in the middle of February, he was not well received.

He demanded the complete restoration of the Sardinian kingdom, and he said that he had the full support of both Russia and Prussia. Talleyrand said that the French did not trust the little confidence that the Sardinian monarchy had shown in them, but that, in deference to Paul, they were disposed to "do something advantageous" for the kingdom. The closing of Sardinian ports to the English, however, would have to precede any other agreement. Saint-Marsan was clever enough to object and to ask that Kolychev be informed of this state of affairs. Whereupon Talleyrand, who was offended, broke off the talks.

More than three weeks passed, and on April 12, Bonaparte learned of Paul's death. He immediately ordered that Sardinia be divided into departments suitable for annexation to France, though he antedated the order by ten days. On June 27 the French police ordered Saint-Marsan to leave Paris within four days.[5]

In the case of Naples, the story was similar. Bonaparte attempted to use his liaison with Paul, as interpreted and advertised by Bonaparte himself, to cow the Neapolitan monarchy into a quick submission. He ignored or misrepresented his promises to Paul.

In December the advancing French armies in Italy approached the Kingdom of Naples. The Neapolitans appealed to Paul for protection. Paul sent Levashev to Italy to mediate between them and the French. Soon afterwards, the marquis de Gallo was sent from Naples to Paris to negotiate a peace with France under Kolychev's mediation. Gallo was asked to agree to the closing of all the Neapolitan ports to the English. He refused, saying that he would await Kolychev's arrival. This was apparently just what Bonaparte and Talleyrand had feared, and they suddenly discovered that Gallo's instructions did not explicitly empower him to negotiate under the mediation of the Russians. So Gallo was sent away before Kolychev arrived.

In the meantime, both Levashev, Paul's special envoy, and Italinskii, Russia's ambassador in Naples, asked Bonaparte's commander Murat to suspend the invasion of Naples. Murat politely refused.

When he arrived in Paris, Kolychev immediately protested. He objected both to the mistreatment of Gallo and to the invasion of Naples. He demanded that the invasion be halted and that the negotiations be conducted under his mediation. Talleyrand refused.

On March 24 Bonaparte ordered Murat to proceed with the invasion and occupation of Naples at all possible speed. On March 28 Naples capitulated and signed a peace which closed her ports to the English and allowed the French to garrison her southern ports. All of this arrogant proceeding Bonaparte had misrepresented as consonant with Paul's wishes, but the Neapolitans knew the truth from the Russian diplomats accredited to them.[6]

Kolychev remonstrated vehemently. He and Talleyrand were never likely to agree. Kolychev repeated his request to be relieved from this unpleasant assignment, and Alexander sent Count A. I. Morkov to replace him.

Frustrated suddenly by Russia's intransigence and apprehensive about Alexander's intentions, Bonaparte sent one of his aides-de-camp, General Duroc, to St. Petersburg. Duroc was instructed to talk about the visions of Catherine II, about her designs on the Ottoman Empire, about France's secure position in Egypt, and about Russia's interest in several German princes and in the fate of the German Empire in general. He was to say that Bonaparte had regarded Paul's interests in Italy as personal rather than political. In summary, he was to divert the Russians' attention from Italy to Germany and Turkey.[7]

The Russian principles of negotiation, however, remained approximately the same, except that Alexander was not as interested in Malta. Morkov tried to obtain security for the same four territories that Kolychev had intervened for. It soon became apparent that Alexander would not follow the French orientation that Paul had appeared to follow. And peace with Austria and the beginning of peace talks with England considerably diminished Bonaparte's dependence on the leverage of Russian diplomacy. When peace was at length signed between France and Russia, then, it was Alexander who compromised and Bonaparte who got his way. The treaty stipulated the joint mediation of the indemnities in Germany. It provided only for consultations on affairs in Italy. Bonaparte was permitted to maintain his troops in the Neapolitan ports until "the fate of Egypt is settled." The real extent of the French diplomatic victory is best seen in the miserably innocuous article on Sardinia: "His Majesty the Emperor of all the Russias and the First Consul of the French Republic will take up in a friendly fashion . . . the interests of His Majesty the King of Sardinia with all deference compatible with the actual state of things." Indemnities were to be arranged for Bavaria, Württemberg, and Baden.[8]

The negotiations of the indemnities in Germany required two years. Of Paul's two German client states, Bavaria was traditionally an enemy of Austria and an ally of France. The other, Württemberg, was located near the river Rhine and thus was not far from the new border of France. When Alexander acceded to the throne, he also entered a plea of indemnification for the native land of his own empress (as Paul had done in the case of Württemberg), Baden, a narrow state located directly between Württemberg and France. Alexander's objective in the aggrandizement of these three states was to construct a kind of barrier on the French border as a guarantee against future French expansion. Bonaparte was delighted to play this game, for he saw how to turn the idea around. As chief architect of the reconstruction of Germany, he provided handsome indemnities for all three states and managed to make his own proximity to them more influential than was the patronage of their distant Russian ally. The small states were growing fat on Austrian sacrifices, and Austrian grievances forced them to turn to Bonaparte for protection. In summary, he contrived, by doing literally what the Russians demanded of him, to convert their clients into his satellites. In the next war, all three states fought for France against Russia.[9]

In Italy, Bonaparte's policy was more unilateral and even more ominous. In January 1802 he made himself president of the Cisalpine Republic (Milan), now renamed the Italian Republic and soon to become the Italian Kingdom of Napoleon I. In September 1802 he announced what was already a *fait accompli,* the annexation of Sardinia. In the spring of 1803 the Neapolitan ports, which had been evacuated a year earlier after the Peace of Amiens, were reoccupied.

In addition, Bonaparte had made himself tyrant, by right of conquest, in Switzerland and Holland, had occupied Hanover, and had made very threatening gestures in Egypt. His relentless aggrandizement during peacetime provoked a new war. All the great powers were alarmed, and Russia was especially concerned about the eastern Mediterranean. Late in 1804, Russia, Austria, and England allied again, and the war was joined the following year.

BY THIS TIME, our hero had placed a crown on his head. He was now Napoleon I, emperor of the French. The change of title was quite consonant with the more pretentious spirit of his foreign policy. The Third Coalition was a watershed, not only in Napoleon's Russian policy, but in his entire career. As his victories began to accumulate, a fundamental division of opinion developed between him and Talleyrand; and it was Talleyrand's judgment that proved wise and his own that proved foolish. Talleyrand was horrified by the continuing spectacle of Napoleon's unlimited ambitions, and he undertook to restrain him.

Not even Napoleon, alone, had enough power to keep the whole Continent subdued; he needed an ally. In the fall and winter of 1805 a crucial choice was posed: Should he ally with Austria or with Russia? Talleyrand argued ably for Austria. He was concerned to analyze the reasons for the recurrent hostility of most of the great powers toward France and the formation of constant coalitions against her. He could not very well influence Napoleon by telling him that it was because of his own ambition and French aggression. So he proceeded more indirectly.

Talleyrand suggested that the three other great powers—discounting Prussia—were the inveterate enemies of France because of conflicts that were fundamental and traditional. The issue in the struggle with England was commerce and colonies; with Austria, the balance of power in the borderlands of south and central Germany and Italy; with Russia, the eastern Mediterranean. In these circumstances, England, the paymaster of the coalitions, was easily able to combine the powers against France.

The objective of France should be, then, Talleyrand argued, to divide her enemies among themselves and turn their conflicts to her own advantage. The best way to do it was to achieve a genuine reconciliation with Austria by a policy of mutual disengagement in central Europe and a reorientation of Austrian power toward southeastern Europe by offering large compensations in Bulgaria and Rumania. This policy would have many advantages. It would aggravate the incipient conflict of Russia and Austria in the Balkans, making them natural enemies. France and Austria would then be encouraged to make common cause against Russian imperialism in the Balkans. And Russian hostility to Austria would make her quite dependent on a French alliance. Furthermore, Russia, deprived thus of her goals in the Balkans, would turn her imperialism toward Asia, where she would collide with English colonies, and England would then be deprived of allies on the Continent. The nightmare of coalitions would come to an end.[10]

Admittedly, this was not a simple proposal that could be easily accomplished. The means themselves were grand and even difficult. It assumed a rather radical reshuffling of the map of Europe and the alliance system. However, not even the means were so presumptuous as the actual renovations of Europe that had been undertaken by Napoleon, and the ends are altogether different from his—namely, the sane and sober ends of peace and security. Talleyrand had tried to use a Russian alliance in 1801 to make peace. From that time on, the imperial dreams of Guttin and Napoleon were anathema to him, and his own proposal to Napoleon in the fall of 1805 was a conscious antidote to the scheme that has dominated this story.

Napoleon did not respond to Talleyrand's recommendations. He evidently preferred the more cosmic qualities and the romantic reveries of Guttin's old Russian scheme. In 1807 he succeeded in embodying that scheme in the Treaty of Tilsit. The Tilsit agreement again called for a vast alliance, based on the partition of the Ottoman Empire, and a far-flung Continental System, designed to ruin the commerce of England.

Was he more sincere this time; did he discharge his obligations to the Russians more honestly? The best judgment on this question is Herbert Butterfield's:

> From the vagueness and remoteness of his promises of Turkish partition; from the way in which, when he returned to Paris, he turned round and said "that he saw no advantage for France in the dismemberment of the Ottoman Empire, that he asked for nothing more than to guarantee its integrity"; from the absence of any sign on his part that he had the least intention of carrying out his promises; . . . we can infer that Napoleon was luring the Czar with visions which he never for a moment intended to convert into actualities, that he was quite well aware of how some time he would be found out and would come into collision with Russian policy; we might safely say that he conceived of the arrangement as an interim one, destined to secure him the maritime peace which he desired and to enable him to consolidate his empire in the west, also perhaps to postpone the renewal of the more decisive conflict with Russia.[11]

Napoleon and Talleyrand parted ways after Tilsit. Informed persons well understood that Talleyrand regarded Tilsit as the politics of megalomania and an invitation to disaster. He therefore resigned from the foreign ministry in August 1807.

By the spring of 1808 the Russians had grown impatient with waiting for the benefits promised them at Tilsit. They demanded the implementation of the agreement. In February they sat down with the French ambassador in St. Petersburg to work out the details of partitioning the Ottoman Empire. The Russians naturally expected the realization of their ancient dream, the annexation of the Turkish straits. Bonaparte, however, was not willing to grant them what he had implied that he would. He offered either the Bosporus, without the Dardanelles, or the north shore of the straits without the south shore. Alexander protested that this would be tantamount to not having the keys to one's own house; and the negotiations broke down.[12] Napoleon's proposition was precisely the one that was stipulated in Guttin's memorandum in 1799: "Russia will have for her part the spoils of the Porte up to the left side [*côte gauche*] of the Dardanelles and of the Bosphorus; but France will reserve to herself on the opposite side of the same straits a territory extensive enough to form there an establishment suitable to assure herself the exclusive commerce of the Black Sea."

Napoleon was asking the Russians to make the serious economic sacrifices which the break in their trade with England meant for them; yet he refused to offer any compensation or even to make good on his previous promises. The strain that this produced in the alliance was not long in showing up.

In 1808 Napoleon was deeply engaged in the Spanish rebellion. His entanglement there tempted the Austrians to consider throwing off his hegemony. In this situation, he expected his Russian ally to neutralize Austria and to deter her from challenging France. But the Russians, who were now disaffected, were no longer willing to serve him free of charge. Hence, a grand conference was called between the two sovereigns at Erfurt in October 1808.

Considering how little Napoleon was willing to offer the Russians, the only hope of getting them to do his bidding seemed to be to deceive them again, if that were possible. The most practiced master at the art of deception was Talleyrand; so, in spite of their mutual disaffection, Napoleon asked Talleyrand to accompany him to Erfurt. Talleyrand consented, and the deception that he accomplished there exceeded Napoleon's wildest expectations. The biggest dupe was Napoleon himself.

Talleyrand early made arrangements to meet with Alexander secretly. At one of their first meetings he declared plain treason: "Sire, it is in your power to save Europe, and you will only do so by refusing to give way to Napoleon. The French people are civilised, their sovereign is not. The sovereign of Russia is civilised and his people are not: the sovereign of Russia should therefore be the ally of the French people." Alexander was evidently impressed. He had already decided not to be the pawn of Napoleon. He met with Talleyrand secretly every evening at the home of the sister of the queen of Prussia. Together they reviewed the day's business, and Talleyrand coached Alexander in how to negotiate with Napoleon.

Alexander's position was strong, for Napoleon was, with revolt in Spain and revolt imminent in Austria, overextended. Napoleon eventually felt compelled to offer even material concessions: his own evacuation of the Grand Duchy of Warsaw on the Russian border, and Russian annexation of the Rumanian principalities. Still, Alexander stubbornly refused to wage war against Austria.

Talleyrand advised Alexander not to restrain Austria, and he informed the Austrians that Alexander would not. Thus he spoiled Napoleon's plans. The conference served merely to put a superficially pretty appearance on the alliance: this was all that Napoleon could get. Then he hurried off to Spain.

During Napoleon's absence from Paris, Talleyrand intrigued against him, and not secretly, but publicly and provocatively, in such a way that news of it could not fail to reach him. In January 1809 Napoleon returned to Paris abruptly in order to confront Talleyrand. For half an hour he ranted and raved, in a famous tirade, saying that Talleyrand was nothing more than "shit in a silk stocking." Finally, he threatened: "Talleyrand, you are a traitor, and I ought to have you hanged." Talleyrand, who had maintained his celebrated composure throughout, replied simply, "I don't agree with you, Sire"; and so lived to serve and betray still other sovereigns.[13]

France fought and won the war with Austria without Russian assistance. The war in Spain continued. In December 1810 Alexander quit the Continental System and resumed trade with the English. Napoleon prepared to march to Moscow. Like the pseudo rapprochement of 1801 and the actual alliance of 1807, the war of 1812 belongs among his greatest moments, good and bad, and all of them Russian. As everyone knows, the 1812 campaign ruined him.

IN RETROSPECT, then, did the Guttin memorandums and the body of ideas associated with them represent the constant principles of Napoleon's Russian policy? In any literal sense, no, because he did not want what he and the plan said he wanted—namely, to share equal authority in Germany and Italy and to partition the Ottoman Empire. When dealing with a personality as opportunistic and insatiable as Napoleon's, it is impossible to identify with certainty a grand plan with carefully delineated limits, even at a given moment, much less to show that such a plan stabilized and provided a constant guide to his action over a long period of time.

On the other hand, it is hard to deny that Bonaparte was enchanted during his dreamier moments by some such vision. The romantic reveries and the seductive fancies of this almost cosmic concept of foreign policy did tease his mind and titillate his imagination. Though it would be nonsense to pretend to have discovered a single impulse that actuated the mind of genius, it is nonetheless true that from the spring of 1800 through the campaign of 1812, the substance of Guttin's fantasies provided the *context* and defined the issues, even specious ones, of much of Napoleon's policy. Parts of it were realized; parts only dreamed of; but even the dreams he used in order to seduce the minds of his friends and his enemies—for example, Paul's and Alexander's—perhaps even his own.

In this vaguer, more fluid sense, the Guttin memorandums provide us with little less than a prophetic synopsis of the diplomatic history of Napoleonic Europe.

For, as Pierre Muret has put it so sanely, "the Napoleonic policy is explained, not by a fixed design, but by a state of mind, and this state of mind of Napoleon's . . . transported him to the most grandiose and the least definite conceptions of conquest and domination."[14] Muret's judgment, so far as I can tell, accords perfectly with the findings of my study of Napoleon's Russian policy.

Georges Lefebvre, the greatest modern student of Napoleon, has said that he was a realist, preeminently in the execution of things; and we have seen that this is right. There is a perfectly dazzling fecundity to his mind and his diplomacy—for example, simultaneously he carried on a Russian rapprochement, Austrian negotiations, an English war, an Italian blockade, and an Egyptian rescue operation; still he had the thought for such finesse as the Versailles pistols for Levashev and songs in praise of Peter the Great at the Opera—all this quite apart from a busy domestic policy which gave birth to a concordat with the Church, the end of a civil war, and the *Code Napoléon.*

"And yet," Lefebvre says, "he was a realist in execution only. There lived in him an alter-ego which contained certain features of the hero. . . . Above all he longed to equal the semi-legendary heroes of Plutarch and Corneille. His greatest ambition was glory. 'I live only for posterity,' he exclaimed, 'death is nothing, but to live defeated and without glory is to die every day.' His eyes were fixed on the world's great leaders: Alexander, . . . Caesar, Augustus, Charlemagne." And Lefebvre agrees with Muret:

> From these he did not deduce a precise formulation to be used as a rule. . . . They were for him examples. . . . He was an artist, a poet of action, for whom France and mankind were but instruments. . . .
>
> That is why it is idle to seek for limits to Napoleon's policy, or for a final goal at which he would have stopped: there simply was none. As for his followers who worried about it, he once remarked, "I always told them that I just didn't know," or again, more significantly, despite the triteness of his expression, "To be in God's place? Ah! I would not want it; that would be a cul-de-sac!" Here, then, we see that dynamic temperament which struck us at first glance in its psychological manifestation. It is the romantic Napoleon, a force seeking to expand and for which the world was no more than an occasion for acting dangerously.[15]

Talleyrand was not a romantic. He spent his life to a great degree playing cards, seducing women, taking bribes. All his enemies and most of his friends would have taken at face value his maxim, "The best principle is to have none." Scoundrel, reprobate, Machiavellian, and traitor, he was described by Lady Stafford, an Englishwoman, as "a baddish, tricking character, and supposed not very upright in disposition or heart." Yet he did so little damage in the world. The people whose money he took had plenty of it, and he spent it with more taste and style than they did. The people he ruined were those who designed to ruin nations and continents. Bourrienne, Napoleon's secretary, said of Talleyrand: "I can declare that I never saw him flatter [Napoleon's] dreams of ambition; but, on the contrary, he always endeavoured to make him sensible of his true interests." When his character was denounced in the House of Lords, the duke of Wellington rose to defend him. As far back as 1792, Talleyrand had denounced the policy that would become Napoleon's and had announced his own:

> We have learnt, a little late no doubt, that for States as for individuals real wealth consists not in acquiring or invading the domains of others, but in developing one's own. We have learnt that all extensions of territory, all usurpations, by force or by fraud, which have long been connected by prejudice with the idea of 'rank,' of 'hegemony,' of 'political stability,' of 'superiority' in the order of the Powers, are only the cruel jests of political lunacy, false estimates of power, and that their real effect is to increase the difficulty of administration and to diminish the happiness and security of the governed for the passing interest or for the vanity of those who govern. . . . France ought, therefore, to remain within her own boundaries; she owes it to her glory, to her sense of justice and of reason, to her own interest and to that of the other nations who will become free.[16]

His diplomacy is a record of these principles.

As for the Russians, Talleyrand clearly dreaded them, their despotism, and their imperialism. He used them in 1801 to make peace. He refused to engage with them in 1807 to build an excessive empire. In 1808 he collaborated with their emperor to rid Europe of his own tyrannical master. On the surface his Russian policy seemed highly variable, but it was fundamentally constant and always starkly realistic, even if it was sometimes based on misunderstandings.

If Napoleon had been willing to settle for limited objectives and to share his advantages with the Russians, they might have continued to be his friends and allies. If they had, there is every chance that he would not have been chased off to St. Helena but would have remained to perpetuate his dynasty in France indefinitely. Against a backdrop on this scale of grandeur, perhaps the most ironic thing about his relations with the Russians is that he, hero and revolutionary, by seeking to make the Russians a mere instrument of his policy without extending them an honest quid pro quo that might keep them faithful to the alliance, succumbed to a slightly racier version of the same fatal policy followed by that pathetic prince of the Bourbons, Louis XV, and his oafish King's Secret.

In 1945, as in 1812, Russian armies occupied much of eastern Europe. The Russians in the post-Napoleonic era became, as they did again in our own, the most feared nation in Europe. After 1812, westerners focused on the image of Catherine's and Peter's Russia, a Russia that was bent on conquering Europe. After 1945 they focused on the specter of communism. In both cases, and during most of the period between, an insuperable barrier precluded effective communication through the Russian frontier.

Bonaparte referred to the two sides of that barrier as republican civilization and Cossack civilization. Nicholas I recognized the barrier, too, though he had a different conception of it. He understood the two cultural principles as Russia and revolution. Russia has perceived the West as a place of radical politics and suspect morals. The West has thought of Russia as a land where inhuman persecution sustains a military power that threatens the happier lands of the Continent. The "Testament," which is a symbol of European fears, has continued to be published in the West upon the outbreak of every major conflict with Russia, in 1854, 1878, 1914. It was discussed in displaced persons' camps in Europe in 1946 and at a businessmen's luncheon in New York in 1947. President Truman assumed that it was authentic. In 1979 it cropped up on the front page of the *Christian Science Monitor*.[17]

It may be that the age of Paul and his two sons, Alexander I and Nicholas I, represented the best chance for effecting a reconciliation of these two worlds. As I have pointed out, there were natural obstacles to further Russian expansion in Europe, and there is evidence that Paul and his sons rejected Catherine's goals. Paul's policy first embodied the idea of the concert of Europe, though the name was first used by Alexander's contemporaries. Alexander's Holy Alliance was compatible with Paul's political mystique. Nicholas moved, in the 1830s, to preserve the Ottoman Empire from the rebel Mohammad Ali of Egypt. Nicholas offered aid and protection to the Turks, who were so desperate that they accepted, in the famous Treaty of Unkiar Skelessi (1833). Nicholas had stipulated that the Turks were not to permit foreign warships to pass the straits. Europe bristled, mistakenly assuming that the treaty *did* permit the passage of Russian warships, and Russian warships alone. Britain and France objected to Russia's having a privileged position at the straits. This myth persisted for a hundred years, and it was only exposed by a rare American working in Soviet archives in 1934.[18] In the meantime, Nicholas and his foreign minister, K. R. Nesselrode, in pursuit of concert, offered to let Unkiar Skelessi lapse if the British and the other powers would engage in a general guarantee of the closure of the straits to the warships of all nations except the Turks'. This made a good impression, but when Nicholas attempted to anticipate future eventualities, after the fashion of the concert and in the interest of good order, he was again misunderstood. He wished to preserve the Ottoman Empire, he said, but he did not think that it would be possible. He thought that it was too weak to survive. Thus, he wished the powers to come to an agreement beforehand about what to do with the pieces when they fell apart. He was understood to be pushing for an early partition, and the benefit of his previous proposals was undone.[19] The Crimean War soon followed.

The Crimean War worked a revolution in Russian foreign policy and in Russian attitudes toward western Europe. The nationalist party at the Russian court had been critical of Nesselrode's concert diplomacy for some time. The nationalists contended that it was not a dignified and patriotic policy. After the Crimean War, they pointed out that even the extremes to which Nesselrode had gone to conciliate Europe had failed to blunt its hostility toward Russia. The conclusion that was to be drawn from this state of affairs was, for them, inescapable: it was that Europeans were born with malice in their hearts toward Russia. From that time on, concert languished. The revolution of 1917 changed the language of the conflict, translating it into terms of class struggle, but the spirit of the thing remained much the same. Sometimes overtures of peaceful coexistence or détente were heard, but skeptics—on both sides—have never been convinced that the foundations for reconciliation were solid.

Since the Crimean War, the Pan-Slav poets of the nineteenth century and the Leninist *apparatchiki* of the twentieth have played variations on a common theme of Russian messianism in order to conjure up the phantom of the nations of Europe marching in unison to dismember the fatherland of true religion or proletarian internationalism. The Congress of Berlin, the League of Nations, the Locarno Pact, shuttle diplomacy—in the Russian capital, these are enough to excuse the "Testament" of Peter I. In the meantime, the West is no more comfortable with Russia's twentieth-century mission than it was with that of the eighteenth or nineteenth centuries, and it is quite concerned to learn the real nature of Euro-communism.

Part of the problem is bedrock prejudice. Palmerston, in the 1840s, looked the facts in the face and did not see them. The Bolsheviks did much the same thing at the time of Versailles and the time of Locarno.

A more fundamental part of the problem has to do with cultural attitudes, especially with attitudes toward information. We know what the Russians do with information: they bury it. They bury it, fortunately, more effectively than they bury us, and some of their more stubborn critics have suggested that the one of these things explains the other.

The Russians have historically not only tolerated but encouraged the assimilation of one lone aspect of western culture, the mechanical dimension. All others they have devoted their best resources to filtering out of the inevitable cultural flow that attends even the most strictly controlled international exchanges. Beards, blue jeans, jazz, and, worst of all, liberal ideas—these things threaten to break down the absolutist nature of the Russian state.

In this respect, Paul was as severe as any Russian sovereign. He forbade the entry into Russia of all printed materials whatever, including sheet music. His civil servants broke the codes and read the correspondence of every diplomat in St. Petersburg in 1800. Alexander was not much better, and Nicholas was worse.

Control of information as comprehensive as that achieved by the Russian state poses problems for states that have to deal with it. In the early twentieth century the Russian archivist S. M. Goriainov published a famous study in which he alleged that the Russo-Turkish treaties of 1798 and 1805 gave the Russians standing permission to send warships back and forth through the straits while denying that privilege to all other powers except Turkey.[20] In 1945 Stalin claimed a revision of the straits regime in the spirit of these two treaties and cited them as precedents.

Goriainov had based his findings on the secret articles of the treaties, and though the Russians never published these articles, his work was accepted as authoritative for years both by historians and by diplomats. In 1962 an American scholar, J. C. Hurewitz, found in the Turkish archives the French and Turkish copies of the treaties that Goriainov had cited. He proved conclusively that Russia's right to send warships through the straits had been limited to the duration of the war then in progress and that such passage required the permission of the sultan each time that it took place.[21]

One of the minor facts but major ironies regarding Russian control of information is that the keepers of historical secrets in Moscow today have perpetuated the misunderstanding of Paul's policy that is explained here. They restrict the access of both native and foreign scholars to Russian archives and of native scholars to foreign archives. The rectification of the record of Paul's policy contained herein rests on the use of several Western archival depositories, chiefly Danish, which are never used by Russian scholars on this subject. During six months of working in Moscow I was systematically denied the use of Russian archives.

The interpretation of Paul's policy that is documented in this study is not available in the published documents or the historical literature of either imperial Russian or Soviet scholarship. The Russian records have never been reviewed by anyone who has been free to publish whatever he found in them. We do not know whether appropriate records exist but have been withheld from scholars, whether they have been destroyed, or whether they were never made in the first place. We know all too well that the extraordinary control of information that the Russian state practices today inspires little trust among the states with which it does business and that it works at times to the decided disadvantage of the Russians themselves. It is hard to imagine that a myth like Peter's "Testament" could be perpetuated in a land where the flow of information might ventilate an otherwise hermetic atmosphere of suspicion. The same observation applies to Anglo-Austrian suspicion of Paul's foreign policy, to Anglo-French suspicion of Nicholas' treaty of Unkiar Skelessi, and to American suspicion of the Soviet role in the Yom Kippur War.

We have seen here, though not without difficulty, the real nature of Paul's foreign policy. It was endowed with an ambitious mission, it was perhaps not thoroughly sane, it was full of pious illusions, and it was morally immaculate.

We would be very much surprised today, if we could look at Soviet foreign policy unvarnished and undisguised, to find it morally immaculate. But whatever it is—ambitious and messianic, sane or insane, full of doctrinaire illusions—our historians and statesmen alike would perhaps deal with it more realistically and more justly if they were better informed about it. The massive effort of the Russians to keep us ill informed furnishes excuses for our darkest suspicions.

141

NOTES

CHAPTER 1

1. *Correspondance de Napoléon I*, ed. J. P. B. Vaillant et al., 32 vols. (Paris: Plon & Dumaine, 1858–70), vol. 6, nos. 4445, 4446.
2. 30 December 1794, in *The Parliamentary History of England from the Earliest Period to the Year 1803*, ed. William Cobbett, 36 vols. (London: Hansard, 1806–20), vol. 31, col. 1036.
3. Edouard Driault, *Napoléon et l'Europe: La Politique extérieure du premier consul, 1800–1803* (Paris: Alcan, 1910); John Ehrman, *The Younger Pitt* (New York: Dutton, 1969–); John Holland Rose, *William Pitt*, 2 vols. (London: Bell, 1911); Adolphus W. Ward and G. P. Gooch, eds., *The Cambridge History of British Foreign Policy*, vol. 1: *1783–1815* (New York: Macmillan, 1922); John Steven Watson, *The Reign of George III, 1760–1815* (London: Oxford, 1960).
4. *Parliamentary History*, vol. 34, cols. 1198–1200.
5. Alfred von Vivenot, "Thugut und sein politisches System, II," *Archiv für österreichische Geschichte* 43:105–83 (1870); "Thugut," in *Allgemeine Deutsche Biographie* (Leipzig: Duncker & Humblot, 1894), 38:138–58; Albert Sorel, "L'Autriche et le Comité de salut public, avril 1795," *Revue historique* 17:25–63 (September/October 1881).
6. Albert Sorel, *L'Europe et la Révolution française*, 8 vols. (Paris: Plon, Nourrit, 1885–1904), vols. 1–5 passim.

CHAPTER 2

1. Albert Lortholary, *Le Mirage russe en France au XVIIIe siècle* (Paris: Editions contemporaines, n.d.); Dmitri Sergius von Mohrenschildt, *Russia in the Intellectual Life of Eighteenth-Century France* (New York: Columbia University Press, 1936).
2. Albert Vandal, *Louis XV et Elisabeth de Russie* (Paris: Plon, 1882), pp.

424–25.

3. Ministère des Affaires étrangères, Mémoires et documents, Russie 31, no. 37.
4. Ibid.
5. Ministère des Affaires étrangères, Correspondance politique, Russie supplément 17, nos. 42, 43. The order and the phraseology of this version are quite different from those of the other three, all of which are more or less alike; but the contents are the same.
6. Ministère des Affaires étrangères, Mémoires et documents, Russie 35, no. 26; Michel Sokolnicki, "A propos du centenaire de 1812: Le Testament de Pierre le Grand," *Revue des sciences politiques* 27:88–98 (1912).
7. Ministère des Affaires étrangères, Mémoires et documents, Russie 1, no. 7.
8. Eon de Beaumont, Charles Geneviève Louis Auguste André Timothée d', *Mémoires du chevalier d'Eon,* ed. Fréderic Gaillardet, 2 vols. (Paris: Editions de Saint-Clair, 1967); E. N. Danilova, "Zaveshchanie Petra Velikogo," *Trudy istoriko-arkhivnogo instituta* 2:205–70 (1946).
9. Instruction to Baron Breteuil, 16 March 1760, in *Recueil des instructions données aux ambassadeurs et ministres de France depuis les traités de Westphalie jusqu'à la Révolution française: Russie,* ed. Alfred Rambaud, 2 vols. (Paris: Alcan, 1890–91), 2:125, 132.
10. Broglie to the King, 7 June 1772, in *Correspondance secrète inédite de Louis XV sur la politique étrangère . . . ,* ed. Edgard Boutaric, 2 vols. (Paris: Plon, 1866), vol. 1, no. 360.
11. Broglie to the King, summer 1773, in ibid., vol. 2, no. 366.
12. Louis Antoine Fauvelet de Bourrienne, *Mémoires de M. de Bourrienne, ministre d'état; sur Napoléon, le Directoire, le Consulat, l'Empire et la Restauration . . . ,* 10 vols. (Paris: Ladvocat, 1829), 2:223. This source is controversial.
13. *Manuel de politique étrangère* (Paris: Belin, 1900).
14. Edouard Driault, *Napoléon et l'Europe,* 5 vols. (Paris: Alcan, 1910–27).
15. See, for example, the recent comment of the dean of Napoleonic scholars in France today, Jacques Godechot, "La Rêve oriental de Bonaparte," *Revue de défense nationale* 25:1622–34 (October 1969).
16. Clarence Crane Brinton, *The Lives of Talleyrand* (New York: Norton, 1963). Duff Cooper, in *Talleyrand* (London: Jonathan Cape, 1932), agrees; his is a much stronger biography. Georges Lacour-Gayet's *Talleyrand, 1754–1838,* 4 vols. (Paris: Payot, 1928–34), is relentlessly pejorative. Jean Orieux's *Talleyrand* (Paris: Flammarion, 1970) contains more up-to-date research.
17. Alexander Bankier Rodger, *The War of the Second Coalition, 1798–1801* (Oxford: Clarendon Press, 1965), chaps. 4 and 5.
18. Georges Lefebvre, *The French Revolution from 1793 to 1799,* trans. John Hall Stewart (New York: Columbia University Press, 1964), p. 219. Lefebvre says that the note fell into the hands of the Directory, which suppressed it. He does not identify his source, and I have not been able to find any other information on this provocative point. See also J. Christopher Herold, *Bonaparte in Egypt* (New York: Harper & Row, 1962).
19. Alexis François Artaud de Montor, *Histoire de la vie et des travaux politiques du comte d'Hauterive,* 2d ed. (Paris: Adrien le Clere, 1839).
20. Alice Chevalier, *Claude-Carloman de Rulhière, premier historien de la Pologne* (Paris: Domat-Montschrestien, 1939), passim. Rulhière died in 1791, and his work was published posthumously: *Histoire de l'anarchie de Pologne et du démembrement de cette république,* 4 vols. (Paris: Desenne, 1807).

21. Charles-Louis Lesur, *Des progrès de la puissance russe, depuis son origine jusqu'au commencement du XIX siècle* (Paris: Fantin, 1812).
22. Message to the Senate, 29 January 1807, in *Correspondance de Napoléon I*, vol. 14, no. 11722. Cf. point 14 of Peter's "Testament."
23. 22 April 1799, in Ministère des Affaires étrangères, Mémoires et documents, Russie 31, no. 53.
24. Artaud de Montor, *Histoire de la vie et des travaux politiques du comte d'Hauterive*, pp. 172–74.
25. Ministère des Affaires étrangères, Correspondance politique, Russie supplément 17, no. 43.
26. Norman Saul, *Russia and the Mediterranean, 1797–1807* (Chicago: University of Chicago Press, 1970), pp. 23–52. See also Roderick E. McGrew, "Paul I and the Knights of Malta," in *Paul I: A Reassessment of His Life and Reign*, ed. Hugh Ragsdale (Pittsburgh, Pa.: The University Center for International Studies, University of Pittsburgh, 1979), pp. 44–75.
27. July 1798, in *Correspondance diplomatique de Talleyrand: Le Ministère Talleyrand sous le Directoire*, ed. Georges Pallain (Paris: Plon, Nourrit, 1891), pp. 245–46.
28. Ministère des Affaires étrangères, Mémoires et documents, Russie 5, no. 14, and Russie 31, no. 56; Archives nationales, AF 3, carton 79 (Russie), 325, plaquette 1.
29. The many undated ones refer to events of about this time.
30. January–October 1799, in Ministère des Affaires étrangères, Correspondance politique, Russie 139, no. 170; ibid., Mémoires et documents, Russie 31, nos. 39, 57, and Russie 35, no. 40.
31. 13 October 1799, in Ministère des Affaires étrangères, Correspondance politique, Russie 139, no. 171.
32. 31 January 1800, in ibid., Mémoires et documents, Russie 32, no. 1.
33. 28 June 1800, in ibid., Correspondance politique, Russie 139, no. 193.
34. 27 July 1800, in ibid., no. 198.
35. Undated, in ibid., no. 194. There is, of course, no satisfactory way to translate such a thing: "Vous nous avez entretenu depuis alors dans l'esperance sertaine d'ettre employe. . . . Vous nous observe que Vous ete encore plus victime que nous puisque Vous n'avez pas recu un centime. . . . Votre mal ne fait pas notre bien l'on nous a conseille de porter de plaintes contre Vous au ministre nous le feron si Vous ne nous rendre pas justice. Salut et fraternite Lewontoski."
36. Ibid., Russie 139, no. 175; Mémoires et documents, Russie 5, 31, 35, passim; Archives nationales, AF 3, carton 79 (Russie), 325, plaquette 1.
37. 26 October 1799, in Ministère des Affaires étrangères, Correspondance politique, Russie 139, no. 175; ibid., Mémoires et documents, Russie 31, no. 39. Though this document is dated, in a hand different from the one on the text of the document, Ventose an 4 (February/March 1796), the text refers to Paul in the coalition and to Bonaparte in Egypt. Hence, it must have been written between March and October 1799.
38. 22 April 1799, in ibid., Mémoires et documents, Russie 31, no. 53.
39. Paul to Francis, 22 October 1799, in Dmitrii A. Miliutin, *Istoriia voiny 1799 goda mezhdu Rossiei i Frantsiei v tsarstvovanie imperatora Pavla I*, 2d ed., 5 vols. (St. Petersburg: Imperatorskaia Akademiia nauk, 1852–53), 3:332.
40. Public Record Office, London, FO 65 (Russia), vols. 46 and 47.

41. 13 February 1800, March 1800, Public Record Office, FO 65/46; 14 March 1800, FO 65/47.
42. Dispatches of Lord Minto, in *Life and Letters of Sir Gilbert Elliott, First Earl of Minto, from 1751 to 1806*, ed. Emma Eleanor Elizabeth Elliott, 3 vols. (London: Longmans, Green, 1874), 3:83–89, 93–95, 134.
43. Copy of Paul to Vorontsov, 12 February 1800, Public Record Office, FO 65/46; Rostopchin to Vorontsov, 3 June 1800, in *Arkhiv kniazia Vorontsova*, ed. Petr Ivanovich Bartenev, 40 vols. (St. Petersburg: Universitetskaia tipografiia, 1870–95), 28:214.
44. 21 January 1800, in *Correspondance de Napoléon I*, vol. 6, no. 4542.
45. Ministère des Affaires étrangères, Correspondance politique, Russie 139, no. 209. Though Talleyrand's note is undated, I agree with Bailleu, who regards it as a response to Bonaparte's query, rather than with Trachevskii, who accepts the dating "end of the Year VIII" (August or September 1800). See Paul Bailleu, ed., *Preussen und Frankreich von 1795 bis 1807*, 2 vols. (Leipzig: Hirzel, 1881–87), vol. 1, no. 520; and Aleksandr A. Trachevskii, ed., *Diplomaticheskiia snosheniia Rossii s Frantsiei v epokhu Napoleona I*, 4 vols. (St. Petersburg: Stasiulevich, 1890–93), 1:650.
46. *Correspondance de Napoléon I*, vol. 6, nos. 4703, 4705.
47. Talleyrand to Bonaparte, 19 and 23 May and early July 1800, in "Correspondance de Talleyrand avec le Premier Consul pendant la campagne de Marengo," ed. Count Boulay de la Meurthe, *Revue d'histoire diplomatique* 6:263, 267, 303 (1892).
48. Archives nationales, AF 4, 1696, first dossier.
49. 30 September 1800, in *Correspondance de Napoléon I*, vol. 6, no. 5118.
50. Ibid., vol. 30 (*Mémoires*), p. 473.

CHAPTER 3

1. Bailleu, *Preussen und Frankreich*, vol. 1, nos. 324, 325, 328.
2. Ibid., nos. 310, 312, 334; "Correspondance de Talleyrand," p. 275. Paul's response, whatever it may mean, was: "Quant au rapprochement avec la France, Je ne demanderai pas mieux que de la voir venir à Moi, et surtout *en contrepoid contre l'Autriche*." See Miliutin, *Istoriia voiny 1799 g.*, 5:293. Italics in original.
3. Bonaparte to Talleyrand, 1 and 4 June 1800, in *Correspondance de Napoléon I*, vol. 6, nos. 4860, 4873; Talleyrand to Bonaparte, 10 June 1800, "Correspondance de Talleyrand," p. 286.
4. *Diplomaticheskiia snosheniia*, pp. 1–3.
5. Bonaparte to Talleyrand, 4 July 1800, in *Correspondance de Napoléon I*, vol. 6, no. 4965; Talleyrand to Panin, 26 August 1800, in Ministère des Affaires étrangères, Correspondance politique, Russie 139, no. 208.
6. *Correspondance de Napoléon I*, vol. 30 (*Mémoires*), pp. 473–74; Charles Maurice de Talleyrand, *Memoirs*, 5 vols. (New York: Putnam, 1891–92), 1:210.
7. Copy of Carnot to General Gilot, commandant of Fourth Division, in Miliutin, *Istoriia voiny 1799 g.*, 5:501–2; *Moniteur*, 2me jour complémentaire an 8 (19 September 1800).
8. Ministère des Affaires étrangères, Correspondance politique, Russie 139, no. 141; Archives nationales, AF 4, 1696, first dossier.

9. The story is told by Abbé Jean François Georgel, in *Voyage à St.-Pétersbourg, en 1799–1800* (Paris: Eymery, 1818), and by the Jesuit historian Jacques Crétineau-Joly, in *Histoire religeuse, politique et littéraire de la Compagnie de Jésus*, 6 vols. (Paris: Le Coffre, 1859), 5:396. Also Mikhail Moroshkin, *Iezuity v Rossii: S tsarstvovaniia Ekateriny II i do nashego vremeni*, 2 vols. (St. Petersburg: II otdel Imper. kantseliarii, 1867–70), 1:379–80; and Nikolai K. Schilder, *Imperator Pavel Pervyi: Istoriko-biograficheskii ocherk* (St. Petersburg: Suvorin, 1901), p. 421.

10. Ministère des Affaires étrangères, Mémoires et documents, Russie 31, no. 43.

11. Beurnonville to Talleyrand, in Ministère des Affaires étrangères, Correspondance politique, Prusse 227, no. 51; Bourgoing to Talleyrand, in Ministère des Affaires étrangères, Correspondance politique, Hambourg 115, nos. 9, 31, 50, 56, 66, 78; Talleyrand to Bourgoing, in ibid., no. 41.

12. Panin to Baron Kriudener, 10 February 1800, in Nikita Petrovich Panin, *Materialy dlia zhizneopisaniia grafa Nikity Petrovicha Panina*, ed. Alexander Brückner, 7 vols. (St. Petersburg: Imperatorskaia Akademiia nauk, 1888–92), 5:185.

13. Ibid., pp. 602–6.

14. Jean Marie Collot d'Herbois (1750–96), an actor and theater director by profession, became a member of the Committee of Public Safety and introduced the Terror in Lyons in its most severe form.

15. The biography of Chevalier is recounted briefly in most major French encyclopedias and biographical dictionaries. Georgel, *Voyage à St.-Pétersbourg*, p. 358. François-Gabriel de Bray, "La Russie sous Paul Iᵉʳ," *Revue d'histoire diplomatique* 23:600–601 (1909).

16. Rostopchin to S. R. Vorontsov, 8 April 1801, in *Arkhiv kniazia Vorontsova*, 8:276.

17. *Russkii arkhiv*, 1878, 1:103–10.

18. Ibid., p. 110.

19. Ministère des Affaires étrangères, Correspondance politique, Russie supplément 17, no. 42.

20. Beurnonville to Talleyrand, 16 September and 22 October 1800, in Ministère des Affaires étrangères, Correspondance politique, Prusse 224, nos. 202 and 228. Paul was allied with Naples and Bavaria. His empress was from the royal house of Württemberg. His policy was to protect these small states from the ravages of either the Revolution or Austrian imperialism.

21. *Diplomaticheskiia snosheniia*, p. 14.

22. Sprengporten to Paul, 1 November 1800, in Nikolai K. Schilder, *Imperator Aleksandr Pervyi: Ego zhizn' i tsarstvovanie*, 4 vols. (St. Petersburg: Suvorin, 1897–98), 1:344.

23. Instructions to Sprengporten, 10 October 1800, in *Diplomaticheskiia snosheniia*, pp. 11–12; Clarke to Bonaparte, 10 December 1800, in ibid., pp. 14–20.

24. Miliutin, *Istoriia voiny 1799 g.*, 1:270–72.

25. Beurnonville to Talleyrand, 25 December 1800, in Ministère des Affaires étrangères, Correspondance politique, Prusse 228, no. 128.

26. Talleyrand to Rostopchin, 21 December 1800, in *Diplomaticheskiia snosheniia*, pp. 26–27.

27. Bonaparte to Paul, 21 December 1800, in *Correspondance de Napoléon I*, vol. 6, no. 5232.

28. Paul to Bonaparte, 29 December 1800, in Ministère des Affaires étrangères, Correspondance politique, Russie supplément 17.
29. Letters of 21 and 27 January 1801, in *Correspondance de Napoléon I*, vol. 6, nos. 5315 and 5327.
30. 20 January 1801, in ibid., no. 5312.
31. *Diplomaticheskiia snosheniia*, pp. 31–32.
32. *Polnoe sobranie zakonov Rossiiskoi imperii*, 45 vols. (St. Petersburg: Kantseliariia, 1830–42), vol. 26, no. 19746.
33. Ministère des Affaires étrangères, Correspondance politique, Russie 140, no. 77.
34. Ibid., Russie supplément 17.
35. Carysfort to Grenville, 4 November and 27 December 1800, Public Record Office, FO 64/59; Correspondence of the Oddy brothers, 16 December 1800, Public Record Office, FO 65/47; Dreyer to Bernstorff, 24 October 1800, Copenhagen Rigsarkivet, Dpt. f. u. A. Frankrig 2, Depecher 1800, no. 78.
36. Madame Guttin to Talleyrand, 24 October 1800, in Ministère des Affaires étrangères, Correspondance politique, Russie 140, no. 5; Beurnonville to Talleyrand, 8 November 1800, in ibid., Prusse 228, no. 44.
37. E. Despréaux, "Louis XVIII en Courlande," *Monde slave*, n.s., 5th year, 3:406–7, 418 (1928); Ernest Daudet, *L'Histoire de l'émigration pendant la révolution française*, 2d ed., 3 vols. (Paris: Hachette, 1904–7), 3:207–8.
38. Artaud de Montor, *Histoire de la vie et des travaux politiques de comte d'Hauterive*, p. 103.
39. Alexandre d'Hauterive, *De l'état de la France à la fin de l'an VIII* (Paris: Henrics, 1800), pp. 112–25, 138–49, 160–71, and passim.
40. Carysfort to Grenville, 13 February 1801, in *The Manuscripts of J. B. Fortescue Preserved at Dropmore*, ed. Walter Fitzpatrick, 7 vols. (London: Historical Manuscripts Commission, 1892–1910), 6:446. This collection will hereinafter be referred to as *Manuscripts at Dropmore*.
41. Hauterive, *State of the French Republic at the End of the Year VIII* (London: Jordan, 1801).
42. Friedrich von Gentz, *Von dem Politischen Zustande von Europa vor und nach der Französischen Revoluzion* (Berlin: Frölich, 1801); *On the State of Europe before and after the French Revolution; Being an Answer to "L'Etat de la France à la fin de l'an VIII,"* trans. John Charles Herries (London: Hatchard, 1802).
43. *Moniteur universel*, 29 germinal, 8 messidor, 25 thermidor, an 8, 9 vendémiaire, 14 vendémiaire, 9 frimaire, 11 frimaire, and 18 pluviose, an 9.
44. "Tableau de la situation, Ministère de police," 30 November 1800, in *Paris sous le consulat*, ed. François Aulard, 4 vols. (Paris: Cerf, 1903–9), vol. 2, nos. 380, 401.
45. *Moniteur universel*, 20 pluviose, an 9 (9 February 1801).
46. Carysfort to Grenville, 29 November and 5 December 1800, in *Manuscripts at Dropmore*, 6:396, 404.
47. La Palue to Stamford, 2 December 1800, in Maurice H. Weil, *Un Agent inconnu de la coalition: Le Général de Stamford, d'après sa correspondance inédite, 1793–1806* (Paris: Payot, 1923), p. 420.
48. Public Record Office, FO 79/19.
49. John Malcolm to Lord Elgin, 23 March 1801, in *Manuscripts at Dropmore*, 7:376–81.
50. William Hunter, *A Short View of the Political Situation of the Northern Powers;*

Founded on Observations made during a Tour through Russia, Sweden, and Denmark in the last seven months of the year 1800 (London: Stockdale, 1801), pp. 89–90.

51. Dreyer to Bernstorff, 2 March 1801, Copenhagen Rigsarkivet, Dpt. f. u. A. Frankrig 2, Depecher 1801, no. 23.
52. Adams to Secretary of State, 10 February and 14 March 1801, U.S. National Archives, record group 59, no. 172.
53. Lucien to Napoleon, 4 April 1801, in Lucien Bonaparte, *Mémoires*, 2 vols. (Paris: Charpentier, 1822), 2:247.
54. Paul to Sprengporten, 23 January 1801, Archives nationales, AF 4, 1696, first dossier.

CHAPTER 4

1. Adolf Beer, *Die orientalische Politik Oesterreichs seit 1774* (Leipzig: Freytag, 1883); Nikolai N. Bantysch-Kamenskii, *Obzor vneshnikh snoshenii Rossii po 1800 g.* (Moscow: Lissner & Roman, 1894), vol. 1.
2. Roderick E. McGrew, "A Political Portrait of Paul I from the Austrian and English Diplomatic Archives," *Jahrbücher für Geschichte Osteuropas,* n.s. 18: 503–29 (December 1970).
3. Instructions to Cobenzl, 14 October 1800, in Johann Amadeus Franz de Paula von Thugut, *Vertrauliche Briefe,* 2 vols. (Vienna: Braumüller, 1872), 2:468.
4. Talleyrand to Joseph, 25 October 1800, in *Histoire des négociations diplomatiques relatives aux traités de Mortfontaine, de Lunéville, et d'Amiens,* comp. Albert Du Casse, 3 vols. (Paris: Dentu, 1855), 2:45–46.
5. Ibid., pp. 68–69.
6. Ibid., pp. 102, 120.
7. Ibid., p. 73.
8. Thugut to Foreign Minister Colloredo, 19 October 1800, in Thugut, *Vertrauliche Briefe,* vol. 2, no. 1147; Colloredo to Cobenzl, 24 October 1800, in ibid., no. 1156.
9. Talleyrand to Joseph, 18 November 1800, in *Histoire des négociations diplomatiques,* p. 101.
10. Joseph to Talleyrand, 11 December 1800, in ibid., p. 168.
11. Joseph to Talleyrand, 10 December 1800, in ibid., pp. 164–65, 167.
12. Joseph to Talleyrand, 23 December 1800, in ibid., p. 179.
13. Report of Archduke Charles to the Emperor, 20 December 1800, the day after he assumed command of the army, in *Quellen zur Geschichte der Kriege von 1799 und 1800,* ed. Hermann Hüffer, 2 vols. (Leipzig: Teubner, 1900–1901), 2:490–92. Of course the archduke had been the outspoken advocate and leader of the peace party for nearly a year, and his assessment of the situation was anticipated. But the gravity of the crisis is amply corroborated in the other sources cited below.
14. Ernest Picard, *Hohenlinden* (Paris: Charles-Lavauzelle, 1909), pp. 42, 235–36, is the fullest work on any phase of the campaign. A. Schleifer, *Die Schlacht bei Hohenlinden* (Erding: Hauser, 1885), p. 46; Arthur Chuquet, "La Bataille de Hohenlinden," in *Etudes d'histoire* (Paris: Fontemoing, 1903–), vol. 6, pp. 161–95; Vincent J. Esposito and John Robert Etting, eds., *A Military History and Atlas of the Napoleonic Wars* (New York: Praeger, 1964), map 44, the

emphasis of which reflects the historiography of the campaign in that the day of Marengo receives several times more attention than the remainder of the year. Bonaparte's well-known jealousy of Moreau may have played a part in the historiography of the German campaign. Baron Henri de Jomini, *Histoire critique et militaire des guerres de la Révolution*, new ed., 15 vols. (Paris: Anselin & Pochard, 1820–24), vol. 14; Emile Bourdeau, *Campagnes modernes, 1792–1815*, vol. 1: *L'Epopée républicaine* (Paris: Charles-Lavauzelle, 1912); Friedrich Franz Xaver von Hohenzollern-Hechingen (a participant), "Beitrage zur Kriegsgeschichte in Italien, Jahrgang 1800 und 1801," in *Quellen zur Geschichte der Kriege*, 2:145–90; "La Campagne des français en Allemagne, 1800," in *Mémorial du dépôt de la guerre*, ed. Marquis de Carrion-Nisas, vol. 5 (Paris, 1829). The armistice conventions are in *Recueil des traités et conventions conclus par l'Autriche avec les puissances étrangères depuis 1763 jusqu'à nos jours*, ed. Leopold Neumann, 8 vols. (Leipzig: Imprimerie de la Cour, 1877–88), 1:601–32. The memoirs of Marshals Guillaume Brune and Alexandre Macdonald and the several slight works on Moreau are of little use.

15. Dispatch to Archduke Charles, in *Quellen zur Geschichte der Kriege*, 2:488–89.
16. "La Campagne des français en Allemagne, 1800," pp. 416–17.
17. Moreau to General Reynier, 23 January 1801, in ibid., p. 423.
18. Paul to Kutuzov, in Mikhail I. Kutuzov, *M. I. Kutuzov: Dokumenty*, vol. 1 (Moscow: Voenizdat, 1950), no. 833.
19. Ibid., no. 840; "Acte de démarcation relatif à la Pologne," 2 July 1796, in *Recueil des traités et conventions conclus par la Russie avec les puissances étrangères*, ed. Fedor F. Martens, 15 vols. (St. Petersburg: Böhnke, 1874–1909), vol. 6, no. 234; I. C. M. Reinecke, ed., *Charte des ganzen Russischen-Reichs* (Weimar: Verlag des Industrie Comptoirs, 1800); *Voenno-topograficheskaia karta Rossii*, ser. 21, list 3: *G. Volynskoi i Liublinskoi* (Moscow: Upravlenie voennykh topografov, 1911), and ser. 18, list 2: *Grodnenskoi i Sedletskoi g.* (Moscow: Upravlenie voennykh topografov, 1870).
20. *Histoire des négociations diplomatiques*, pp. 174–75.
21. Joseph to Talleyrand, 18 December 1800, in ibid., p. 176.
22. Cobenzl to Thugut, 23 December 1800, in Thugut, *Vertrauliche Briefe*, vol. 2, no. 1215.
23. Cobenzl to Thugut, 27 December 1800, in ibid., no. 1216.
24. Joseph to Talleyrand, 31 December 1800, in *Histoire des négociations diplomatiques*, pp. 204, 205.
25. Cobenzl to Colloredo, 6 January 1801, in Thugut, *Vertrauliche Briefe*, vol. 2, no. 1228.
26. Talleyrand to Joseph, 7 December 1800, in *Histoire des négociations diplomatiques*, p. 160. The duke of Modena, an Este prince, was closely connected to Vienna by a Habsburg marriage. A cadet branch of the Habsburgs ruled in Tuscany. The duke of Parma was the Bourbon scion of Bonaparte's Spanish ally. The Romagna and the Legations belonged to the Papal States.
27. Joseph to Talleyrand, 26 December 1800, in ibid., pp. 185–88.
28. Cobenzl to Colloredo, 6 January 1801, in Thugut, *Vertrauliche Briefe*, vol. 2, no. 1228.
29. Summary of the protocol of 11 January 1801, in *Histoire des négociations diplomatiques*, p. 224.
30. Summary of the protocol of 15 January 1801, in ibid., pp. 228–30.

31. Cobenzl to Colloredo, 16 January 1801, in Thugut, *Vertrauliche Briefe,* vol. 2, no. 1242.
32. 21 January 1801, in *Correspondance de Napoléon I,* vol. 6, no. 5315.
33. Talleyrand to Joseph, 20 January 1801, in *Histoire des négociations diplomatiques,* pp. 236–39.
34. Cobenzl to Colloredo, 22 January 1801, in Thugut, *Vertrauliche Briefe,* vol. 2, no. 1254.
35. Treaty of Lunéville, in *Recueil des traités de la France, publié sous les auspices du Ministère des Affaires étrangères,* ed. Alexandre Jehan Henry de Clercq and Jules de Clercq, 23 vols. (Paris: Ministère des Affaires étrangères, 1880–1917), 1:424–29.
36. 27 February 1801, in *Correspondance de Napoléon I,* vol. 7, no. 5417.
37. Kaiser Francis to Cobenzl, 23 December 1800, in Thugut, *Vertrauliche Briefe,* 2:476.
38. Ibid., no. 1230.
39. See, e.g., ibid., nos. 1203 and 1207.
40. Ibid., nos. 1268 and 1272.
41. Ibid., no. 1316.
42. Ibid., no. 1331.
43. *Diplomaticheskiia snosheniia,* p. xlvii.

CHAPTER 5

1. Richard Hakluyt, *The Principal Navigations, Voyages, Traffiques & Discoveries of the English Nation* . . . , 8 vols. (London: Dent, 1907; first published in 1589), 2:98–108. Parts of several letters are selected here. The cited passages are from pp. 98, 107, and 103.
2. John Milton, *The Works of John Milton,* 18 vols. (New York: Columbia University Press, 1931–38), 10:339–42.
3. Joshua Jepson Oddy, *European Commerce* (London: Richardson, 1805); Serafin A. Pokrovskii, *Vneshniaia torgovlia i vneshniaia torgovaia politika Rossii* (Moscow: Mezhdunarodnaia kniga, 1947); Iosif M. Kulisher, *Ocherk istorii russkoi torgovli* (St. Petersburg [sic]: Atenei, 1923); Sergei V. Voznesenskii, *Ekonomika Rossii XIX-XX vv. v tsifrakh* (Leningrad: GUBONO, 1924), vol. 1; Werner Schlote, *British Overseas Trade from 1700 to the 1930s* (Oxford: Blackwell, 1952).
4. David M. Griffiths, "Russian Court Politics and the Question of an Expansionist Foreign Policy under Catherine II, 1762–1783" (Ph.D. diss., Cornell University, 1967); Isabel de Madariaga, *Britain, Russia, and the Armed Neutrality of 1780* (New Haven, Conn.: Yale University Press, 1962).
5. Eduard Fuchs and Hans Kraemer, *Die Karikatur der europäischen Völker vom Altertum bis zur Neuzeit* (Berlin: Hofmann, 1901), p. 252.
6. Whitworth to Grenville, mid March 1800, Public Record Office, FO 65/46.
7. Eli Heckscher, *The Continental System: An Economic Interpretation* (Oxford: Clarendon Press, 1922), p. 36.
8. James Brown Scott, ed., *The Armed Neutralities of 1780 and 1800: A Collection of Official Documents* (New York: Oxford University Press, 1918), p. 485.
9. *Parliamentary History,* vol. 21, col. 1153; vol. 10, col. 483; vol. 8, col. 636.
10. Quoted in Heckscher, *Continental System,* p. 208.

11. Quoted in Georges Lefebvre, *Napoleon: From Tilsit to Waterloo, 1807–1815,* trans. J. E. Anderson (New York: Columbia University Press, 1969), p. 6.
12. Constantine John Colombos, *The International Law of the Sea,* 5th ed. (London: Longmans, 1962); *Neutrality, Its History, Economics and Law,* 4 vols. (New York: Columbia University Press, 1936), especially vol. 2: Walter Allison Phillips and Arthur H. Reede, *The Napoleonic Period;* Evgenii V. Tarle, *Kontinentalnaia blokada* (Moscow: Akademiia nauk, 1958); Watson, *Reign of George III;* Frank E. Melvin, *Napoleon's Navigation System: A Study of Trade Control during the Continental Blockade* (New York: Appleton, 1919); Heckscher, *Continental System.*
13. O. P. Markova, "O neitralnoi sisteme i franko-russkikh otnosheniiakh (Vtoraia polovina XVIII v.)," *Istoriia SSSR,* no. 6, pp. 42–55 (1970).
14. Rosenkrantz to Bernstorff, 23 August 1800, Copenhagen Rigsarkivet, Dpt. f. u. A. Rusland 2, Depecher 1800.
15. Beurnonville to Talleyrand, spring 1800, in Ministère des Affaires étrangères, Correspondance politique, Prusse 227, no. 128 bis; *Diplomaticheskiia snosheniia,* pp. xvi–xvii.
16. Desaugier (Copenhagen) to Talleyrand, 27 and 31 May 1800, in Ministère des Affaires étrangères, Correspondance politique, Danemark 176, nos. 70, 75; Talleyrand to Bonaparte, 5 June 1800, "Correspondance de Talleyrand avec le Premier Consul," pp. 279–80.
17. Alexander de Conde, *The Quasi-War: The Politics and Diplomacy of the Undeclared War with France, 1797–1801* (New York: Scribner, 1966), pp. 241–42, 447.
18. Convention of 29 August 1800, *Danske Tractater efter 1800,* 3 vols. (Copenhagen: Schultz, 1871–75), vol. 1, no. 1.
19. Bernstorff to Whitworth, 26 August 1800, in *Supplément au Recueil des principaux traités . . . des puissances et états de l'Europe,* ed. Georg Friedrich von Martens, 20 vols. (Göttingen: Dieterich, 1802–42), 2:336.
20. Rosenkrantz to Panin, 20 August 1800, Copenhagen Rigsarkivet, Dpt. f. u. A. Rusland 2, Depecher 1800; Gustavus Adolphus IV to Paul, 20 August 1800, in Miliutin, *Istoriia voiny 1799 g.,* 5:495.
21. Scott, *Armed Neutralities,* pp. 489–92.
22. Paul to General Svechin, governor of St. Petersburg, 4 and 10 September 1800, *Russkaia starina,* January 1882, pp. 195–97.
23. Bernstorff to Rosenkrantz, 6 September 1800, Copenhagen Rigsarkivet, Gesandtskabsarkiver Rusland 1, Ordrer 1800; Ehrenheim (chancellor) to Stedingk (ambassador), 12 September 1800, Stockholm Riksarkivet, Ur Moscovitica 498, Samtliga Handlingar 1800; Kriudener to Panin, 23 October 1800, in Brückner, *Materialy dlia zhizneopisaniia grafa N. P. Panina,* 5:487.
24. *Recueil des principaux traités,* 6:556–61.
25. R. N. Mordvinov, ed., *Admiral Ushakov: Sbornik dokumentov,* 3 vols. (Moscow: Voenizdat, 1951–56), vol. 3, nos. 242, 243, 271, 304.
26. Paget to Italinskii (Russian ambassador at Naples), 1 July 1800, and Paget to Pigot, 12 August 1800, in *The Paget Papers: Diplomatic and Other Correspondence of the Right Hon. Sir Arthur Paget, G.C.B., 1794–1807,* ed. A. B. Paget, 2 vols. (London: Heinemann, 1896), 1:236–37, 265–66.
27. Ibid., pp. 274–75.
28. Grenville to Carysfort, 7 November 1800, in *Manuscripts at Dropmore,* 6:373.
29. Admiralty to St. Vincent, 11 May 1799, in *The Keith Papers,* ed. W. G. Perrin

and Christopher Lloyd, 3 vols. (London: Navy Records Society, 1927–55), 2:159–60. I am indebted to Professor Clara Tucker of the State University of New York at Albany for clarification of this point.

30. Paul's orders to Governor of St. Petersburg, *Russkii arkhiv*, 1876, p. 32, and 1882, pp. 201–2; Reports of British consul Stephen Shairp, 30 October, 21 November, and 1 December 1800, Public Record Office, FO 65/47.

31. *Materialy dlia istorii russkago flota*, 17 vols. (St. Petersburg: Morskoe ministerstvo, 1865–1904), vol. 16, nos. 702, 719, 737, and passim.

32. Talleyrand to Dreyer, 3 September 1800, Copenhagen Rigsarkivet, Dpt. f. u. A. Frankrig 2, Depecher 1800.

33. The Treaty of Mortfontaine, 3 October 1800; see Conde, *Quasi-War*, pp. 257, 297.

34. *Correspondance de Napoléon I*, vol. 6, no. 5208.

35. *Supplément au Recueil des principaux traités*, 2:375–79.

36. 13 and 16 December 1800, in Ministère des Affaires étrangères, Correspondance politique, Danemark 176, nos. 147, 148.

37. *Supplément au Recueil des principaux traités*, 2:417.

38. Bernstorff to Bourke (ambassador in Stockholm), 19 September 1800, Copenhagen Rigsarkivet, Gesandtskabsarkiver Sverig 1, Ordrer 1800.

39. Carysfort to Grenville, 21 January 1801, Public Record Office, FO 64/60.

40. Scott, *Armed Neutralities*, pp. 531–49.

41. Dispatches 179 and 181, 31 January and 17 February 1801, U.S. National Archives, record group 59.

42. Bonaparte to Paul, 27 February 1801, in *Correspondance de Napoléon I*, vol. 7, no. 5417.

43. Cesáreo Fernández Duro, *Armada española desde la unión de los reinos de Castilla y de León*, 9 vols. (Madrid: Est. tipográfico "Successores de Rivadeneyra," 1895–1903), 8:217.

44. *Times* (London), 20 January 1801.

45. *Diplomaticheskiia snosheniia*, pp. 32–33.

46. Edouard Desbrière, *1795–1805: Projets et tentatives de débarquement aux Îles britanniques*, 4 vols. (Paris: Chapelot, 1900–1902), 2:337–415.

47. Contrary to Kazimierz Waliszewski, *Paul the First of Russia* (London: Heinemann, 1913), pp. 370 ff.

48. Dreyer to Bernstorff, 16 January 1801, Copenhagen Rigsarkivet, Dpt. f. u. A. Frankrig 2, Depecher 1801, no. 5.

49. Paul to General Orlov, 24 January 1801, *Russkaia starina*, 1873, 8:409.

50. Crawford to Hawkesbury, 4 April 1801, Public Record Office, FO 33/21.

51. *Correspondance de Napoléon I*, vol. 7, no. 5417.

52. *Polnoe sobranie zakonov Rossiiskoi imperii*, vol. 26, nos. 19747, 19755, 19775.

53. Murat to Levashev, 23 January 1801, and Murat to Bonaparte, 24 January 1801, in *Lettres et documents pour servir à l'histoire de Joachim Murat, 1767–1815*, ed. Joachim Napoléon Murat, 8 vols. (Paris: Plon, Nourrit, 1908–14), vol. 1, nos. 171, 172.

54. *Correspondance de Napoléon I*, vol. 7, no. 5337; *Lettres et documents pour servir à l'histoire de Joachim Murat*, vol. 1, no. 216; *Paget Papers*, 1:313.

55. *Recueil des traités de la France*, 1:424–29.

56. Dispatches of Thomas Appleton, 15 March 1801, U.S. National Archives, record group 59.

57. *Correspondance de Napoléon I*, vol. 7, no. 5311; Bailleu, *Preussen und Frankreich*, vol. 2, nos. 14, 20.
58. Oddy, *European Commerce*, p. 452; Guy Stanton Ford, *Hanover and Prussia, 1795–1803: A Study in Neutrality* (New York: Columbia University Press, 1903), pp. 231–35 and passim; Dispatches nos. 174, 181 of J. Q. Adams, 8 December 1800 and 17 February 1801, U.S. National Archives, record group 59.
59. Lowendal to Bernstorff, 7 March 1801, Copenhagen Rigsarkivet, Dpt. f. u. A. Rusland 2, Depecher 1801. Language and expression as in the original.
60. Paul to Kriudener, 23 March 1801, in Schilder, *Imperator Aleksandr Pervyi*, 1:341; *Diplomaticheskiia snosheniia*, p. 672; Ford, *Hanover and Prussia*, pp. 231–35.
61. Baudissin to Bernstorff, 29 March 1801, Copenhagen Rigsarkivet, Dpt. f. u. A. Preussen 2, Depecher 1801.
62. *Supplément au Recueil des principaux traités*, 2:451–52; Miliutin, *Istoriia voiny 1799 g.*, 5:510; Scott, *Armed Neutralities*, pp. 592–94; Public Record Office, FO 33/21.
63. Norway was at this time part of the Kingdom of Denmark. My phrase "Adriatic to the Arctic" requires one modest qualifier. While it is true that there was not, so far as I know, any formal Swedish legislation that excluded British commerce from entry into Sweden or that prohibited Swedish exports to England, Swedish trade with England was carried on through Baltic ports, and hence the whole thrust of the Northern League, and especially the naval arrangements attendant on it, effectively ended that trade, with or without the formalities on which Paul insisted in the case of Denmark.
64. François Crouzet, *L'Economie britannique et le blocus continental, 1806–1813*, 2 vols. (Paris: Presses universitaires de France, 1958); also Tarle, *Kontinentalnaia blokada*, and Heckscher, *Continental System*.
65. Crouzet, *L'Economie britannique*, 1:383–84.
66. Ibid., p. 91.
67. Whitworth to Grenville, 14 April 1800, Public Record Office, FO 65/46.
68. Ibid.
69. Ibid., pp. 93–94; Robert G. Albion, *Forests and Sea Power: The Timber Problem of the Royal Navy* (Cambridge, Mass.: Harvard University Press, 1926), pp. 139–41. Yards are the crosspieces on masts. Spars are small masts.
70. Albion, *Forests and Sea Power*, p. 338.
71. R. E. Prothero, baron Ernle, *English Farming, Past and Present*, ed. A. D. Hall, 5th ed. (London: Longmans, Green, 1936), p. 267; Watson, *Reign of George III*, pp. 10–11.
72. Crouzet, *L'Economie britannique*, 1:98–101; William Freeman Galpin, *The Grain Supply of England during the Napoleonic Period*, vol. 6 of University of Michigan Publications, History and Political Science (New York: Macmillan, 1925), p. 127.
73. Arthur Young, *The Question of Scarcity Plainly Stated and Remedies Considered* (London: McMillan, 1800), pp. iii–iv, 18–19.
74. Galpin, *Grain Supply*, pp. 10–19.
75. Bonaparte to Berthier, 22 November 1800, in *Correspondance de Napoléon I*, vol. 6, no. 5191; Stephen Shairp to Grenville, 1 December 1800, Public Record Office, FO 65/47; George Brown to Grenville, 18 December 1800, in ibid.
76. *Parliamentary History*, vol. 35, col. 495.

77. Ibid., cols. 748, 754, 777–78, 781–82, 811, 820–21; Galpin, *Grain Supply,* pp. 14–15, 18, 203–6.
78. Public Record Office, BT (8), minutes (5), no. 12k, pp. 60, 77; Galpin, *Grain Supply,* p. 127.
79. Galpin, *Grain Supply,* pp. 127, 256.
80. Copenhagen Rigsarkivet, Øresunds Told Bog (Sound Dues Toll Book).
81. Galpin, *Grain Supply,* pp. 249, 250, 256.
82. Public Record Office, BT (8), miscellanea (6), no. 136, corn, foreign, imported weekly into England, 1797–1802.
83. Galpin, *Grain Supply,* pp. 213 ff.; Arthur D. Gayer, W. W. Rostow, and Anna Jacobson Schwartz, *The Growth and Fluctuation of the British Economy, 1790–1850,* 2 vols. (Oxford: Clarendon Press, 1953), 1:468, table 39; Brian R. Mitchell, with Phyllis Deane, *Abstract of British Historical Statistics* (Cambridge, Eng.: Cambridge University Press, 1962), pp. 484–87. This was the highest nominal price for grain in England until after 1950 (156s. 2d. per quarter of wheat), and perhaps the highest real price in history; see Mitchell, *Abstract,* and *Encyclopedia Britannica,* 15th ed. (Chicago, 1970), 18:494.
84. Thomas Tooke and William Newmarch, *A History of Prices and of the State of the Circulation from 1792 to 1856,* 6 vols. (reprint of the 1838–57 edition; New York: Adelphi, 1928), 1:252–53.
85. John Marshall, *A Digest of all the accounts relating to the population, productions, revenues, financial operations, manufactures, shipping, colonies, commerce . . . presented to Parliament during the last thirty-five years* (London: Haddon, 1833), pt. 1, pp. 23, 31.
86. Geoffrey C. Bolton, *The Passing of the Irish Act of Union* (Oxford: Oxford University Press, 1966).
87. George suffered from porphyria, an inherited metabolic disturbance which produces, among other things, mental derangement. Ida Macalpine and Richard Hunter, *George III and the Mad-Business* (London: Allen Lane, 1969).
88. Baudissin to Bernstorff, 29 March 1801, Copenhagen Rigsarkivet, Dpt. f. u. A. Preussens 2, Depecher 1801.
89. Rufus King to Secretary of State, 13 December 1800 and 6 February 1801, U.S. National Archives, Dispatches of United States Ministers to Great Britain, vols. 8 and 9, record group 59.
90. 4 December 1800 and 18 March 1801, in *Parliamentary History,* vol. 35, cols. 710, 1064.
91. Thomas Grenville to William Grenville, 9 October 1800, in *Manuscripts at Dropmore,* 6:344.
92. Hawkesbury to Otto, 20 and 21 March 1801, Public Record Office, FO 27/66.
93. Hawkesbury to Carysfort, 24 March 1801, Public Record Office, FO 64/60.

CHAPTER 6

1. Francis to Cobenzl, 31 March 1801, in Beer, *Orientalische Politik Oesterreichs,* pp. 774–75.
2. Ministère des Affaires étrangères, Mémoires et documents, Russie 31, no. 49.
3. Lucchesini to Haugwitz, 2 February 1801, in Bailleu, *Preussen und Frankreich,* vol. 2, no. 15.
4. Scott, *Armed Neutralities,* pp. 557, 570; Public Record Office, Admiralty 3,

minutes, 15 January 1801; Instructions to Crawford (in Hamburg), 15 January 1801, in ibid., FO 33/21.

5. Spencer to St. Vincent, 9 February 1801, in *The Private Papers of George, Second Earl Spencer, First Lord of the Admiralty, 1794–1801*, ed. Julian S. Corbett, 4 vols. (London: Navy Records Society, 1913–24), 3:383.

6. Oliver Warner, *Nelson's Battles* (New York: Macmillan, 1965), p. 109.

7. Geoffrey J. Marcus, *The Age of Nelson: The Royal Navy, 1793–1815* (New York: Viking, 1971), p. 174.

8. St. Vincent to Parker, 11 March 1801, in *Letters of Admiral of the Fleet, the Earl of St. Vincent*, ed. David B. Smith, 2 vols. (London: Navy Records Society, 1922–27), 1:86.

9. Marcus, *Age of Nelson*, pp. 173–74.

10. *The Dispatches and Letters of Vice-Admiral Lord Viscount Nelson*, ed. Nicholas Harris Nicolas, 7 vols. (London: Colburn, 1845–46), 4:296–98.

11. *Manuscripts at Dropmore*, 6:425.

12. Letter to his brother, 3 April 1801, in *Logs of the Great Sea Fights, 1794–1805*, ed. Thomas Sturges Jackson, 2 vols. (London: Navy Records Society, 1895–1900), 2:103; *Dispatches*, 4:309, quoting from James S. Clarke and John M'Arthur, *Life of Lord Nelson*, 2:266–67.

13. Warner, *Nelson's Battles*, p. 110. Bligh also had two other mutinies on his record.

14. Marcus, *Age of Nelson*, p. 184.

15. My account of the Baltic expedition and the Battle of Copenhagen is based on *The Dispatches and Letters of Vice-Admiral Lord Viscount Nelson*, which includes Colonel Stewart's account; *Logs of the Great Sea Fights*, 2:83–135, which includes Parker's own logbook; William James, *The Naval History of Great Britain, from the Declaration of War by France in 1793, to the Accession of George IV*, new ed., 6 vols. (London: Bentley, 1837), vol. 3, chap. 2; Roger C. Anderson, *Naval Wars in the Baltic during the Sailing-ship Epoch, 1522–1850* (London: Gilbert-Wood, 1910), chap. 14; William Laird Clowes et al., *The Royal Navy: A History from the Earliest Times to the Present*, 7 vols. (London: Low, Marston, 1897–1903), vol. 4; Captain Alfred Thayer Mahan, *The Life of Nelson*, 2d ed., rev. (New York: Greenwood, 1968), vol. 2; Dudley Pope, *The Great Gamble: Nelson at Copenhagen* (New York: Simon & Schuster, 1972); and the other accounts cited above.

16. This is probably a reference to Panin and Suvorov. When the latter returned from the campaigns of 1799, he was received in disgrace, due to the tattered appearance of his troops. In April 1800 he responded to a peremptory summons from Paul to go to St. Petersburg, but sickened and died as he arrived.

17. *Arkhiv kniazia Vorontsova*, 11:380.

18. Schilder, *Imperator Pavel Pervyi*; Evgenii S. Shumigorskii, *Imperator Pavel I: Zhizn' i tsarstvovnie* (St. Petersburg: Smirnov, 1907); Aleksandr Brückner, *Smert' Pavla I* (Moscow: Pirozhkov, 1907).

19. Lucchesini to court, 17 April 1801, in Bailleu, *Preussen und Frankreich*, vol. 2, no. 30.

20. *Moniteur universel*, 27 germinal, an 9.

21. James J. Kenney, Jr., "Lord Whitworth and the Conspiracy against Tsar Paul I: The New Evidence of the Kent Archive," *Slavic Review* 36:205–19 (June 1977).

22. *Vneshniaia politika Rossii XIX i nachala XX veka*, ed. A. L. Narochnitskii et al. (Moscow: Gospolitizdat, 1960–), ser. 1, vol. 1, nos. 1, 2.

23. Alexander to S. R. Vorontsov, 6 April 1801, in *Arkhiv kniazia Vorontsova,* 28:417–21.
24. *Vneshniaia politika Rossii,* ser. 1, vol. 1, no. 9.
25. Cornwallis to Major-General Ross, 13 and 22 February 1802, in *Correspondence of Charles, First Marquis Cornwallis,* ed. Charles Ross, 3 vols. (London: Murray, 1859), 3:457, 460.
26. 12 February 1802, in ibid., p. 457.
27. Adapted from Edouard Driault, *Napoléon et l'Europe: La Politique extérieure du premier consul,* pp. 201–2.

CHAPTER 7

1. *Diplomaticheskiia snosheniia,* pp. 45–113.
2. Ibid., pp. 43–44.
3. Ibid., pp. 45–113.
4. Quoted in Driault, *Napoléon et l'Europe: La Politique extérieure du premier consul,* p. 174.
5. *Russkii arkhiv,* 1874, vol. 2, cols. 961–64.
6. The most thorough debunking is done by Danilova, in "Zaveshchanie Petra Velikogo," the timing of which (1946) is interesting. Danilova did not use the papers of the Quai d'Orsay. The most recent comment on the Testament is by the distinguished Soviet scholar N. I. Pavlenko, "Tri tak nazyvaemykh zaveshchaniia Petra I," *Voprosy istorii* 2:129–44 (1979). It is a rudimentary and cursory review. The author has not used the manuscripts in Paris, and he presents nothing new.
7. By a descendant of the general, Sokolnicki, "A propos du centenaire de 1812: Le Testament de Pierre le Grand," pp. 88–98.
8. Orest Subtelny, " 'Peter I's Testament': A Reassessment," *Slavic Review* 33:663–78 (December 1974).
9. Vasilii O. Kliuchevskii, *Sochineniia,* vol. 4: *Kurs russkoi istorii,* vol. 4 (Moscow: Sotsekizdat, 1958), p. 50.
10. On this point see the recent research of Roderic H. Davison, " 'Russian Skill and Turkish Imbecility': The Treaty of Kuchuk Kainardji Reconsidered," *Slavic Review* 35:463–83 (September 1976).
11. Miliutin, *Istoriia voiny 1799 g.,* 5:312–20.
12. Rosenkrantz to Bernstorff (Danish chancellor), 30 August 1800, Copenhagen Rigsarkivet, Dpt. f. u. A. Rusland 2, Depecher.
13. Rosenkrantz to Bernstorff, 31 October 1800, in ibid.
14. Stedingk to Ehrenheim (Swedish chancellor), 14 October 1800, Stockholm Riksarkivet, Ur Muscovitica, 464.
15. *Diplomaticheskiia snosheniia,* pp. 10–11.
16. Memorandum by Haugwitz (Prussian chancellor), 12 August 1800, Deutsche Zentralarchiv, Historische Abteilung 2, Merseburg (DDR), Ministerium für auswärtige Angelegenheiten, AA I Rep. 4, no. 487.
17. Report of Baron Stedingk, 20 August 1800, Stockholm Riksarkivet, Ur Muscovitica, 464.
18. Rosenkrantz to Bernstorff, 5 December 1800, Copenhagen Rigsarkivet, Dpt. f. u. A. Rusland 2, Depecher.
19. Rosenkrantz to Bernstorff, 13 December 1800, in ibid.

20. Rosenkrantz to Bernstorff, 12 November 1800, in ibid.
21. Rosenkrantz to Bernstorff, 13 December 1800, in ibid.
22. *Diplomaticheskiia snosheniia*, pp. 26–27.
23. His instructions were not perfectly clear on whether he insisted on the territorial integrity of the old Sardinian kingdom as well as further indemnification, but Kolychev in Paris did so insist.
24. *Russkii arkhiv*, 1874, vol. 2, cols. 961–64.
25. With the sole exception, so far as I know, of Sorel, *L'Europe et la Révolution française*, which ignores it.
26. Duc Albert de Broglie, "La Politique de la Russie en 1800 d'après un document inédit," *Revue d'histoire diplomatique* 3:1–12 (1889).
27. H. B. Maret, duc de Bassano (1763–1830), publicist and editor of *Le Moniteur universel*, became foreign minister in the spring of 1811 and went to Russia in 1812.
28. Emile Bourgeois, "L'Alliance de Bonaparte et de Paul I (1800–1801)," *Revue des travaux et comptes rendus, Académie des sciences morales et publiques*, n.s. 197:274–75 (1922).
29. Agathon Jean François Fain, *Manuscrit de mil huit cent douze, contenant le précis des événemens de cette année . . .* , 2 vols. (Paris: Delaunay, 1827), and *Mémoires du baron Fain* (Paris: Plon, Nourrit, 1908).
30. Bourgoing to Talleyrand, 29 November 1800, in Ministère des Affaires étrangères, Correspondance politique, Danemark 176.
31. See note 54 of chap. 3.
32. French possession of Egypt had, of course, been recommended in Rostopchin's alliance project.
33. Sprengporten to Paul, 28 March 1801, in *Diplomaticheskiia snosheniia*, pp. 93–95.
34. Bray, "La Russie sous Paul Ier," pp. 594–96.
35. I am preparing a psychological study of Paul.

CHAPTER 8

1. Report of Sandoz-Rollin to court, 7 August 1800, in Bailleu, *Preussen und Frankreich*, vol. 1, no. 348.
2. Paul Marmottan, ed., "Lucchesini ambassadeur de Prusse à Paris (1800–1801)," *Revue d'histoire diplomatique* 43:76 (1929).
3. Bailleu, *Preussen und Frankreich*, vol. 2, no. 19.
4. Guttin to Foreign Ministry, an 9 (1800), in Ministère des Affaires étrangères, Mémoires et documents, Russie 35, no. 42.
5. *Correspondance de Napoléon I*, vol. 6, no. 5137, vol. 7, no. 5468, and passim; Albert Pingaud, *La Dominance française dans l'Italie du Nord, 1796–1805*, 2 vols. (Paris: Perrin, 1914), 1:270; Edouard Driault, *Napoléon en Italie, 1800–1812* (Paris: Alcan, 1906), pp. 99–114.
6. *Correspondance de Napoléon I*, vol. 7, nos. 5433, 5483, 5459; *Lettres et documents pour servir à l'histoire de Joachim Murat*, vol. 1, no. 286; *Correspondance de Joachim Murat*, ed. Alberto Lumbroso (Turin: Roux Frassati, 1899), p. 55; *Diplomaticheskiia snosheniia*, pp. 44–45; *Recueil des traités de la France*, 1:432–35; Miliutin, *Istoriia voiny 1799 g.*, 5:278–79; André Bonnefons, *Une*

Ennemie de la Révolution et de Napoléon: Marie-Caroline, reine des Deux-Siciles, 1768–1814 (Paris: Perrin, 1905), pp. 227–28.

7. Correspondance de Napoléon I, vol. 7, no. 5545.

8. Recueil des traités et conventions conclus par la Russie, vol. 13, no. 489.

9. Herbert A. L. Fisher, Studies in Napoleonic Statesmanship: Germany (Oxford: Clarendon Press, 1903), pp. 39–45; E. D. Verbitskii, "Germanskii vopros v russko-frantsuzskikh otnosheniiakh 1800–1803 gg.," Uchenye zapiski Khersonskogo pedagogicheskogo instituta, issue 4, pp. 1–58 (1949); Uta Krüger-Löwenstein, Russland, Frankreich und das Reich, 1801–1803: Zur Vorgeschichte der 3. Koalition (Wiesbaden: Steiner, 1972), esp. pp. 103–12.

10. Talleyrand to Bonaparte, 17 October 1805, Revue historique 39:64–68 (January/February 1889).

11. Herbert Butterfield, The Peace Tactics of Napoleon, 1806–1808 (Cambridge, Eng.: Cambridge University Press, 1929), p. 272.

12. Albert Vandal, Napoléon et Alexandre 1er, 3 vols. (Paris: Plon, Nourrit, 1893–96), 1:291 ff. See also Vernon J. Puryear, Napoleon and the Dardanelles (Berkeley: University of California Press, 1951).

13. On Talleyrand see especially Vandal, Napoléon et Alexandre 1er; and Cooper, Talleyrand.

14. Pierre Muret, "Une Conception nouvelle de la politique étrangère de Napoléon I," Revue d'histoire moderne et contemporaine 18:380 (1913).

15. Georges Lefebvre, Napoleon: From 18 Brumaire to Tilsit, 1799–1807, trans. Henry F. Stockhold (New York: Columbia University Press, 1969), pp. 63–67.

16. Cooper, Talleyrand, p. 66.

17. Dmitry V. Lehovich, "The Testament of Peter the Great," American Slavic and East European Review 7:111–24 (April 1948). In an unpublished paper entitled "President Truman and Peter the Great's Will," J. Garry Clifford shows that Truman, in formulating his attitudes and policy with regard to Russia in 1948, assumed that Peter's "Testament" was authentic. Christian Science Monitor, 31 December 1979.

18. Philip E. Mosely, Russian Diplomacy and the Opening of the Eastern Question in 1838 and 1839 (Cambridge, Mass.: Harvard University Press, 1934).

19. Harold N. Ingle, Nesselrode and the Russian Rapprochement with Britain, 1836–1844 (Berkeley: University of California Press, 1976).

20. Sergei M. Goriainov, Le Bosphore et les Dardanelles (Paris: Plon, Nourrit, 1910).

21. J. C. Hurewitz, "Russia and the Turkish Straits: A Revaluation of the Origins of the Problem," World Politics 14:605–32 (July 1962).

SELECTED BIBLIOGRAPHY

In addition to using the archival manuscripts cited below, I requested permission to use the Russian manuscripts in Soviet archives, but my request was denied. Significant portions of the Russian diplomatic correspondence have been published in *Diplomaticheskiia snosheniia Rossii s Frantsiei v epokhu Napoleona I*, edited by A. S. Trachevskii, and in Dmitrii A. Miliutin's *Istoriia voiny 1799 g.*, which, though it is a history, contains long documentary appendixes.

Portions of the Austrian archives were published in *Vertrauliche Briefe des Freiherrn von Thugut*, edited by Alfred von Vivenot, and in *Quellen zur Geschichte der Kriege von 1799 und 1800*, edited by Hermann Hüffer.

I have also read the diplomatic correspondence in the old Prussian archives now at Merseburg, German Democratic Republic, and that in the Swedish Riksarkivet in Stockholm. Both sets of papers are full of good information on Russian policy, but the Franco-Prussian correspondence has been published, *Preussen und Frankreich von 1795 bis 1807*, edited by Paul Bailleu; and the Swedes did not have diplomatic relations with the French during the period of this study. Hence I will wait to use these materials when I write my study of Paul's foreign policy; therefore they have not been listed here.

Two titles merit special mention because they contain a brief but more or less accurate account of the Talleyrand-Bourgoing-Chevalier-Rostopchin intrigue. The mysterious author of *Mémoires tirés des papiers d'un homme d'état*, edited by Armand François d'Allonville, who has long been the subject of historical controversy, was well placed and well informed about Paul and Bonaparte. *Historia de Carlos IV*, by Andrés Muriel (1776–?), also has all the essential information about the court intrigue in St. Petersburg and the Indian expedition which was allegedly prompted by Bonaparte. Muriel was a Spanish professor of philosophy and a churchman who served in Joseph Bonaparte's educational administration. He left Spain with Joseph in 1812 and spent the rest of his life, so far as is known, in Paris. Neither of these accounts, however, is completely credible without the documentation of the Ministère des Affaires étrangères, which they do not cite.

Finally, in the bibliography of this subject, it is interesting to observe historiography being used in the service of politics. Much of the literature and much of the publication of sources on the rapprochement of 1801 as well as on the Treaty of Tilsit was occasioned by the Franco-Russian alliance of 1894. See, for example, the works of Trachevskii, Tatishchev, and Vandal, which appear below.

UNPUBLISHED SOURCES

France

Archives du Ministère des Affaires étrangères, Paris
Correspondance politique
Russie
Fond 139: 1793 to 1800
Fond 140: 1800 to 1801
Fond Supplément 17: 1789 to 1812
Prusse
Fond 226: September 1799 to March 1800
Fond 227: March to September 1800
Fond 228: September 1800 to March 1801
Fond 229: March to September 1801
Hambourg
Fond 115: 1800 to 1802
Mémoires et documents
Russie
Fond 5: 1721 to 1804
Fond 31: 1760 to 1799
Fond 32: 1800 to 1813
Fond 35: 1789 to 1828
France: "Fonds Ernest Daudet" (copies of Russian archives)
Fond 1891: Moscow archives, 1780 to 1804
Fond 1892: St. Petersburg archives, 1792 to 1820
Archives nationales, Paris
AF 3: Carton 79 (Russie)
AF 4: Carton 1696, Relations extérieures, Russie, Mémoires, rapports, correspondance, An VIII–1814.

England

Public Record Office, London
Foreign Office, General Correspondence
Russia (65)
Vol. 46: January through April 1800
Vol. 47: May through December 1800
Vol. 48: January through July 1801
France (27)
Vol. 66: March 1801 through May 1803
Prussia and Germany (64)
Vol. 58: August through October 1800
Vol. 59: November through December 1800
Vol. 60: January through March 1801
Vol. 61: April through December 1801
Hamburg and the Hanse Towns (33)
Vol. 21: 1801

Admiralty
    Outletters (2)
        Vol. 140: 20 June 1800 to 7 January 1801
        Vol. 141: 7 January 1801 to 15 July 1801
    Board of Trade (8)
    Minutes (5)
        Vol. 12: April 1800 to December 1801
    Miscellanea (6)
        Vol. 136: Corn, foreign, imported weekly into England,
           26 September 1799 to 1802

Denmark

    Rigsarkivet [State Archive], Copenhagen
      Division 1: Gesandtskabsarkiver; Ordrer [Legation Records; Outgoing
      Instructions]
        Rusland [Russia]
          1800
          1801
        Frankrig [France]
          1800
          1801
        Preussen [Prussia]
          1800
          1801
        Sverige [Sweden]
          1800
          1801
      Division 2: Department for udenrigske Anliggender, Depecher
      [Department for Foreign Affairs, Incoming Dispatches]
        Rusland [Russia]
          1800
          1801
        Frankrig [France]
          1800
          1801
        Preussen [Prussia]
          1800
          1801
        Sverige [Sweden]
          1800
          1801
        Øresunds Told Bog [Sound Dues Toll Book]
          1800
          1801
          1802

United States

    National Archives, Washington, D.C.
      Record Group 59

Selected Bibliography

Dispatches of U.S. Ministers to Prussia
   Vol. 1: 1799 to 1801
Dispatches of U.S. Ministers to Great Britain
   Vol. 8: January 1799 through December 1800
   Vol. 9: January through December 1801
Dispatches of U.S. Consuls in Hamburg
   Vol. 1: 1790 to 1808
Dispatches of U.S. Consuls in Copenhagen
   Vol. 1: 1792 to 1811
Dispatches of U.S. Consuls in Leghorn
   Vol. 1: 1793 to 1812

PUBLISHED SOURCES

Books

Addington, Henry, first viscount Sidmouth. *The Life and Correspondence of the Right Hon. Henry Addington, First Viscount Sidmouth*. Edited by George Pellew. 3 vols. London: Murray, 1847.

Allonville, Armand François, comte d', ed. *Mémoires tirés des papiers d'un homme d'état, sur les causes secrètes qui ont déterminé la politique des cabinets dans la guerre de la révolution, depuis 1792 jusqu'en 1815*. 13 vols. Paris: Ponthieu, 1828–38.

Annual Register . . . for the Year 1801, The. London: Otridge, 1813.

Aulard, François Victor Alphonse, ed. *Paris sous le consulat*. 4 vols. Paris: Cerf, 1903–9.

Austria, Treaties. *Recueil des traités et conventions conclus par l'Autriche avec les puissances étrangères depuis 1763 jusqu'à nos jours*. Edited by Freiherr Leopold von Neumann. 8 vols. Leipzig: Imprimerie de la Cour, 1877–88.

Bailleu, Paul, ed. *Preussen und Frankreich von 1795 bis 1807*. 2 vols. Leipzig: Hirzel, 1881–87.

Bartenev, Petr Ivanovich, ed. *Arkhiv kniazia Vorontsova* [The archives of the Princes Vorontsov]. 40 vols. Moscow: Universitetskaia tipografiia, 1870–95.

Bode-Kolychev, M. I., ed. *Boiarskii rod Kolychevykh* [The Boyar family Kolychev]. Moscow: Sinodal'naia tipografiia, 1886.

Bonaparte, Lucien. *Mémoires*. 2 vols. Paris: Charpentier, 1882.

Bourrienne, Louis Antoine Fauvelet de. *Mémoires de M. de Bourrienne, ministre d'état; sur Napoléon, le Directoire, le Consulat et la Restauration. . . .* 10 vols. Paris: Ladvocat, 1829.

Broglie, Albert, duc de, ed. *Le Secret du roi: Correspondance secrète de Louis XV avec ses agents diplomatiques, 1752–1774*. 2 vols. Paris: Levy, 1878.

Cornwallis, Charles Cornwallis, first marquis. *Correspondence of Charles, First Marquis Cornwallis*. Edited by Charles Ross. 3 vols. London: Murray, 1859.

Dalrymple, William. *A Treatise on the Culture of Wheat*. London: Becket, 1801.

Denmark, Treaties. *Danske Tractater efter 1800* [Danish treaties after 1800]. 3 vols. Copenhagen: Schultz, 1871–75.

Djuvara, Trandafir, G., ed. *Cent projets de partage de la Turquie (1281–1913)*. Paris: Alcan, 1914.

Du Casse, Albert, baron, comp. *Histoire des négociations diplomatiques relatives aux traités de Mortfontaine, de Lunéville, et d'Amiens*. 3 vols. Paris: Dentu, 1855.

Eon de Beaumont, Charles Geneviève Louis Auguste André Timothée d'. *Mémoires du chevalier d'Eon.* Edited by Frédéric Gaillardet. 2 vols. Paris: Editions de Saint-Clair, 1967.

Fain, Agathon Jean François. *Manuscrit de mil huit cent douze, contenant le précis des événmens de cette année.* . . . 2 vols. Paris: Delaunay, 1827.

————. *Mémoires du baron Fain.* Paris: Plon, Nourrit, 1908.

France, Commission des archives diplomatiques. *Recueil des instructions données aux ambassadeurs et ministres de France depuis les traités de Westphalie jusqu'à la Révolution française: Russie.* Edited by Alfred Rambaud. 2 vols. Paris: Alcan, 1890–91.

France, Treaties. *Recueil des traités de la France, publié sous les auspices du Ministère des Affaires étrangères.* Edited by Alexandre Jehan Henry de Clercq and Jules de Clercq. 23 vols. Paris: n.p., 1880–1917.

George III, king of England. *The Later Correspondence of George III.* Edited by Arthur Aspinall. 4 vols. to date. Cambridge, Eng.: Cambridge University Press, 1962–.

Georgel, Jean François. *Voyage à St.-Pétersbourg, en 1799–1800.* Paris: Eymery, 1818.

Glenbervie, Sylvester Douglas, baron. *The Diaries of Sylvester Douglas (Lord Glenbervie).* Edited by Francis Bickley. 2 vols. London: Constable, 1928.

Grech, Nikolai Ivanovich. *Zapiski o moei zhizni* [Notes on my life]. St. Petersburg: Suvorin, 1880.

Grenville, William Wyndham Grenville, baron. *The Manuscripts of J. B. Fortescue, esq., Preserved at Dropmore.* Edited by Walter Fitzpatrick. 7 vols. London: Historical Manuscripts Commission, 1892–1910.

Hauterive, Alexandre Maurice Blanc de Lanaulte, comte d'. *De l'état de la France à la fin de l'an VIII.* Paris: Henrics, 1800.

Hüffer, Hermann, ed. *Quellen zur Geschichte der Kriege von 1799 und 1800.* 2 vols. Leipzig: Teubner, 1900–1901.

Hunter, William. *A Short View of the Political Situation of the Northern Powers: Founded on Observations Made during a Tour through Russia, Sweden, and Denmark, in the Last Seven Months of the Year 1800.* London: Stockdale, 1801.

Jackson, Thomas Sturges, ed. *Logs of the Great Sea Fights, 1794–1805.* 2 vols. London: Navy Records Society, 1895–1900.

Joachim Murat, king of Naples. *Correspondance de Joachim Murat.* Edited by Alberto Lumbroso. Turin: Roux Frassati, 1899.

————. *Lettres et documents pour servir à l'histoire de Joachim Murat, 1767–1815.* Edited by Joachim Napoléon Murat. 8 vols. Paris: Plon, Nourrit, 1908–14.

Keith, George Keith Elphinstone, viscount. *The Keith Papers.* Edited by W. G. Perrin and Christopher Lloyd. 3 vols. London: Navy Records Society, 1927–55.

King, Rufus. *The Life and Correspondence of Rufus King.* Edited by Charles R. King. 6 vols. New York: Putnam, 1894–1900.

Kutuzov, Mikhail I. *M. I. Kutuzov: Dokumenty.* Edited by L. G. Beskrovnyi. 5 vols. Moscow: Voenizdat, 1950–54.

Lesur, Charles-Louis. *Des progrès de la puissance russe, depuis son origine jusqu'au commencement du XIX siècle.* Paris: Fantin, 1812.

Louis XV, king of France. *Correspondance secrète inédite de Louis XV sur la politique étrangère.* . . . Edited by Edgard Boutaric. 2 vols. Paris: Plon, 1866.

Macpherson, David. *Annals of Commerce, Manufactures, Fisheries and Navigation,*

. . . *containing the commercial transactions of the British Empire and other countries, from the earliest accounts to . . . January, 1801.* 4 vols. London: Nichols & Son, 1805.

Manuel de politique étrangère. Paris: Belin, 1900.

Marshall, John. *A Digest of all the accounts relating to the population, productions, revenues, financial operations, manufactures, shipping, colonies, commerce . . . of the United Kingdom, Great Britain and Ireland, diffused through more than 600 volumes of journals, reports, and papers, presented to Parliament during the last thirty-five years.* London: Haddon, 1833.

Martens, Georg Friedrich von, ed. *Recueil des principaux traités . . . conclus par les puissances de l'Europe . . . depuis 1761 jusqu'à présent.* 7 vols. Göttingen: Dieterich, 1791–1801.

————, ed. *Supplément au Recueil des principaux traités.* . . . 20 vols. Göttingen: Dieterich, 1802–42.

Minto, Sir Gilbert Elliot-Murray-Kynymound, first earl of Minto. *Life and Letters of Sir Gilbert Elliot, First Earl of Minto, from 1751 to 1806.* Edited by Emma Eleanor Elizabeth (Hislop) Elliot-Murray-Kynymound, countess of Minto. 3 vols. London: Longmans, Green, 1874.

Mitchell, Brian R., with collaboration of Phyllis Deane. *Abstract of British Historical Statistics.* Cambridge, Eng.: Cambridge University Press, 1962.

Mordvinov, R. N., ed. *Admiral Ushakov: Sbornik dokumentov.* 3 vols. Moscow: Voenizdat, 1951–56.

Napoléon I. *Correspondance de Napoléon I.* Edited by J. P. B. Vaillant et al. 32 vols. Paris: Plon & Dumaine, 1858–70.

————. *Oeuvres littéraires et écrits militaires de Napoléon I.* Edited by Jean Tulard. 3 vols. Paris: Société encyclopédique française, 1967–68.

Narochnitskii, A. L., et al., eds. *Vneshniaia politika Rossii XIX i nachala XX veka* [The foreign policy of Russia in the nineteenth and the beginning of the twentieth century], ser. 1: *1801–1815.* 6 vols. to date. Moscow: Gospolitizdat, 1960–.

Nelson, Horatio, viscount. *The Dispatches and Letters of Vice-Admiral Lord Viscount Nelson.* Edited by Sir Nicholas Harris Nicolas. 7 vols. London: Colburn, 1845–46.

Oddy, Joshua Jepson. *European Commerce, Shewing New and Secure Channels of Trade with the Continent of Europe: Detailing the Produce, Manufactures, and Commerce of Russia, Prussia, Sweden, Denmark, and Germany.* London: Richardson, 1805.

Paget, Sir Arthur. *The Paget Papers: Diplomatic and Other Correspondence of the Right Hon. Sir Arthur Paget, G.C.B., 1794–1807.* Edited by A. B. Paget. 2 vols. London: Heinemann, 1896.

Panin, Nikita Petrovich. *Materialy dlia zhizneopisaniia grafa Nikity Petrovicha Panina* [Materials for the biography of Count N. P. Panin]. Edited by Alexander Brückner. 7 vols. St. Petersburg: Imperatorskaia Akademiia nauk, 1888–92.

Parliamentary History of England from the Earliest Period to the Year 1803, The. Edited by William Cobbett. 36 vols. London: Hansard, 1806–20.

Piggott, Sir Francis Taylor, and Omond, G. W. T. *Documentary History of the Armed Neutralities.* London: University of London Press, 1919.

Reinicke, I. C. M., ed. *Charte des ganzen Russischen-Reichs.* Weimar: Verlag des Industrie Comptoirs, 1800.

Russia, Laws. *Polnoe sobranie zakonov Rossiiskoi imperii* [Complete collection of laws of the Russian Empire]. 45 vols. *Sobranie I: 1649–1825.* St. Petersburg: Kantseliariia, 1830.

Russia, Morskoe ministerstvo. *Materialy dlia istorii russkago flota* [Materials on the history of the Russian fleet]. 17 vols. St. Petersburg: Morskoe ministerstvo, 1865–1904.

Russia, Treaties. *Recueil des traités et conventions conclus par la Russie avec les puissances étrangères.* Edited by Fedor Fedorovich Martens. 15 vols. St. Petersburg: Böhnke, 1874–1909.

St. Vincent, John Jervis. *Letters of Admiral of the Fleet, the Earl of St. Vincent.* Edited by David Bonner Smith. 2 vols. London: Navy Records Society, 1922–27.

Scott, James Brown, ed. *The Armed Neutralities of 1780 and 1800: A Collection of Official Documents Preceded by the Views of Representative Publicists.* New York: Oxford University Press, 1918.

Spain, Treaties. *Tratados, convenios y declaraciones de paz y de comercio que han hecho con las potencias estranjeras los monarcos españoles de la casa de Borbon.* Edited by Alejandro del Cantillo. Madrid: Alegria & Charlain, 1843.

Spencer, George John Spencer, second earl Spencer. *Private Papers of George, Second Earl Spencer, First Lord of the Admiralty, 1794–1801.* Edited by Julian S. Corbett. 4 vols. London: Navy Records Society, 1913–24.

Stedingk, Curt Bogislaus Ludwig Kristoffer von. *Mémoires posthumes.* 3 vols. Paris: Bertrand, 1844–47.

Talleyrand-Périgord, Charles Maurice de. *Correspondance diplomatique de Talleyrand: Le Ministère de Talleyrand sous le Directoire.* Edited by Georges Pallain. Paris: Plon, Nourrit, 1891.

———. *Memoirs of the Prince de Talleyrand.* 5 vols. New York: Putnam, 1891–92.

Thugut, Johann Amadeus Franz de Paula, freiherr von. *Vertrauliche Briefe des Freiherrn von Thugut.* Edited by Alfred von Vivenot. 2 vols. Vienna: Braumüller, 1872.

Trachevskii, Aleksandr S., ed. *Diplomaticheskiia snosheniia Rossii s Frantsiei v epokhu Napoleona I* [Diplomatic relations of Russia with France in the epoch of Napoleon I]. 4 vols. St. Petersburg: Stasiulevich, 1890–93. (Vols. 70, 77, 82, and 88 of the *Sbornik* Russkago istoricheskago obshchestva.)

Turgenev, Aleksandr Ivanovich, ed. *La Cour de Russie il y a cent ans 1725–1783: Extraits des dépêches des ambassadeurs anglais et français.* Paris: Dentu, 1858.

United States, Bureau of the Census. *Historical Statistics of the United States.* Washington, D.C.: Government Printing Office, 1960.

Vasilchikov, Aleksandr Alekseevich, ed. *Semeistvo Razumovskikh* [The Razumovskii family]. 5 vols. St. Petersburg: Stasiulevich, 1880–94.

Young, Arthur. *The Question of Scarity Plainly Stated and Remedies Considered.* London: McMillan, 1800.

Documents in Periodicals

Bertrand, Pierre, ed. "M. de Talleyrand, l'Autriche, et la question d'Orient en 1805." *Revue historique* 39:63–75 (1889).

Bray, François-Gabriel de. "La Russie sous Paul Ier." *Revue d histoire diplomatique* 23:580–609 (1909) and 25:559–90 (1911).

Broglie, Albert, duc de. "La Politique de la Russie en 1800 d'après un document inédit." *Revue d'histoire diplomatique* 3:1–12 (1889).

Selected Bibliography

Carrion-Nisas, Marquis de, ed. "La Campagne des Français en Allemagne, 1800." *Memorial du dépôt de la guerre* 5:1–433 (1829).

Marmottan, Paul, ed. "Joseph Bonaparte diplomate (Lunéville-Amiens)." *Revue d'histoire diplomatique* 41:276–300 (1927).

———, ed. "Lucchesini ambassadeur de Prusse à Paris (1800–1801)." *Revue d'histoire diplomatique* 42:323–48 (1928), 43:65–87 (1929), and 44:450–61 (1930).

Paul I, emperor of Russia. "Instruction secrète donnée par l'empereur Paul 1-er au conseiller privé actuel Kalitscheff." *Russkii arkhiv*, 1874, pp. 961–70.

Rostopchin, F. V., count. "Zapiska grafa F. V. Rostopchina o politicheskikh otnosheniiakh Rossii v posliednye miesiatsy pavlovskago tsarstvovaniia" [A note of Count F. V. Rostopchin on the political relations of Russia in the last months of the reign of Paul]. *Russkii arkhiv*, 1878, pp. 103–10.

Talleyrand-Périgord, Charles Maurice de. "Correspondance de Talleyrand avec le Premier Consul pendant la campagne de Marengo." Edited by Count Boulay de la Meurthe. *Revue d'histoire diplomatique* 6:244–309 (1892).

Newspapers

Le Moniteur universel (Paris)
Sanktpeterburgskiia vedomosti [St. Petersburg News]
Times (London)

SECONDARY ACCOUNTS

Books

Albion, Robert G. *Forests and Sea Power: The Timber Problem of the Royal Navy.* Cambridge, Mass.: Harvard University Press, 1926.

Anderson, Roger C. *Naval Wars in the Baltic during the Sailing-ship Epoch, 1522–1850.* London: Gilbert-Wood, 1910.

Artaud de Montor, Alexis François. *Histoire de la vie et des travaux politiques du comte d'Hauterive.* 2d ed. Paris: Adrien le Clere, 1839.

Ayling, Stanley Edward. *George the Third.* London: Collins, 1972.

Bamford, Paul W. *Forests and French Sea Power, 1660–1789.* Toronto: Toronto University Press, 1956.

Bantysh-Kamenskii, Nikolai N. *Obzor vneshnikh snoshenii Rossii po 1800 g.* [Survey of the foreign relations of Russia through 1800]. Vol. 1. Moscow: Lissner & Roman, 1894.

Beer, Adolph. *Die orientalische Politik Oesterreichs seit 1774.* Leipzig: Freytag, 1883.

Bezobrazov, Pavel V. *O snosheniiakh Rossii s Frantsiei* [Franco-Russian relations]. Moscow: Universitetskaia tipografiia, 1892.

Bignon, Louis Pierre. *Histoire de France, depuis le 18 brumaire (novembre 1799) jusqu'à la paix de Tilsitt (juillet 1807).* 14 vols. Paris: Béchet, 1829–50.

Bolton, Geoffrey C. *The Passing of the Irish Act of Union.* Oxford: Oxford University Press, 1966.

Bonnefons, André. *Une Ennemie de la Révolution et de Napoléon: Marie-Caroline, reine des Deux-Siciles, 1768–1814.* Paris: Perrin, 1905.

Bourdeau, Emile Hippolyte. *Campagnes modernes, 1792–1815.* 3 vols. Paris: Charles-Lavauzelle, 1912–21.

168

Selected Bibliography

Bourgeois, Emile. *Manuel historique de politique étrangère.* 4 vols. Paris: Belin, 1927–29.

Bowman, Hervey Meyer. *Preliminary Stages of the Peace of Amiens: The Diplomatic Relations of Great Britain and France from the Fall of the Directory to the Death of Emperor Paul of Russia, November 1799–March 1801.* Toronto: Toronto University Library, 1899.

Brandt, Otto. *England und die napoleonische Weltpolitik, 1800–1803.* Heidelberg: Winter, 1916.

Brinton, Clarence Crane. *The Lives of Talleyrand.* New York: Norton, 1963.

Brückner, Aleksandr. *Smert' Pavla I* [The death of Paul I]. Moscow: Pirozhkov, 1907.

Bruun, Geoffrey. *Europe and the French Imperium, 1799–1814.* New York: Harper, 1938.

Butterfield, Herbert. *The Peace Tactics of Napoleon, 1806–1808.* Cambridge, Eng.: Cambridge University Press, 1929.

Chevalier, Alice. *Claude-Carloman de Rulhière, premier historien de la Pologne.* Paris: Domat-Montchrestien, 1939.

Chevalier, Louis Edouard. *Histoire de la marine française sous le Consulat et l'Empire.* Paris: Hachette, 1886.

Chuquet, Arthur. *Etudes d'histoire.* Vol. 6. Paris: Fontemoing, n.d.

Clowes, William Laird, et al. *The Royal Navy: A History from the Earliest Times to the Present.* 7 vols. London: Low, Marston, 1897–1903.

Colombos, Constantine John. *The International Law of the Sea.* 5th ed. London: Longmans, 1962.

Conde, Alexander de. *The Quasi-War: The Politics and Diplomacy of the Undeclared War with France, 1797–1801.* New York: Scribner, 1966.

Cooper, Duff. *Talleyrand.* London: Jonathan Cape, 1932.

Corbet, Charles. *A l'ère des nationalismes: L'Opinion française face à l'inconnue russe, 1799–1894.* Paris: Didier, 1967.

Cretineau-Joly, Jacques. *Histoire religieuse, politique et littéraire de la Compagnie de Jesus.* 6 vols. Paris: Le Coffre, 1859.

Crosby, Alfred W., Jr. *America, Russia, Hemp, and Napoleon: American Trade with Russia and the Baltic, 1783–1812.* Columbus: Ohio State University Press, 1965.

Crouzet, François. *L'Economie britannique et le blocus continental, 1806–1813.* 2 vols. Paris: Presses universitaires de France, 1958.

Daudet, Ernest. *L'Histoire de l'émigration pendant la révolution française.* 2d ed. Paris: Hachette, 1905–7.

Desbrière, Edouard. *1795–1805: Projets et tentatives de débarquement aux îles britanniques.* 4 vols. Paris: Chapelot, 1900–1902.

Deutsch, Harold C. *The Genesis of Napoleonic Imperialism.* Cambridge, Mass.: Harvard University Press, 1938.

Driault, Edouard. *Napoléon en Italie, 1800–1812.* Paris: Alcan, 1906.

———. *Napoléon et l'Europe.* 5 vols. Paris: Alcan, 1910–27.

Ehrman, John. *The Younger Pitt.* New York: Dutton, 1969.

Ernle, Rowland Edmund Prothero, baron. *English Farming, Past and Present.* Edited by Sir A. D. Hall. 5th ed. London: Longmans, Green, 1936.

Esposito, Vincent J., and Etting, John Robert. *A Military History and Atlas of the Napoleonic Wars.* New York: Praeger, 1964.

Fernández Duro, Cesáreo. *Armada española desde la unión de los reinos de Castilla*

y de León. 9 vols. Madrid: Est. tipográfico "Successores de Rivadeneyra,"
1895–1903.

Fisher, Herbert A. L. *Studies in Napoleonic Statesmanship: Germany.* Oxford:
Clarendon Press, 1903.

Flassan, Gaëtan de Rexis de. *Histoire générale et raisonnée de la diplomatie française, ou de la politique de la France, depuis la fondation de la monarchie,
jusqu'à la fin du règne de Louis XVI.* 2d ed. 7 vols. Paris: Treuttel &
Würtz, 1811.

Ford, Guy Stanton. *Hanover and Prussia, 1795–1803: A Study in Neutrality.* New
York: Columbia University Press, 1903.

Fournier, August. *Napoleon I.* 2d ed. 2 vols. London: Longmans, Green, 1914.

Fuchs, Eduard, and Kramer, Hans. *Die Karikatur der europäischen Völker vom
Altertum bis zur Neuzeit.* Berlin: Hofmann, 1901.

Fugier, André. *Napoléon et l'Espagne, 1799–1808.* 2 vols. Paris: Alcan, 1930.

———. *Napoléon et l'Italie.* Paris: Janin, 1947.

———. *La Révolution française et l'Empire napoléonien.* Paris: Hachette, 1954.

Galpin, William F. *The Grain Supply of England during the Napoleonic Period.*
Vol. 6 of University of Michigan Publications, History and Political Science.
New York: Macmillan, 1925.

Gayer, Arthur D., Rostow, W. W., and Schwartz, Anna Jacobson. *The Growth
and Fluctuation of the British Economy, 1790–1850.* 2 vols. Oxford: Clarendon
Press, 1953.

Gentz, Friedrich von. *Von dem Politischen Zustande von Europa vor und nach der
Französischen Revoluzion.* Berlin: Frölich, 1801.

———. *On the State of Europe before and after the French Revolution; Being an
Answer to "L'Etat de la France à la fin de l'an VIII."* Translated by John
Charles Herries. London: Hatchard, 1802.

Godechot, Jacques Léon. *La Contre-révolution: Doctrine et action, 1789–1804.*
Paris: Presses universitaires de France, 1961.

Goriainov, Sergei M. *Le Bosphore et les Dardanelles.* Paris: Plon, Nourrit, 1910.

Griffiths, David M. "Russian Court Politics and the Question of an Expansionist
Foreign Policy under Catherine II, 1762–1783." Ph.D. dissertation, Cornell
University, 1967.

Grunwald, Constantin de. *Les Alliances franco-russes: Neuf siècles de malentendus.*
Paris: Plon, 1965.

Guyot, Raymond. *Le Directoire et la paix de l'Europe: Des traités de Bâle à la
deuxième coalition, 1795–1799.* Paris: Alcan, 1911.

Hakluyt, Richard. *The Principal Navigations, Voyages, Traffiques & Discoveries of
the English Nation . . . .* 8 vols. London: Dent, 1907; first published in 1589.

Haumant, Emile. *La Culture française en Russie, 1700–1900.* Paris: Hachette, 1910.

Heckscher, Eli Filip. *The Continental System: An Economic Interpretation.* Edited
by Harald Westergaard. Oxford: Clarendon Press, 1922.

Heils, Kirsten. *Les Rapports économiques franco-danois sous le Directoire, le Consulat et l'Empire: Contribution a l'étude du système continental.* Paris: Presses
de la Cité, 1958.

Herold, J. Christopher. *Bonaparte in Egypt.* New York: Harper & Row, 1962.

Hill, Charles E. *The Danish Sound Dues and the Command of the Baltic.* Durham,
N.C.: Duke University Press, 1926.

Holm, Peter Edvard. *Danmark-Norges udenrigske Historie under den Franske
Revolution og Napoleons krige fra 1791 til 1807* [The history of Danish foreign

policy in the time of the French Revolutionary and Napoleonic Wars, 1791–1807]. 2 vols. Copenhagen: Gad, 1875.

Hunt, William. *The History of England from the Accession of George III, to the Close of Pitt's First Administration (1760–1801)*. London: Longmans, Green, 1930.

Ingle, Harold N. *Nesselrode and the Russian Rapprochement with Britain, 1836–1844*. Berkeley: University of California Press, 1976.

James, William. *The Naval History of Great Britain, from the Declaration of War by France in 1793, to the Accession of George IV*. New ed. 6 vols. London: Bentley, 1837.

Jomini, Henri de, baron. *Histoire critique et militaire des guerres de la Révolution*. New ed. 15 vols. Paris: Anselin & Pochard, 1820–24.

Kirchner, Walther. *Commercial Relations between Russia and Europe, 1400 to 1800*. Bloomington: Indiana University Press, 1966.

Kliuchevskii, Vasilii O. *Sochineniia* [Works], vol. 4: *Kurs russkoi istorii* [The course of Russian history], vol. 4. Moscow: Sotsekizdat, 1958.

Krüger-Löwenstein, Uta. *Russland, Frankreich und das Reich, 1801–1803: Zur Vorgeschichte des 3. Koalition*. Wiesbaden: Steiner, 1972.

Kulisher, Iosif M. *Ocherk istorii russkoi torgovli* [A survey of the history of Russian trade]. St. Petersburg: Atenei, 1923.

Lacour-Gayet, Georges. *Talleyrand, 1754–1838*. 4 vols. Paris: Payot, 1928–34.

Lefebvre, Armand Edouard. *Histoire des cabinets de l'Europe pendant le consulat et l'empire*. 3 vols. Paris: Gosselin, 1845–47.

Lefebvre, Georges. *The French Revolution from 1793 to 1799*. Translated by John Hall Stewart. New York: Columbia University Press, 1964.

———. *Napoleon: From 18 Brumaire to Tilsit, 1799–1807*. Translated by Henry F. Stockhold. New York: Columbia University Press, 1969.

———. *Napoleon: From Tilsit to Waterloo, 1807–1815*. Translated by J. E. Anderson. New York: Columbia University Press, 1969.

Levasseur, Emile. *Histoire du commerce de la France*. 2 vols. Paris: Rousseau, 1911–12.

Lortholary, Albert. *Le Mirage russe en France au XVIIIe siècle*. Paris: Bouvin, [1951].

Macalpine, Ida, and Hunter, Richard. *George III and the Mad-Business*. London: Allen Lane, 1969.

Madariaga, Isabel de. *Britain, Russia, and the Armed Neutrality of 1780*. New Haven, Conn.: Yale University Press, 1962.

Mahan, Alfred Thayer. *The Influence of Sea Power upon the French Revolution and Empire, 1793–1812*. 2 vols. Boston: Little, Brown, 1892.

———. *The Life of Nelson*. 2d ed., rev. 2 vols. New York: Greenwood, 1968.

Manfred, Albert Zakharovich. *Napoleon Bonapart*. Moscow: Mysl', 1971.

Marcus, Geoffrey Jules. *The Age of Nelson: The Royal Navy, 1793–1815*. New York: Viking, 1971.

Marmoiton, Pierre. *Le Maréchal Brune et la maréchale Brune*. Paris: Lethielleux, 1900.

Masson, Frédéric. *Le Département des Affaires étrangères pendant la révolution, 1787–1804*. Paris: Plon, 1877.

Matheson, Cyril. *The Life of Henry Dundas, First Viscount Melville, 1742–1811*. London: Constable, 1933.

Melvin, Frank E. *Napoleon's Navigation System: A Study of Trade Control during the Continental Blockade.* New York: Appleton, 1919.

Miliutin, Dmitrii A. *Istoriia voiny 1799 goda mezhdu Rossiei i Frantsiei v tsarstvovanie imperatora Pavla I* [A history of the War of 1799 between Russia and France in the reign of Emperor Paul I]. 5 vols. St. Petersburg: Imperatorskaia Akademiia nauk, 1852–53.

Milton, John. *The Works of John Milton.* 18 vols. New York: Columbia University Press, 1931–38.

Mitchell, Harvey. *The Underground War against Revolutionary France: The Missions of William Wickham, 1794–1800.* Oxford: Clarendon Press, 1965.

Mohrenschildt, Dmitri Sergius von. *Russia in the Intellectual Life of Eighteenth-Century France.* New York: Columbia University Press, 1936.

Moroshkin, Mikhail. *Iezuity v Rossii: S tsarstvovaniia Ekateriny II i do nashego vremeni* [The Jesuits in Russia from the reign of Catherine II to our time]. 2 vols. St. Petersburg: II otdel Imper. kantseliarii, 1867–70.

Mosely, Philip E. *Russian Diplomacy and the Opening of the Eastern Question in 1838 and 1839.* Cambridge, Mass.: Harvard University Press, 1934.

Mouravieff, Boris. *Le Testament de Pierre le Grand: Légende et réalité.* Neuchâtel: Baconnière, 1949.

Mowat, Robert B. *The Diplomacy of Napoleon.* London: Arnold, 1924.

Muriel, Andrés. *Historia de Carlos IV.* 6 vols. Madrid: Tello, 1893–94.

Naryshkina, Nataliia Fedorovna. *1812: Le Comte Rostopchine et son temps.* St. Petersburg: Golicke & Willborg, 1912.

Oddy, Joshua Jepson. *European Commerce.* London: Richardson, 1805.

Orieux, Jean. *Talleyrand: ou, Le Sphinx incompris.* Paris: Flammarion, 1970.

Parkinson, Cyril Northcote. *Trade in the Eastern Seas, 1793–1813.* Cambridge, Eng.: Cambridge University Press, 1937.

———. *War in the Eastern Seas, 1793–1815.* London: Allen & Unwin, 1954.

Phillips, Walter Allison, and Reede, Arthur H. *Neutrality: Its History, Economics and Law.* Vol. 2: *The Napoleonic Period.* New York: Columbia University Press, 1936.

Picard, Ernest. *Bonaparte et Moreau.* Paris: Plon, Nourrit, 1905.

———. *Hohenlinden.* Paris: Charles-Lavauzelle, 1909.

Pietri, François. *Lucien Bonaparte à Madrid, 1801.* Paris: Grasset, 1951.

Pingaud, Albert. *La Dominance française dans l'Italie du Nord, 1796–1805.* 2 vols. Paris: Perrin, 1914.

Pingaud, Léonce. *Un Agent secret sous la révolution et l'empire: Le Comte d'Antraigues.* 2d ed. Paris: Plon, Nourrit, 1894.

———. *Choiseul-Gouffier: La France en Orient sous Louis XVI.* Paris: Picard, 1887.

———. *Les Français en Russie et les Russes en France.* Paris: Perrin, 1886.

Pokrovskii, Serafin A. *Vneshniaia torgovlia i vneshniaia torgovaia politika Rossii* [The foreign trade and the foreign-trade policy of Russia]. Moscow: Mezhdunarodnaia kniga, 1947.

Pope, Dudley. *The Great Gamble: Nelson at Copenhagen.* New York: Simon & Schuster, 1972.

Puryear, Vernon J. *Napoleon and the Dardanelles.* Berkeley: University of California Press, 1951.

Rain, Pierre. *La Diplomatie française d'Henri IV à Vergennes.* Paris: Plon, 1945.

———. *La Diplomatie française de Mirabeau à Bonaparte.* Paris: Plon, 1950.

Rodger, Alexander Bankier. *The War of the Second Coalition, 1798–1801.* Oxford: Clarendon Press, 1964.

Rodocanachi, Emmanuel Pierre. *Bonaparte et les îles Ioniennes.* Paris: Alcan, 1899.

Rose, John Holland. *William Pitt and the Great War.* London: Bell, 1911.

————. *William Pitt and the National Revival.* London: Bell, 1911.

Ross, Steven T. "The War of the Second Coalition." Ph.D. dissertation, Princeton University, 1963.

Rulhière, Claude-Carloman de. *Histoire de l'anarchie de Pologne et du démembrement de cette république.* 4 vols. Paris: Desenne, 1807.

Saul, Norman E. *Russia and the Mediterranean, 1797–1807.* Chicago: University of Chicago Press, 1970.

Savant, Jean. *Les Espions de Napoléon.* Paris: Hachette, 1957.

————. *Les "Fonds secrets" de Napoléon.* Paris: Editions Académie, 1952.

Schilder, Nikolai K. *Imperator Aleksandr Pervyi: Ego zhizn' i tsarstvovanie* [Emperor Alexander the First: His life and reign]. 4 vols. St. Petersburg: Suvorin, 1897–98.

————. *Imperator Pavel Pervyi: Istoriko-biograficheskii ocherk* [Emperor Paul the First: A historical and biographical study]. St. Petersburg: Suvorin, 1901.

Schleifer, A. *Die Schlacht bei Hohenlinden.* Erding: Hauser, 1885.

Schlote, Werner. *British Overseas Trade from 1700 to the 1930s.* Oxford: Blackwell, 1952.

Seeley, John Robert. *The Growth of British Policy.* 2 vols. Cambridge, Eng.: Cambridge University Press, 1895.

Ségur, Anatole Henri Philippe, comte de. *Vie du comte Rostopchine.* Paris: Bray & Retaux, 1871.

Shumigorskii, Evgenii S. *Imperator Pavel I: Zhizn' i tsarstvovanie* [Emperor Paul I: Life and reign]. St. Petersburg: Smirnov, 1907.

Sirotkin, Vladlen G. *Duel' dvukh diplomatii* [The duel of two diplomacies]. Moscow: Nauka, 1966.

Sorel, Albert. *L'Europe et la Révolution française.* 8 vols. Paris: Plon, Nourrit, 1885–1904.

Stanislavskaia, Avgusta M. *Russko-angliiskie otnosheniia i problemy sredizemnomoria, 1798–1807* [Russo-English relations and problems of the Mediterranean, 1798–1807]. Moscow: Akademiia nauk, 1962.

Tarle, Evgenii V. *Kontinental'naia blokada* [The Continental blockade]. Moscow: Akademiia nauk, 1958.

————. *Napoleon.* Moscow: Zhurnal'no-gazetnoe obedinenie, 1939.

————. *Taleiran* [Talleyrand]. Moscow: Akademiia nauk, 1948.

Thiers, Louis Adolphe. *Histoire du consulat et de l'empire.* 21 vols. Paris: Paulin, 1845–74.

Tooke, Thomas, and Newmarch, William. *A History of Prices and of the State of the Circulation from 1792 to 1856.* Reprint of 1838–57 edition. 6 vols. New York: Adelphi, 1928.

Tramond, Joannès. *Manuel d'histoire maritime de la France des origines à 1815.* 2d ed., rev. and enl. Paris: Société d'éditions géographiques, maritimes et coloniales, 1927.

Vandal, Albert. *Louis XV et Elisabeth de Russie.* Paris: Plon, 1882.

————. *Napoléon et Alexandre 1er.* 3 vols. Paris: Plon, Nourrit, 1893–96.

Verbitskii, E. D. "Russko-frantsuzskie otnosheniia v 1800–1803 gg." [Russo-French relations in 1800–1803]. Candidate dissertation, Kherson Pedagogical Institute, 1950.

Voenno-topograficheskaia karta Rossii [Military-topographical map of Russia]. Ser. 18, pl. 2: *Grodnenskoi i Sedletskoi g.* [Map of Grodnenskaia and Sedletskaia gubernii]. Moscow: Upravlenie voennykh topografov, 1870.

————. Ser. 21, pl. 3: *G. Volynskoi i Liublinskoi* [Map of Volynskaia and Liublinskaia gubernii]. Moscow: Upravlenie voennykh topografov, 1911.

Voenskii, Konstantin. *Bonapart i russkie plennye* [Bonaparte and the Russian prisoners]. St. Petersburg: Tipografiia glavnago upravleniia udelov, 1907.

Voznesenskii, Sergei V. *Ekonomika Rossii XIX–XX vv. v tsifrakh* [The economy of Russia in the eighteenth and nineteenth centuries in figures]. Leningrad: GUBONO, 1924.

Waliszewski, Kazimierz. *Paul the First of Russia.* London: Heinemann, 1913.

Ward, Adolphus W., and Gooch, G. P., eds. *The Cambridge History of British Foreign Policy, 1783–1919.* 3 vols. New York: Macmillan, 1922–23.

Warner, Oliver. *Nelson's Battles.* New York: Macmillan, 1965.

Watson, John Steven. *The Reign of George III, 1760–1815.* Oxford: Clarendon Press, 1960.

Weil, Maurice H. *Un Agent inconnu de la coalition: Le Général de Stamford, d'après sa correspondance inédite, 1793–1806.* Paris: Payot, 1923.

Zorin, Valerian A., et al. *Istoriia diplomatii* [History of diplomacy]. 2d ed. 3 vols. Moscow: Gospolitizdat, 1959–65.

Articles

Blanc, Simone. "Histoire d'une phobie: Le Testament de Pierre le Grand." *Cahiers du monde russe et soviétique* 9:265–93 (1968).

Bourgeois, Emile. "L'Alliance de Bonaparte et de Paul I (1800–1801)." *Revue des travaux et comptes-rendus, Académie des sciences morales et publiques,* n.s. 197: 273–90 (1922).

Boyer, Ferdinand. "Présents du gouvernement consulaire aux négociateurs étrangers (1800–1802)." *Revue d'histoire diplomatique* 83:70–76 (1969).

Buchholz, Gustav. "Die Napoleonische Weltpolitik und die Idee des französisch-russischen Bundes." *Preussische Jahrbücher* 84:385–402 (1896).

Danilova, E. N. "Zaveshchanie Petra Velikogo" [The Testament of Peter the Great]. *Trudy istoriko-arkhivnogo instituta* 2:205–70 (1946).

Davison, Roderic H. "'Russian Skill and Turkish Imbecility': The Treaty of Kuchuk Kainardji Reconsidered." *Slavic Review* 35:463–83 (September 1976).

Despréaux, E. "Louis XVIII en Courlande." *Monde slave,* n.s., 5th year, vol. 3, no. 9, pp. 403–22 (1928).

Godechot, Jacques. "La Rêve orientale de Bonaparte." *Revue de défense nationale* 25:1622–34 (1969).

Hurewitz, J. C. "Russia and the Turkish Straits: A Revaluation of the Origins of the Problem." *World Politics* 14:605–32 (July 1962).

Imlah, A. H. "Real Values in British Foreign Trade." *Journal of Economic History* 8:133–52 (1948).

Kazakov, N. I. "Napoleon glazami ego russkikh sovremennikov" [Napoleon in the eyes of his Russian contemporaries]. *Novaia i noveishaia istoriia,* 1970, no. 3, pp. 31–47, and no. 4, pp. 42–55.

Kenney, James J., Jr. "Lord Whitworth and the Conspiracy against Tsar Paul I:

Selected Bibliography

The New Evidence of the Kent Archive." *Slavic Review* 36:205–19 (June 1977).
Lehovich, Dmitry V. "The Testament of Peter the Great." *American Slavic and East European Review* 7:111–24 (April 1948).
McGrew, Roderick E. "Paul I and the Knights of Malta." In *Paul I: A Reassessment of His Life and Reign*, edited by Hugh Ragsdale, pp. 44-75. Pittsburgh, Pa.: The University Center for International Studies, University of Pittsburgh, 1979.
———. "A Political Portrait of Paul I from the Austrian and English Diplomatic Archives." *Jahrbücher für Geschichte Osteuropas*, n.s. 18:503–29 (December 1970).
Manfred, A. Z. "Poiski soiuza s Rossiei, 1800–1801" [In search of an alliance with Russia, 1800–1801]. *Istoriia SSSR*, 1971, no. 4, pp. 38–59.
Markova, O. P. "O neitralnoi sisteme i franko-russkikh otnosheniiakh (Vtoraia polovina XVIII v.)" [On the neutral system and Franco-Russian relations: The second half of the eighteenth century]. *Istoriia SSSR*, 1970, no. 6, pp. 42–55.
Muret, Pierre. "Une Conception nouvelle de la politique étrangère de Napoléon I." *Revue d'histoire moderne et contemporaine* 8:177–200 and 353–80 (1913).
Pavlenko, N. I. "Tri tak nazyvaemykh zaveshchaniia Petra I" [Three so-called Testaments of Peter I]. *Voprosy istorii* 2:129–44 (1979).
Philippson, Martin. "La Paix d'Amiens et la politique générale de Napoléon I." *Revue historique* 75:286–318 (1901).
Ragsdale, Hugh. "A Continental System in 1801: Paul I and Bonaparte." *Journal of Modern History* 42:70–89 (1970).
———. "The Origins of Bonaparte's Russian Policy." *Slavic Review* 27:85–90 (1968).
———. "Russian Influence at Lunéville." *French Historical Studies* 5:274–84 (1968).
Roberts, L. M. "The Negotiations Preceding the Peace of Lunéville, 1801." *Transactions of the Royal Historical Society*, n.s. 15:47–130 (1901).
Ruppenthal, Roland. "Denmark and the Continental System." *Journal of Modern History* 15:7–23 (1943).
Silberling, Norman J. "British Prices and Business Cycles, 1779–1850." *Review of Economic Statistics*, 5th suppl., pp. 219–62 (1923).
———. "Financial and Monetary Policy of Great Britain during the Napoleonic Wars." *Quarterly Journal of Economics* 38:214–33 and 397–439 (1924).
Sokolnicki, Michel. "A propos du centenaire de 1812: Le Testament de Pierre le Grand." *Revue des sciences politiques* 27:88–98 (1912).
Sorel, Albert. "L'Autriche et le Comité de salut public, avril 1795." *Revue historique* 17:25–63 (September/October 1881).
Subtelny, Orest. " 'Peter I's Testament': A Reassessment." *Slavic Review* 33:663–78 (December 1974).
Tatishchev, Sergei. "Paul I et Bonaparte." *Nouvelle revue* 47:631–65 (1887), 48:41–58 (1888), 49:233–60 and 754–85 (1889).
"Thugut." *Allgemeine Deutsche Biographie*. Vol. 38, pp. 138–58. Leipzig: Duncker & Humblot, 1894.
Trachevskii, Aleksandr S. "Franko-russkii soiuz v epokhu Napoleona I" [The Franco-Russian Alliance in the epoch of Napoleon I]. *Istoricheskii viestnik* 44:568–93 (1891).
Verbitskii, E. D. "Germanskii vopros v russko-frantsuzskikh otnosheniiakh 1800–

Selected Bibliography

1803 gg." [The German question in Russo-French relations, 1800–1803]. *Uchenye zapiski Khersonskogo pedagogicheskogo instituta*, issue 4 (1949), pp. 1–58.

———. "Pervoe soglashenie dvorianskoi Rossii i burzhuaznoi Frantsii: Mirnyi dogovor i sekretnaia konventsiia 1801 g." [The first settlement of seigneurial Russia and bourgeois France: The peace treaty and secret convention of 1801]. *Uchenye zapiski Kishinevskogo universiteta*, 1963, vol. 65 (Istoricheskii), pp. 71–86.

———. "Russko-frantsuzskie otnosheniia v kontse 1799–1800 gg.: Povorot ot voiny k miru" [Russo-French relations in 1799–1800: The transition from war to peace]. *Ezhegodnik nauchnykh rabot Khersonskogo sel'sko-khoziaistvennogo instituta*, 1961 issue, pp. 47–55.

———. "Vtoraia popytka primireniia dvorianskoi Rossii i burzhuaznoi Frantsii: Peregovory o mire i soiuze (sentiabr' 1800 g.–mart 1801 g.)" [The second attempt of seigneurial Russia and bourgeois France to make peace: The negotiations on peace and alliance (September 1800–March 1801)]. *Ezhegodnik nauchnykh rabot Khersonskogo sel'sko-khoziaistvennogo instituta*, 1961 issue, pp. 56–67.

Vivenot, Alfred von. "Thugut und sein politisches System, II." *Archiv für österreichische Geschichte* 43:105–83 (1870).

INDEX